THIRD EDITION

Learning Swift
Building Apps for macOS, iOS, and Beyond

Jon Manning, Paris Buttfield-Addison, Tim Nugent

Beijing · Boston · Farnham · Sebastopol · Tokyo

Learning Swift

by Jonathon Manning, Paris Buttfield-Addison, and Tim Nugent

Copyright © 2018 Secret Lab. All rights reserved.

Published by O'Reilly Media, Inc., 1005 Gravenstein Highway North, Sebastopol, CA 95472.

O'Reilly books may be purchased for educational, business, or sales promotional use. Online editions are also available for most titles (*http://oreilly.com/safari*). For more information, contact our corporate/institutional sales department: 800-998-9938 or *corporate@oreilly.com*.

Editor: Rachel Roumeliotis	**Indexer:** Ellen Troutman-Zaig
Production Editor: Melanie Yarbrough	**Interior Designer:** David Futato
Copyeditor: Rachel Head	**Cover Designer:** Karen Montgomery
Proofreader: Kim Cofer	**Illustrator:** Rebecca Demarest

March 2018:   Third Edition

Revision History for the Third Edition
2018-03-26:   First Release

See *http://oreilly.com/catalog/errata.csp?isbn=9781491987575* for release details.

978-1-491-98757-5

[LSI]

Table of Contents

Preface. ix

Part I.   Welcome to Swift

1. Getting Started.   3
    Xcode   3
       Getting Xcode   4
       Creating Your First Project   4
    Working with the Xcode Interface   6
       The Editor   6
       The Toolbar   8
       The Navigator   10
       Utilities   11
       The Debug Area   13
    Running Your Code   13
       The iOS Simulator   14
       Running on a Device   15
       Distributing Your Apps   16
    The Interface Builder   16
       Interfaces in iOS   18
    Conclusion   19

2. The Swift Programming Language. 21
    The Swift Language   22
       Swift 3 Versus 4   24
    Playgrounds and Swift   24
    Comments   26

Imports   27
Variables   28
Operators   30
Collections   31
  Arrays   31
  Tuples   32
  Dictionaries   33
Control Flow   34
  Loops   35
  Switches   37
Types   39
  Working with Strings   40
  Sets   42
  Enumerations   44
  Type Safety and Conversion   46
  Optionals   48
  Type Casting   52
Functions and Closures   53
  Using Functions as Variables   56
  Closures   58
Convenience Features   59
  The defer Keyword   59
  The guard Keyword   60
Making Your Code Swifty   61
Conclusion   61

3. Object-Oriented Development in Swift. 63
Classes and Objects   63
  Initialization and Deinitialization   64
  Properties   66
  Inheritance   69
  Protocols   70
  Extensions   72
  Access Control   75
  Operator Overloading and Custom Operators   78
  Subscripts   80
  Generics   81
Structures   82
Error Handling   84
Memory Management   87
Design Patterns in Swift   91
  Model–View–Controller   92

    Delegation   93
   Swift Libraries   96
     Structuring an App   97
   Swift Package Manager   101
   Conclusion   107

Part II. Building Selfiegram

4. Setting Up Our App. **111**
   Designing Selfiegram   112
   Creating the Project   115
   The Structure   118
   Renaming the Views   120

5. Building the Model Object. **123**
   The Selfie Object   123
   The SelfieStore   127
   Testing the SelfieStore   130
   Filling Out the Method Stubs   136

6. Building the Selfie List UI. **145**
   Creating the Selfie List   145
   Improving the Selfie List   151

7. Adding and Deleting Selfies. **155**
   Deleting Selfies   155
   Taking New Selfies   157

8. Viewing and Editing Selfies. **165**
   The Selfie Viewer   165
    Connecting the Code and the UI   167
   Editing a Selfie   172

9. Adding Location Info to the Selfies. **175**
   Updating the Model   175
   Testing Our New Model   178
   Showing a Selfie's Location   179
   Expanding the Map   183
   Determining Locations   186
    Configuring the App to Support Location   186
    Talking to the Location Hardware   188

10. Building a Settings View... **193**

    Building the Settings UI   193

        Connecting the Settings into Our Hierarchy   195

        Hooking Up the Settings   196

    Implementing the Settings   197

11. Reminders and Notifications.. **201**

    Adding a Reminder to the Settings   201

    Creating a Notification   203

Part III. Polishing Selfiegram

12. Theming and Sharing Selfiegram.. **213**

    Custom Fonts   214

    Making the Theme   217

    Sharing Selfies   222

        Sharing from the Detail View Controller   223

        Sharing from the List View Controller   224

13. Custom Views and View Controllers....................................... **227**

    A Camera View   228

    The Camera View Controller   231

        Building the UI   231

        Connecting the UI   234

        Talking to the Camera   234

    Calling the Capture View Controller   240

14. Image Overlays.. **245**

    Creating the Overlay Model   245

    Testing the Overlay Manager   252

        Writing the Tests   252

        Returning Available Overlays   255

        Downloading Overlay Information   256

        Downloading Overlay Images   258

15. Overlay UI... **263**

    Building the UI   263

        Hooking Up the UI   266

    Creating the Overlay View   266

    Presenting the Overlays   268

        Initial Setup   268

     Drawing Eyebrows   271
     Vision and Image Detection   274
   Connecting It into the App   279

16. Localization and Internationalization. **283**
   Internationalization   284
     Generating the String Table   286
   Localization   287
     Translating the Strings   290
   Testing Locales   290
     Pseudolanguages   292
     Previewing Localizations   294
   Conclusion   296

Part IV.　Beyond Developing Selfiegram

17. Debugging. **299**
   The Debugger   299
     Breakpoints   300
     Inspecting Code   304
     Controlling Program Flow   307
   Performance   309
     Instruments   310

18. UI Tests. **313**
   UI Testing Classes   313
   Writing UI Tests   314
     A Basic Test   314
     Recording UI Actions   315
     Checking if Elements Exist   318
     Handling UI Interruptions   319

19. Automating Chores with Fastlane. **321**
   The Fastlane Tools   322
   Installing Fastlane   323
     Installing via Homebrew   324
     Installing via RubyGems   324
     Installing via Direct Download   324
   Setting Up a Project   324
   Doing a Build   325
   Configuring a Fastfile   327

20. Using Fastlane's Tools. **329**

    Code Signing with match   329

      The Problem That Match Solves   329

      match's Solution   332

    Generating Screenshots Using snapshot   333

    Using Boarding to Add Testers to TestFlight   337

    Managing Your App's Presence on the App Store Using deliver   339

      Getting the Metadata   340

      Submitting New Metadata   340

    Looking Further   341

Index. **343**

Preface

Welcome to *Learning Swift*! This book will help you put the Swift programming language into practice by walking you through the development of a complete application for iOS that features a wide array of features, including camera access, working with the filesystem, face detection, and the iOS graphics system. Along the way, we'll also introduce you to new and advanced topics in the Swift programming language.

Swift is a pretty amazing modern language, taking the best from other newer languages without reinventing the wheel. Swift is easy to write, easy to read, and hard to make big mistakes in.

Our philosophy is that the best way to learn Swift is to build apps using it! To build apps, though, you need a great framework, and Apple has one of the best ones for building high-quality, featureful software: Cocoa Touch. This book could quite easily be titled *Learning Cocoa Touch with Swift*, or something similar, because the frameworks are just as important as the language itself. At the time of writing, Swift is currently at version 4, and has a bright future ahead of it.

Resources Used in This Book

We recommend following along with the book by writing code yourself as you progress through each chapter. If you get stuck, or just want to archive a copy of the code, you can find what you need via our website (*http://www.secretlab.com.au/books/learning-swift-3e*).

Audience and Approach

This book is solely focused on Swift 4 and does not cover the use of Objective-C. We might mention it occasionally, but we don't expect you to know how to use it. We first cover the basics of the Swift 4 language, and then move on to teach as much of the language as we can, as well as the use of Cocoa Touch, through the construction of *Selfiegram*, a photo-taking app for iOS.

This book's approach differs from that of other programming books that you may have encountered. As we've mentioned, we believe that the best way to learn Swift is to build something using it. We assume that you're a reasonably capable programmer, but we don't assume you've ever developed for iOS or used Swift or Objective-C before. We also assume that you're fairly comfortable navigating macOS and iOS as a user.

Organization of This Book

In this book, we'll be talking about Cocoa Touch, the framework used for developing iOS applications. Along the way, we'll also be covering Swift, including its syntax and features.

In Part I, *Welcome to Swift*, we begin with a look at the tools used for programming with Swift, as well as the Apple Developer Program. Then we move on to the basics of the Swift programming language and structuring a program for Apple's platforms, as well as common design patterns.

In Part II, *Building Selfiegram*, we start building Selfiegram, the iOS photo-taking application that's the focus of the book. In this part, we'll build the foundational features, like the ability to take photos and store them on disk.

In Part III, *Polishing Selfiegram*, we add a number of particularly interesting features, including a custom camera view, face detection, network access, and theming the app.

In Part IV, *Beyond Developing Selfiegram*, we discuss a number of features and tools that can help you in your further development work, including Xcode's debugging and profiling tools, as well as third-party tools that can make your life easier.

Conventions Used in This Book

The following typographical conventions are used in this book:

Italic
> Indicates new terms, URLs, email addresses, filenames, and file extensions.

`Constant width`
> Used for program listings, as well as within paragraphs to refer to program elements such as variable or function names, databases, data types, environment variables, statements, and keywords. Also used for commands and command-line output.

This element signifies a tip or suggestion.

 This element signifies a general note.

 This element indicates a warning or caution.

Using Code Examples

Supplemental material (code examples, exercises, errata, etc.) is available for download at our website (*http://www.secretlab.com.au/books/learning-swift-3e*).

This book is here to help you get your job done. In general, if example code is offered with this book, you may use it in your programs and documentation. You do not need to contact us for permission unless you're reproducing a significant portion of the code. For example, writing a program that uses several chunks of code from this book does not require permission. Selling or distributing a CD-ROM of examples from O'Reilly books does require permission. Answering a question by citing this book and quoting example code does not require permission. Incorporating a significant amount of example code from this book into your product's documentation does require permission.

We appreciate, but do not require, attribution. An attribution usually includes the title, author, publisher, and ISBN. For example: "*Learning Swift*, 3rd Edition, by Jonathon Manning, Paris Buttfield-Addison, and Tim Nugent (O'Reilly). Copyright 2018 Secret Lab, 978-1-491-98757-5."

If you feel your use of code examples falls outside fair use or the permission given above, feel free to contact us at *permissions@oreilly.com*.

O'Reilly Safari

 *Safari* (formerly Safari Books Online) is a membership-based training and reference platform for enterprise, government, educators, and individuals.

Members have access to thousands of books, training videos, Learning Paths, interactive tutorials, and curated playlists from over 250 publishers, including O'Reilly Media, Harvard Business Review, Prentice Hall Professional, Addison-Wesley Professional, Microsoft Press, Sams, Que, Peachpit Press, Adobe, Focal Press, Cisco Press, John Wiley & Sons, Syngress, Morgan Kaufmann, IBM Redbooks, Packt, Adobe Press, FT Press, Apress, Manning, New Riders, McGraw-Hill, Jones & Bartlett, and Course Technology, among others.

For more information, please visit *http://oreilly.com/safari*.

How to Contact Us

Please address comments and questions concerning this book to the publisher:

O'Reilly Media, Inc.
1005 Gravenstein Highway North
Sebastopol, CA 95472
800-998-9938 (in the United States or Canada)
707-829-0515 (international or local)
707-829-0104 (fax)

We have a web page for this book, where we list errata, examples, and any additional information. You can access this page at *http://bit.ly/learning-swift-3e*.

To comment or ask technical questions about this book, send email to *bookquestions@oreilly.com*.

For more information about our books, courses, conferences, and news, see our website at *http://www.oreilly.com*.

Find us on Facebook: *http://facebook.com/oreilly*

Follow us on Twitter: *http://twitter.com/oreillymedia*

Watch us on YouTube: *http://www.youtube.com/oreillymedia*

Acknowledgments

Jon thanks his mother, father, and the rest of his crazily extended family for their tremendous support.

Paris thanks his mother, without whom he wouldn't be doing anything nearly as interesting, let alone writing books.

Tim thanks his parents and family for putting up with his rather lackluster approach to life.

We'd all like to thank Rachel Roumeliotis, whose skill and advice were invaluable to completing the book. Likewise, all the O'Reilly Media staff we've interacted with over the course of writing the book have been the absolute gurus of their fields.

A huge thank you to Tony Gray and the Apple University Consortium (AUC) (*http://www.auc.edu.au*) for the monumental boost they gave us and others listed on this page. We wouldn't be writing this book if it weren't for them. And now you're writing books, too, Tony—sorry about that!

Thanks also to Neal Goldstein, who deserves full credit and/or blame for getting us into the whole book-writing racket.

We're thankful for the support of the goons at MacLab (who know who they are and continue to stand watch for Admiral Dolphin's inevitable apotheosis), as well as professor Christopher Lueg, Dr. Leonie Ellis, and the rest of the staff at the University of Tasmania for putting up with us. "Apologies" to Mark Pesce. He knows why.

Additional thanks to Mars G., Dave J., Rex S., Nic W., Andrew B., Jess L., and everyone else who inspires us and helps us. And very special thanks to Steve Jobs, without whom this book (and many others like it) would not have reason to exist.

Thanks also to our tech reviewers, with special thanks to Chris Devers and Nik Saers for their thoroughness and professionalism.

Finally, thank *you* very much for buying our book—we appreciate it! And if you have any feedback, please let us know. You can email us at *lab@secretlab.com.au* and find us on Twitter at @thesecretlab (*http://twitter.com/thesecretlab*).

PART I

Welcome to Swift

CHAPTER 1

Getting Started

Welcome to *Learning Swift*! In this book, we'll take you from knowing nothing about the Swift programming language to building a full-featured app for iOS 11. Along the way, we'll explore the libraries, frameworks, and features available to you as a developer of software for iPhones and iPads. We'll be covering practical solutions to common problems, as well as the details of the Swift language itself.

We'll begin with some important setup work that needs to be done before you can start using the developer tools. In particular, we'll take a look at the Apple Developer Program, and how to get your account set up so that you can build your app on a device.

 This book assumes that you've got access to two things: a Mac and an iOS device of some kind (that is, an iPhone or iPad).

The Mac is mandatory; without it, you can't run Xcode, which is the tool for writing your code, designing your interfaces, and building and running your code. Your Mac will need to be capable of running Xcode 9.2 or newer, which means that it needs to run macOS 10.12 or higher.

The iOS device is not absolutely mandatory, but you won't be able to follow all of the book without it, because the app that we're making in this book makes use of hardware features that aren't present in the iOS simulator. The device you use needs to be able to run iOS 11 or later.

Xcode

Xcode is the development environment used for all development work done on Apple platforms. As you work through this book, you'll be spending most of your time inside Xcode. With that in mind, we'll be spending the rest of this chapter getting a copy of Xcode, setting it up, and getting familiar with the interface.

Getting Xcode

Xcode is available via the App Store. To get a copy, search the App Store for Xcode or go to Apple's developer downloads page (*https://developer.apple.com/download/*), find Xcode, and click the Download button.

 If you prefer not to use the App Store, you can download it directly via Apple's Downloads for Apple Developers (*https://devel oper.apple.com/download/more/*) page. This page lists *all* versions of Xcode, so be sure to get the most recent one.

Once it's installed, go ahead and launch it. You'll be greeted by the welcome screen seen in Figure 1-1.

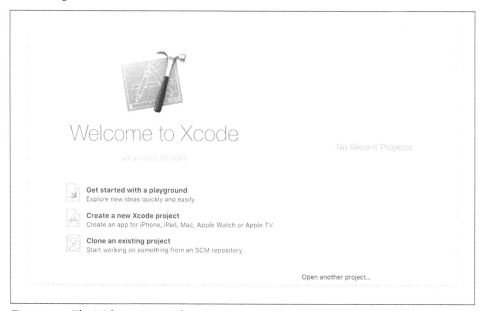

Figure 1-1. The Welcome to Xcode screen

Creating Your First Project

Since we want to take a tour of Xcode, we'll start by creating an empty project (we'll repeat this step in Chapter 4, when we start building this book's main app):

1. Click "Create a new Xcode project." The template chooser (seen in Figure 1-2) will appear.

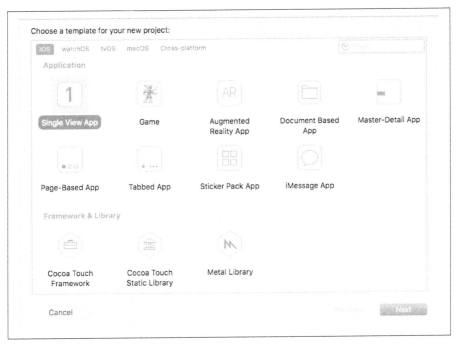

Figure 1-2. The Xcode template chooser

2. Select Single View App, and click Next.

   Xcode will ask you to provide some initial information describing the app. Because you'll just be using this app as a way to get used to Xcode, rather than actually work on the code itself, it doesn't matter much what you put in this field, though this will be different in Chapter 4.

3. When you're done, click Next, and choose where to save the project.

   You'll now be looking at Xcode's main interface, as seen in Figure 1-3.

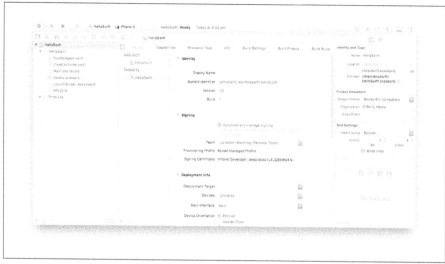

Figure 1-3. Xcode's main interface

Working with the Xcode Interface

Xcode shows your entire project in a single window, which is divided into a number of sections. You can open and close each section at will, depending on what you want to see.

Let's take a look at each of these sections and examine what they do.

The Editor

The Xcode editor is where you'll be spending most of your time. All source code editing, interface design, and project configuration takes place in this section of the application, which changes depending on which file you have open.

If you're editing source code, the editor is a text editor, with code completion, syntax highlighting, and all the usual features that developers have come to expect from an integrated development environment. If you're modifying a user interface, the editor becomes a visual editor, allowing you to drag around the components of your interface. Other kinds of files have their own specialized editors as well.

When you first create a project, the editor will start by showing the project settings, as seen in Figure 1-4.

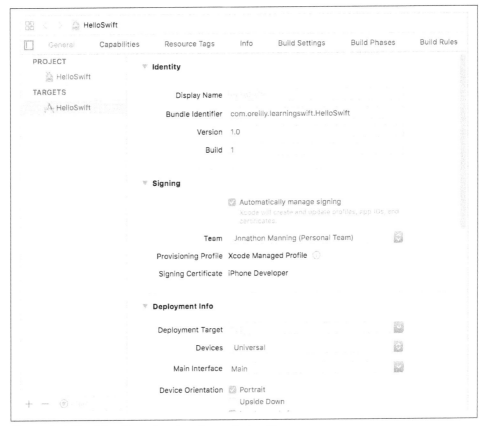

Figure 1-4. Xcode's editor, showing the project settings

The editor can also be split into a *main editor* and an *assistant editor* through the *editor selector*. The assistant shows files that are related to the file open in the main editor. It will continue to show files that have a relationship to whatever is open, even if you open different files.

For example, if you open an interface file and then open the assistant, the assistant will, by default, show related code for the interface you're editing. If you open another interface file, the assistant will show the code for the newly opened file.

At the top of the editor, you'll find the *jump bar*. The jump bar lets you quickly jump from the content that you're editing to another piece of related content, such as a file in the same folder. The jump bar is a fast way to navigate your project.

The Toolbar

The Xcode toolbar (Figure 1-5) acts as mission control for the entire interface. It's the only part of Xcode that doesn't significantly change as you develop your applications, and it serves as the place where you can control what your code is doing.

Figure 1-5. Xcode's toolbar

From left to right, after the macOS window controls, the toolbar features the following items:

Run button (Figure 1-6)
Clicking this button instructs Xcode to compile and run the application.

Depending on the kind of application you're running and your currently selected settings, this button will have different effects:

- If you're creating a Mac application, the new app will appear in the Dock and will run on your machine.
- If you're creating an iOS application, the new app will launch either in the iOS simulator or on a connected iOS device, such as an iPhone or iPad.

Additionally, if you click and hold this button, you can change it from Run to another action, such as Test, Profile, or Analyze. The Test action runs any unit tests that you have set up; the Profile action runs the Instruments application (we cover this much later, in Chapter 17); and the Analyze action checks your code and points out potential problems and bugs.

Figure 1-6. The run button

Stop button (Figure 1-7)
Clicking this button stops any task that Xcode is currently doing—if it's building your application it stops, and if your application is running in the debugger it quits it.

Figure 1-7. The stop button

Scheme selector (Figure 1-8)

> Schemes are what Xcode calls build configurations—that is, what's being built, how, and where it will run (i.e., on your computer or on a connected device).
>
> Projects can have multiple apps inside them. When you use the scheme selector, you choose which app, or *target*, to build.
>
> To select a target, click the lefthand side of the scheme selector.
>
> You can also choose where the application will run. If you are building a Mac application, you will almost always want to run the application on your Mac. If you're building an iOS application, however, you have the option of running the application on an iPhone simulator or an iPad simulator. (These are in fact the same application; it simply changes shape depending on the scheme that you've selected.) You can also choose to run the application on a connected iOS device if it has been set up for development. This is discussed in some more detail in "Running Your Code" on page 13.

Figure 1-8. The scheme selector

Status display (Figure 1-9)

> The status display shows what Xcode is doing—building your application, downloading documentation, installing an application on an iOS device, and so on.
>
> If there is more than one task in progress, a small button will appear on the lefthand side, which cycles through the current tasks when clicked.

Figure 1-9. The status display

Editor selector (Figure 1-10)

> The editor selector determines how the editor is laid out. You can choose to display either a single editor, the editor with the assistant, or the versions editor, which allows you to compare different versions of a file if you're using a revision control system like Git or Subversion.

Figure 1-10. The editor selector

We don't have anywhere near the space needed to talk about using version control in your projects in this book, but it's an important topic. We recommend Jon Loeliger and Matthew McCullough's *Version Control with Git*, 2nd Edition (O'Reilly).

View selector (Figure 1-11)

The view selector controls whether the navigator, debug, and utility panes appear on screen. If you're pressed for screen space or simply want less clutter, you can quickly summon and dismiss these parts of the screen by clicking each of the elements.

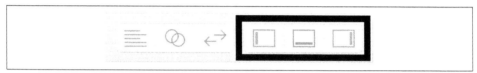

Figure 1-11. The view selector

The Navigator

The lefthand side of the Xcode window is the *navigator*, which presents information about your project (Figure 1-12).

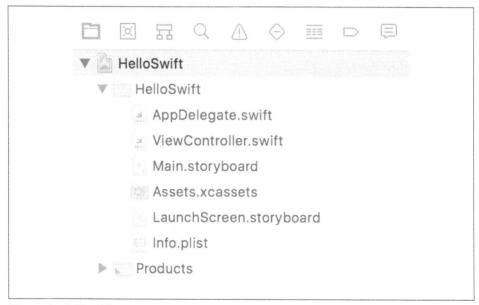

Figure 1-12. Xcode's navigator pane

The navigator is divided into eight tabs, from left to right:

Project navigator
> Lists all the files that make up your project. This is the most commonly used navigator, as it determines what is shown in the editor. Whatever is selected in the project navigator is opened in the editor.

Symbol navigator
> Lists all the classes and functions that exist in your project. If you're looking for a quick summary of a class or want to jump directly to a method in that class, the symbol navigator is a handy tool.

Search navigator
> Allows you to perform searches across your project if you're looking for specific text. (The shortcut is ⌘-Shift-F. Press ⌘-F to search the current open document.)

Issue navigator
> Lists all the problems that Xcode has noticed in your code. This includes warnings, compilation errors, and issues that the built-in code analyzer has spotted.

Test navigator
> Shows all the unit tests associated with your project. Unit tests used to be an optional component of Xcode but are now built into Xcode directly. Unit tests are discussed later, in "Testing the SelfieStore" on page 130.

Debug navigator
> Activated when you're debugging a program; allows you to examine the state of the various threads that make up your program.

Breakpoint navigator
> Lists all of the breakpoints that you've set for use while debugging.

Report navigator
> Lists all the activity that Xcode has done with your project (such as building, debugging, and analyzing). You can go back and view previous build reports from earlier in your Xcode session, too.

Utilities

The utilities pane (Figure 1-13) shows additional information related to what you're doing in the editor. If you're editing a Swift source file, for example, the utilities pane allows you to view and modify settings for that file.

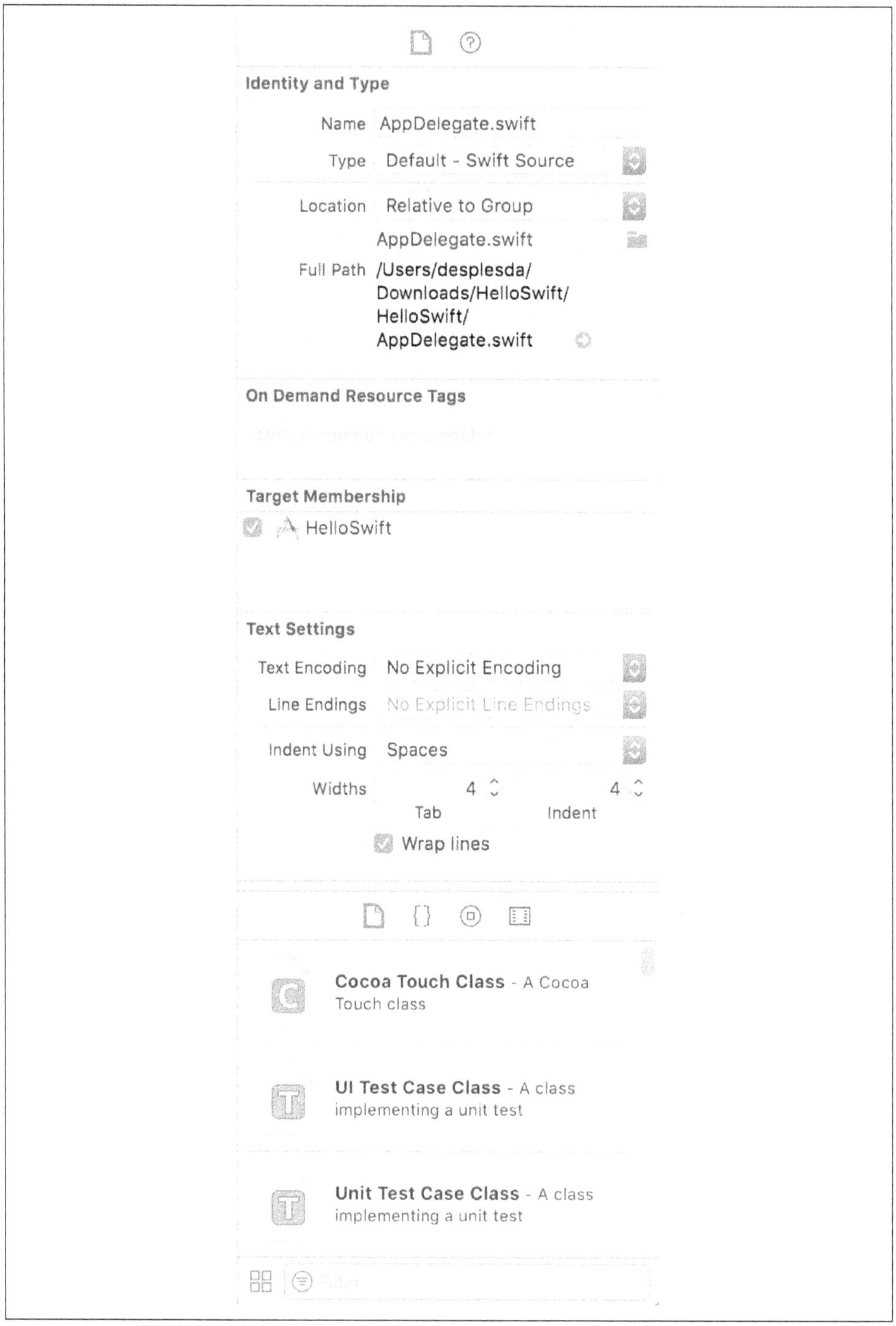

Figure 1-13. The utilities pane, showing information for a source file

The utilities pane is split into two sections: the *inspector*, which shows extra details and settings for the selected item; and the *library*, which is a collection of items that you can add to your project. The inspector and the library are most heavily used when you're building user interfaces; however, the library also contains a number of useful items, such as file templates and code snippets, which you can drag and drop into place.

The Debug Area

The debug area (Figure 1-14) shows information reported by the debugger when the program is running. Whenever you want to see what the application is reporting while running, you can view it in the debug area. By default the debug area is not shown unless there is a program running.

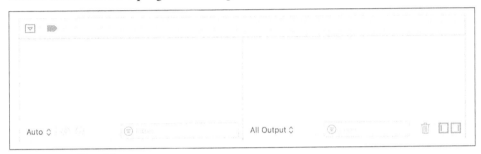

Figure 1-14. The debug area

The area is split into two sections: the lefthand side shows the values of local variables when the application is paused; the righthand side shows the ongoing log from the debugger, which includes any logging that comes from the debugged application.

You can show or hide the debug area by clicking the middle button of the Xcode toolbar's view selector, at the top right of the window (see Figure 1-15).

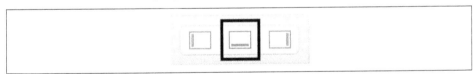

Figure 1-15. The central button in the view selector, which hides and shows the debug area

Running Your Code

When you're building an iOS app, you're writing code that isn't intended to run on the computer that you're developing it on. Instead, your code is designed to run on iOS, which means that you have two options for testing your code: running it on the iOS simulator, or running it on a real device.

The iOS Simulator

We'll start with the iOS simulator, since it doesn't require any setup.

Xcode comes with a number of simulators, and each one is designed to mimic the properties of a current or recent iPhone or iPad.

To build your app for the simulator, open the scheme selector and choose a simulator from the list (seen in Figure 1-16). Click the Build button, or press Command-R, to build your app; when it's done, the app will launch in the simulator.

Figure 1-16. The list of simulators built into Xcode 9.2

The simulator can be quite different to a real device, in a few key ways. The simulator is not an emulator; when you build and run code that runs on the simulator, you're actually running a version of your code that's built for the Intel chip that runs your Mac, and not for the ARM chip that runs iOS devices.

This means that the processing performance of an app in the simulator can be quite different to one running on the device. Additionally, the simulator frequently has much more memory available. If your app runs fine in the simulator, that's not a guarantee of great performance on a real device.

Finally, the simulator lacks several hardware features that a real device has. For example, the simulator doesn't have a camera, which is something that's pretty important for the app we'll be building in the rest of this book.

Running on a Device

The scheme selector also allows you to select a connected iOS device to build and run your app on. Running on a real device is almost as easy as running in the simulator, with one catch—code that runs on a device must be *signed* with a developer certificate.

A developer certificate identifies the person or company who wrote the code. iOS devices will only run code that's been signed using a certificate that itself has been signed by Apple.

Xcode will automatically generate a certificate for you when you sign in with the Apple ID you want to use for development. To do this, follow these steps:

1. Open the Xcode menu, and choose Preferences.
2. Go to the Accounts tab, and click the + button.
3. Sign in to your account.

Once you've signed into an account, you need to associate your app with a *team*. Teams are how Xcode organizes developers and their certificates; if you're an individual developer, your team will contain just yourself.

To set this up, follow these steps:

1. Select the project at the top of the project navigator. (It's the item at the very top, with a blue document icon.)
2. In the Signing section of the main editor, select a team from the Team drop-down menu.

Xcode will do some work to set up code signing, and then you'll be ready to start running your app on your device.

When you associate a project with a team, Xcode will automatically generate a certificate for you, if you don't already have one, as well as a *provisioning profile*—a file that links the app to your certificate. In addition to letting Xcode manage this for you, you can also manually manage it through the Apple developer website (*https://developer.apple.com/account/ios/certificate/*). We'll be discussing code signing in more detail in "Code Signing with match" on page 329.

To build and run your app, follow these steps:

1. Ensure that your device is connected to your Mac.
2. Select your device from the scheme selector, and click the Run button (or press Command-R).

Distributing Your Apps

Running code on your own devices is free, and doesn't require you to sign up for anything besides an Apple ID, which is something you likely have already from when you set up your iPhone or Mac.

However, if you want to distribute your app to others, such as via Apple's TestFlight or the App Store, you'll need to enroll in the Apple Developer Program (*https://developer.apple.com/programs/*). At the time of writing, this costs $99 per year and grants you access to tools like TestFlight, which allows you to distribute beta versions of your app to testers, and iTunes Connect, which is the control panel that allows you to submit apps to the App Store.

 You don't need to be enrolled in the Apple Developer Program in order to follow along with building the example app in this book, but you will need to be in order to get the most out of Chapter 19 and Chapter 20.

The Interface Builder

In addition to writing code, Xcode also serves as the app where you'll design the interfaces for your apps. Since interface design is as important to iOS apps as the code that powers them, we'll spend some time getting used to the interface builder.

To bring up the interface builder, you'll need to select a storyboard file from the project navigator. Select the *Main.storyboard* file now. Xcode will show the interface builder, as seen in Figure 1-17.

Figure 1-17. The interface builder

There are a few important features of the interface builder to know about:

- On the lefthand side of the editor, you'll find the *outline*. The outline contains a list of all objects in the document, and also shows their structure.
- The righthand side of the Xcode window will adjust to show properties specific to the objects in the interface. In addition, the *library* (at the bottom of the utilities pane) contains the list of UI elements that you'll use to build your interface; you can access this list by clicking the Object Library button, which is the circular icon that's second from the right in the selector bar at the top of the library pane (Figure 1-18).

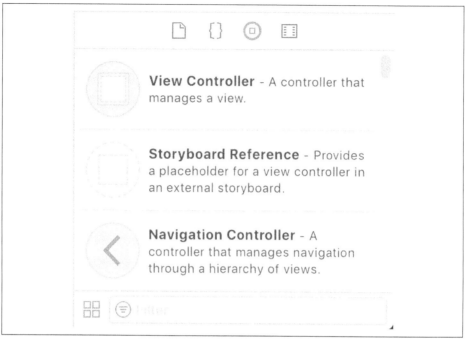

Figure 1-18. The object library

Interfaces in iOS

In iOS, everything that's visible is called a *view*. That is, anything that's on the screen and viewable or interactable with by the user, including buttons, labels, and text fields, is a view.

Views can also be embedded inside other views. This fact underlies the fundamental design philosophy of iOS applications, since each "screen" of content that you're looking at on a device is a view that contains other views.

This top-level view is managed by an object called a *view controller*; to make a screen of content, you create a subclass of UIViewController, which overrides certain functions that are called during the lifecycle of a screen of content, and include methods that are specific to the functionality of the screen you're building. Additionally, you create and set up the interface for the view controller in the interface builder, and link that interface to the name of the class that you've added.

Over the course of this book, we'll be spending significant amounts of time jumping in and out of the interface builder, so it's useful to have this fundamental understanding of how interfaces in iOS apps work.

Conclusion

In this chapter, we've set up and reviewed the tools you'll be using to build your apps. In the next chapter, we'll start looking at the Swift programming language itself.

The Swift Programming Language

The Swift programming language was first introduced in June 2014 at Apple's World-wide Developers Conference (WWDC). Swift was a surprise to everyone: Apple had managed to develop an entire language (as well as all of the supporting libraries, developer tools, and documentation) and make it work seamlessly with the existing Objective-C language. And on top of that, it was a really good "1.0" language.

Swift was open sourced on December 3, 2015 and is now as much a community-run project as it is run by Apple. We can expect Swift to evolve over time, in line with the developments in the Swift Open Source project (*https://swift.org*).

 Xcode supports having multiple versions of the Swift language installed. You might have a different version of the language if, for example, you've downloaded a copy of Swift from the open source project. For information on how to get a copy and use it in Xcode, go to the Swift project's download page (*https://swift.org/download/*).

Swift 3.0 was released in September 2016. This was a very big deal in the Swift community, and the new version included numerous changes to the language as well as to the standard library. At the time of writing, we're now up to Swift 4.0, released in September 2017. Compared to switching from Swift to Swift 3.0, which had huge amounts of code-breaking changes, moving from Swift 3 to Swift 4.0 is relatively painless, with most of the changes relating to programming quality of life and performance.

Swift draws upon an extensive history of language design and has a number of very cool design features that make developing software easier, simpler, and safer. We'll begin this chapter with a high-level overview of what Swift aims to do, and how it sets about doing it, before we dive into the details of the language.

 As Swift develops, it's likely that some of the syntax that we use in this book will become out of date (as is true for any programming book). We'll keep the book's page on our website (*https://www.secretlab.com.au/books/learning-swift*) up to date with a changelog for the latest Swift for as long as we're able.

Everything we cover in this book will be using Swift version 4.0.

The Swift Language

The Swift programming language has the following goals:

Safety
Swift is designed to be a safe language. Many of the pitfalls of C, such as accidentally working with null pointers, are much harder to encounter. Swift is very strongly typed, and objects aren't allowed to be null except under very specific circumstances.

Modernity
Swift contains a large number of modern language features designed to make it easy to express the logic of your code. These include pattern-matching `switch` statements (see "Switches" on page 37), closures (see "Closures" on page 58), and the concept of all values being objects to which you can attach properties and functions (see "Extensions" on page 72).

Power
Swift has access to the entire Objective-C runtime and is seamlessly bridged to Objective-C's classes as well as its own standard library. This means that you can use Swift right away to write full iOS and macOS apps—you don't need to wait for anyone to port any features from Objective-C to Swift. And if you've never used Objective-C, then you don't need to worry about Objective-C! You can do everything you need to develop for Apple platforms using Swift.

So, what does Swift look like?

Here's an example:

```
func sumNumbers(numbers: Int...) -> Int { ❶
    var total = 0 ❷
    for number in numbers { ❸
        total += number ❹
    }
    return total ❺
```

```
}
let sum = sumNumbers(2,3,4,5) ❻
print(sum) ❼
```

This code snippet does the following things:

❶ First, a function called `sumNumbers` is defined. This function takes one or more `Int` values, which are integers (whole numbers), and returns a single `Int`. The `Int...` denotes that the function takes a variable number of `Int` values; you can access these values through the `numbers` variable, which is an array.

❷ Inside the function, the variable `total` is declared. Note that the type isn't explicitly given; the compiler knows that it stores an `Int` because it's being set to the integer value of 0.

❸ Next, a `for-in` loop starts up, which loops over every number that was sent to the method. Notice again that the type of the `number` variable isn't defined—the compiler infers that, given that `numbers` is an array of `Int` values, `number` should itself be an `Int`.

❹ The value of `number` is added to `total`.

❺ When the loop is complete, `total` is returned.

❻ The function `sumNumbers` is called with a collection of integers, and the result is stored in the new variable `sum`. This variable is *constant*: by defining it with the `let` keyword, we tell the compiler that its value never changes. Attempting to change the value of a constant variable is an error.

❼ Finally, we display the value using the `print` function, which prints values out to the console.

There are a few interesting things to note here:

- You usually don't need to define the type of variables. The compiler will do that for you, based on what values you're using.

- Even though the `sumNumbers` function takes a variable number of parameters, there's no weird syntax to deal with it (if you're a C or C++ programmer, you might remember struggling with `va_start` and friends).

- Variables that are declared with the `let` keyword are constants. The language is designed so that any variable that can be a constant should be one to prevent accidental changes later. Importantly, constants in Swift don't have to be known at compile time. Instead, you can think of them as variables that are set only once.

Swift 3 Versus 4

The transition from 3 to 4 is a much smoother and less source code–breaking change than moving from 1 to 2 or 2 to 3, both of which required significant rewrites of code. If you already know Swift 3 and want to quickly get up to speed with 4.0, here's a quick rundown of the main changes:

- Strings have been overhauled to work in a similar but much higher-performance fashion. The new `substring` functionality provides a new way to interface with parts of a string without causing the huge performance hits of the past.
- Collections have been improved. Subscripts are now allowed to be generic and ranges can be one-sided, allowing for faster and easier traversal of collections. There have also been various other quality-of-life changes to collections, including default values in dictionaries.
- There is now support for protocol-based, type-safe serialization and deserialization of classes, structs, and enumerations.
- Various other changes have been made including improvements to the package manager. For a full list, see the Swift 4.0 release page (*https://swift.org/blog/swift-4-0-released/*).

If you have a Swift 3 codebase and are not quite ready to move to Swift 4, you can use the version 3.2 released along with Swift 4.0—although you really ought to be moving to Swift 4 as soon as possible.

Playgrounds and Swift

The easiest way to learn Swift is to use a *playground*. Playgrounds are environments that let you write Swift code and see its results instantly (or pretty close to instantly). You don't need to go to all the effort of setting up an entire project, compiling the code, and running the resulting output just to quickly test something. This means if you want to play around with the language, a function, a class, or even a piece of a larger project, you don't need to make it a part of something much bigger. Playgrounds are designed for exactly this sort of quick messing about and testing.

 Apple recently released Swift Playgrounds for the iPad, so now you can play around with Swift without even needing to fire up your Mac.

The remainder of this chapter (but not the remainder of the book!) is written assuming that the code is being written in a playground. You should get used to working in one if you want to follow along! Playgrounds are really useful, and we strongly recommend you use them when experimenting with and learning Swift.

 It's really useful to have quick access to a playground when you are learning, and even later when developing in Swift. We recommend dragging a playground file (from wherever you saved it in the Finder) into your Dock. That way, you can use it to test Swift code quickly and easily from anywhere in your system.

To start using a playground, you can create one from the "Welcome to Xcode" window that appears when Xcode launches (see Figure 1-1) or by choosing File → New → New Playground from the main menu. For this part we will be working with a blank iOS playground (Figure 2-1).

Figure 2-1. Creating a blank iOS playground

The difference between iOS and macOS playgrounds is mostly around the libraries they have access to. For the purposes of these next few chapters, there's not a huge distinction between the two, but if you were making a playground that specifically tested some iOS code you'd need to create an iOS playground (and the same for macOS applications).

When you first create a playground you will see something that looks like Figure 2-2. On the lefthand side of the window you can type Swift code. On the right side you'll see the results of each line of code that you write. So, let's break down our playground and look at Swift at the same time.

```
//: Playground - noun: a place where people can play

import UIKit

var str = "Hello, playground"                    "Hello, playground"
```

Figure 2-2. Sample blank iOS playground

Comments

The first line in our playground is a comment. Comments in Swift are nonexecutable text. You can use comments as notes, explanations, or reminders to yourself or someone else who will be reading your code. We use comments often in sample code in this book (as you should be doing in your code); they are ignored by the compiler.

You can begin a single-line comment with two forward slashes (//) or open a multi-line comment using a forward slash and an asterisk (/*) and close it using an asterisk followed by a forward slash (*/). Multiline comments can be nested:

```
// this is a single-line comment

/* this is a multiple-
line comment
*/

/* this is a comment

/* this is a comment inside another comment */

still a comment! */
```

Playgrounds support rich text markup within comments that allows you to define headings, lists, and quotes and include images and links. As playgrounds are designed for teaching and exploration, the idea is that this formatting will allow you to explain the code more clearly than you could with simple text comments. Technically, our playground is already doing this; the opening line, `//: Playground - noun: a place where people can play`, is a rich text comment, albeit one without much rich text. To view it in rich text mode, in the menu bar go to Editor → Show Rendered Markup.

For nonplayground code, Xcode supports a subset of the markup for showing what Apple calls Quick Help, designed for explaining your variables and functions. You can write your own Quick Help comments using a triple-slash single-line comment. Quick Help comments can also be used in your playgrounds.

As this is not really a core part of learning Swift we won't be going into more detail about it, but if you are curious it is worth checking out Apple's Markup Formatting Reference (*https://apple.co/2Cp7hRk*).

Imports

The next line is an `import` statement. This is how Swift is able to make use of libraries and external code other than what you have written. Here we are asking the playground to import the UIKit library, which is the standard iOS library; it includes all of the Swift foundational components, such as formatters and timers, as well as the entire iOS UI library, such as buttons and switches. We will talk more about importing and libraries in "Swift Package Manager" on page 101.

Variables

You define a variable in Swift using either the `let` or the `var` keyword. In our playground there is already one variable defined:

```
var str = "Hello, playground"
```

This is a new variable called `str` that has the string value `"Hello, playground"`. We can easily create new variables and constant variables of different types:

```
var myVariable = 123
let myConstantVariable = 123
```

When you define a variable with the `var` keyword, you are allowed to change its value. If you define it with the `let` keyword, it is never allowed to change. This is enforced by the compiler. Swift encourages you to use constants as much as possible, because they are safer—if you know a value can never change, it can't cause a bug by changing without you knowing about it, and the compiler can do all sorts of tricky optimizations with a constant that it can't do with a mutable variable.

```
myVariable += 5
str = "Hello there"
// this is an error
// myConstantVariable = 2
```

Swift is a statically typed language, and a very strongly typed one at that. Once a variable has a type, it cannot be changed—but so far we haven't been writing down any type information. Instead, we've been letting the compiler work out what it should be. This means our variables have been *implicitly typed*. You can also tell the compiler exactly what type you want the variable to be, making it *explicitly typed*:

```
let explicitInt : Int = 5
```

This is especially useful when you know later on you need the variable to be of a type that differs from its initial type, such as for integers and doubles:

```
var explicitDouble : Double = 5
explicitDouble + 0.3
```

In our code we put a space between the variable name, the colon, and the type. This is purely a stylistic choice. In your own code you omit the space before the colon if you prefer.

If we were to use the implicit type here `explicitDouble` would be an `Int` and the call to add `0.3` to it would fail, as integers can't be added to doubles. Most of the time when writing Swift the implicit typing is good enough, though, and we don't need to bother explicitly typing variables.

 The Swift type inference system is extremely powerful and almost always will get you what you want. There will be times, however, when you are aren't sure exactly what is going on with your implicitly typed variables. Luckily, Xcode has a handy tool to give you more information about a variable. If you hold down the Option key and click a variable a small dialog box will appear that will show you the full declaration, including what Swift has determined the type to be and where in the project it was declared. If the variable was documented using the Quick Help system that description will also appear.

Explicitly typed variables are allowed to initially have no value, but you need to assign a value to them before you try to access them:

```
var someVariable : Int
// this is an error
// someVariable += 2

// this works
someVariable = 0
someVariable += 2
```

In other words, if you create a variable with no value, the only thing you can do with it is give it a value. After that, you can use it as normal. This doesn't sound hugely useful, and in a playground it isn't really, but later on when creating your own custom classes in Swift it can be useful to create a variable without a default value that will be given one when the class is initialized.

Unlike many languages, Swift doesn't require you to put a semicolon or other delimiter character at the end of each line to indicate they have ended. If you are missing them you can include them if you want, and that's totally okay.

The exception to the rule of not needing to use semicolons is when you want to put multiple statements on a single line. In those cases you separate each statement with a semicolon:

```
var exampleInteger = 5; print(exampleInteger)
```

This isn't exactly best practice, though, and should be done sparingly.

You can also break up your code over multiple lines without problem, like this:

```
var anotherExampleInt
    = 7
```

We will talk more about types in detail in "Types" on page 39.

Operators

To work with the contents of variables, you use *operators*, some of which we've already been using in the preceding code. There are a wide variety of operators built into Swift, the most common of which are the arithmetic operators, such as addition or division:

```
1 + 7 // 8
6 - 4 // 2
8 / 2 // 4
3 * 5 // 15
```

In almost all cases operators can only be used with two values of the same type. If you try to divide a number by a string, for example, you'll get an error.

In addition to the arithmetic operators, you'll also be frequently working with *equality* operators. These check to see if two values are the same:

```
2 == 2      // true
2 != 2      // false
"yes" == "no" // false
"yes" != "no" // true
```

Related to equality operators are the *comparison* operators. These compare how similar two variables are to one another:

```
5 < 7  // true
1 > 4  // false
2 <= 1 // false
3 >= 3 // true
```

The final common operator you will encounter in Swift is the . operator, which lets you access properties and methods of your variables:

```
true.description  // "true"
4.advanced(by: 3) // 7
```

 We'll be covering methods and properties in more detail in Chapter 3.

Swift supports a whole bunch of other operators in addition to these, such as bitwise operators and logical operators, and you can define your own operators if you wish. However, the ones presented here are the most common ones you'll encounter and the ones you need to know about to continue moving ahead with learning Swift.

Collections

Swift has three main collection types that you will be using quite a lot in your code: arrays, tuples, and dictionaries. The interesting quirk about collections in Swift is that they themselves are also types, so an array of integers is a different type from an array of strings, or an int itself.

Arrays

Arrays are contiguous ordered lists of values. As arrays are common, it is very easy in Swift to quickly create an array using square brackets ([ ]):

```
let intArray = [1,2,3,4,5]
```

This creates an array of ints—the Swift type inference system determines it to be an array of integers because that is the only type inside the array. If we want it to be explicitly typed, we can also do that:

```
let explicitIntArry : [Int] = [1,2,3,4,5]
```

 When you create an array by using a list of comma-separated values surrounded by square brackets, you are initializing it as an array literal. This is just shorthand for the full initializer; [42, 24] actually gets compiled to Array(arrayLiteral: 42, 24).

To get elements out of an array we use their index and the *subscript* operator, which uses the square brackets again, but requires an index:

```
intArray[2] // 3
```

Like in many programming languages, arrays in Swift start at position 0. That means in this example, where we asked for the int at index 2, we were actually after the third element in the array. If we attempt to access an element beyond the range of the array (so, from 0 to the length of the array – 1), Swift will throw an error:

```
// intArray[-1] // this will error if we try and run it
```

As our array here is immutable (defined with `let`), we are unable to add or remove any elements. If we want to modify an array we need to declare it as mutable first:

```
var mutableArray = [1,2,3,4,5]
```

Now we can add elements to and remove elements from this array, and we can do so in a variety of ways:

```
// can append elements to the end of the array
mutableArray.append(6) // [1, 2, 3, 4, 5, 6]
// can remove elements at a specific index
mutableArray.remove(at: 2) // returns 3, array now holds [1, 2, 4, 5, 6]
// can replace elements at a specific index
mutableArray[0] = 3 // returns 3, array now holds [3, 2, 4, 5, 6]
// can insert elements at a specific index
mutableArray.insert(3, at: 2) // array now holds [3, 2, 3, 4, 5, 6]
```

If you need a mutable array but are not able to give it default values, you can declare an empty array in preparation for later use:

```
var emptyArray = [Int]()
// this will create an empty Int array
emptyArray.append(0) // [0]
```

If you need to know how many elements are inside the array, you can use the count property:

```
// returns the number of elements in the array
intArray.count // 5
```

Tuples

A tuple is a simple collection of data. Tuples let you bundle any number of values of any type together into a single value. You create them by wrapping comma-separated values inside parentheses:

```
let fileNotFound = (404,"File Not Found")
```

Once you have a tuple, you can get values out of it by index:

```
fileNotFound.0 // 404
```

As with arrays, a tuple's indexes start at 0. In addition to using indexes to get the values out of a tuple, you can also apply labels to values inside tuples:

```
let serverError = (code:500, message:"Internal Server Error")

serverError.message // "Internal Server Error"
```

One of the main uses of a tuple is when you need to return multiple values from a function. This is also the primary reason to use a tuple given by Apple. Swift functions can only return a single value, but with a tuple you can wrap up as many values as necessary and return that.

 While a tuple can hold any number of values, in practice if you are making tuples with more than six elements you may want to rethink your approach. Tuples are designed for interconnected and related data, not to be placeholders for complex data.

Dictionaries

Dictionaries appear similar to arrays, but are quite different in functionality. A dictionary is a noncontiguous, unordered collection that is indexed by keys. This means that unlike with an array, you can't assume ordering of elements, but you do have a greater amount of flexibility in terms of what the keys are.

You create a dictionary in a manner very similar to an array, using the square bracket syntax again. Say you wanted to store information about the crew of a space station. You could use a dictionary like this:

```
var crew = ["Captain": "Benjamin Sisko",
            "First Officer": "Kira Nerys",
            "Constable": "Odo"]
```

Much like with an array, when you want to access its contents you use the subscript operator—but instead of an index, you pass in the key of the element you are after. For example, to get the "Captain" value from the crew variable, you do this:

```
crew["Captain"] // "Benjamin Sisko"
```

Assuming your dictionary is mutable, as the crew dictionary is, you can add new elements by giving them a key in the dictionary:

```
crew["Doctor"] = "Julian Bashir"
crew["Security Officer"] = "Michael Eddington"
```

And if you want to remove elements, this is also straightforward:

```
crew.removeValue(forKey: "Security Officer")
```

If you ask for a key that doesn't exist, instead of throwing an error like an array, a dictionary will return nil. Similarly, if you set an existing value to nil this has the same effect as removing that element from the dictionary:

```
crew["Science Officer"] = "Jadzia Dax"
crew["Science Officer"] = nil
crew["Science Officer"] // nil
```

nil is a special case in Swift that we will talk more about in "Types" on page 39, but for now you can think of it as "nothing."

The previous examples showed a dictionary that uses String values for both its keys and its values. However, it doesn't have to be set up this way—dictionaries can actually contain almost any values and be indexed by almost any key type. For example, you can make a dictionary use Int values for both keys and values:

```
let arrayDictionary = [0:1,
                       1:2,
                       2:3,
                       3:4,
                       4:5]
arrayDictionary[0] // 1
```

This is in effect a dictionary form of the first array we made earlier.

Both arrays and dictionaries can contain values of different types, but this forces Swift to assume they are collections of unknown types—and this has all sorts of consequences you as the programmer will have to deal with. We'll talk more about dealing with unknown types in "Types" on page 39, but as a general rule of thumb try to have all your collections hold values of a single type.

Control Flow

In every program you write you'll want control over what code gets executed and when. For this, we'll make use of if statements, loops, and so on. The syntax for control flow in Swift is very straightforward, and includes some handy additional features as well.

if statements in Swift are pretty much the same as in any other language, though in Swift there's no need to wrap the expression you're checking in parentheses:

```
if 1+2 == 3 {
    print("The math checks out")
}
// this will print "the math checks out", which is a relief
```

In Swift, the body of all `if` statements—as well as all loops—must be put between two braces ({ and }). In C, C++, Java, and Objective-C, you can omit these braces if you just want to have a single statement in your loop or `if` statement. However, this has led to bugs and security problems in these older languages caused by programmers forgetting to include braces when they're needed, so in Swift they are mandatory.

An `if` by itself is fine, but it is limited in functionality. That is why Swift also has support for `else if` and `else` branches as part of your `if` statements:

```
let ifVariable = 5

if ifVariable == 1 {
    print("it is one")
}
else if ifVariable <= 3 {
    print("it is less than or equal to three")
}
else if ifVariable == 4 {
    print("it is four")
}
else {
    print("it is something else")
}
// this will print "it is something else"
```

Loops

Loops are structures designed to repeat a task a number of times, and loops in Swift are no exception.

When you have a collection of items, such as an array, you can use a `for-in` loop to iterate over every item:

```
let loopArray = [1,2,3,4,5,6,7,8,9,10]
var sum = 0
for number in loopArray {
    sum += number
}
sum // 55
```

The `number` variable used in the loop is implicitly created. You don't need to define a variable elsewhere called `number` to make it work.

You can also use a `for-in` loop to iterate over a range of values. For example:

```
// resetting our counter to 0
sum = 0
for number in 1 ..< 10 {
    sum += number
}
sum // 45
```

Note the `..<` operator on the second line. This is a *range operator*, which Swift uses to describe a range of numbers from one value to another. There are actually two range operators: two dots and a left angle bracket (`..<`) and three dots and no angle bracket (`...`). The *half-range operator*, `<..`, means a range that starts at the first value and goes up to but does not include the last value. For example, the range `5..<9` contains the numbers 5, 6, 7, and 8. If you want to create a range that does include the last number, you instead use the *closed-range operator*, `...`. The range `5...9` contains the numbers 5, 6, 7, 8, and 9. You can use an inclusive range operator in `for-in` loops like so:

```
// resetting our counter to 0
sum = 0
for number in 1 ... 10 {
    sum += number
}
sum // 55
```

You can do a lot with the `for` loop and ranges, but sometimes you need a bit more control over how the loop iterates. This is where *stride* comes into play. The `stride` function allows you to precisely control how you iterate over a sequence. For example, say you wanted to iterate between 0 and 1, going up by 0.1 each time:

```
var strideSum : Double = 0
for number in stride(from: 0, to: 1, by: 0.1) {
    strideSum += number
}
strideSum // 4.5
```

This is the `stride(from: to: by:)` form, which is exclusive of the final number. There is also an inclusive form, `stride(from: through: by:)`:

```
// resetting our counter
strideSum = 0
for number in stride(from: 0, through: 1, by: 0.1) {
    strideSum += number
}
strideSum // 5.5
```

 Depending on your past experience, you might be used to `for` loops looking something more like `for (int i = 0; i <= 10; i++)`. This style of loops used to exist back in Swift 2 but was dropped along with the `++` and `--` operators when Swift 3 came out. Swift is a new language with new rules, and while it tries to stick to existing practices, if it is believed something doesn't work with how the language is designed (such as the old-style `for` loop) it is dropped.

A `while` loop lets you repeatedly run code while a certain condition remains true. For example:

```
var countDown = 5
while countDown > 0 {
    countDown -= 1
}
countDown // 0
```

while loops check to see if the condition at the start of the loop evaluates to true, and if it does, they run the code (and then return to the start). In addition to the regular while loop, the repeat-while loop runs the code at least once and then checks the condition.

Switches

A *switch* is a powerful way to run code depending on the value of a variable. Switches exist in other languages, but Swift kicks them into high gear. To run different code based on the value of an integer, you can use a switch statement like this:

```
let integerSwitch = 3
switch integerSwitch {
case 0:
    print("It's 0")
case 1:
    print("It's 1")
case 2:
    print("It's 2")
default:
    print("It's something else")
} // Prints "It's something else"
```

One of the interesting things about switches in Swift is that they have to be *exhaustive*. This means that the switch statement must cover all possible values. If you're switching using a Bool type, which can either be true or false, you must provide handlers for both values. If you don't, it's a compiler error. However, it's sometimes not possible to cover all cases. In the case of integers, for example, it would take you an awfully long time to write a case for all possible numbers, and you'd likely need an infinite number of monkeys and typewriters. In these cases, you provide a *default* case, which is shorthand for "every other possible value." This is what we did in the preceding switch. So, you either provide a case for all possible values, or you provide a default case.

Another neat little feature of switches in Swift is the ability to use ranges as your cases. This allows you to create code that runs when the value you're testing falls between certain ranges:

```
var someNumber = 15
switch someNumber {
case 0...10:
    print("Number is between 0 and 10")
case 11...20:
```

```
    print("Number is between 11 and 20")
case 21:
    print("Numer is 21!")
default:
    print("Number is something else")
}
// Prints "Number is between 11 and 20"
```

 If multiple cases in a switch statement overlap—for example, case 0...10 and case 5...15—then the first matching case will be used.

Depending on your programming experience, you might be wondering where the break statements in the switch cases have gone. This is something that is different about Swift compared to other languages: a case statement doesn't fall through by default. This means you don't need to add a break to the end of all your cases—but what if you do want your switch to fall through a case to those below? Swift has the fallthrough keyword for this very reason:

```
let fallthroughSwitch = 10
switch fallthroughSwitch {
case 0..<20:
    print("Number is between 0 and 20")
    fallthrough
case 0..<30:
    print("Number is between 0 and 30")
default:
    print("Number is something else")
}
// Prints "Number is between 0 and 20" and then "Number is between 0 and 30"
```

As we've hinted at already, switches in Swift aren't just for numbers. You can switch across all types in swift, with the only caveat being that you have to be exhaustive. For example, a switch statement for a string would look something like the following:

```
let greeting = "Hello"
switch greeting {
case "Hello":
    print("Oh hello there.")
case "Goodbye":
    print("Sorry to see you leave.")
default:
    print("Huh?")
}
// Prints "Oh hello there."
```

When used with tuples, switches really come into their own. This functionality is especially powerful as you can write cases that run when there are partial matches to the tuple's components:

```
let switchingTuple = ("Yes", 123)
switch switchingTuple {
case ("Yes", 123):
    print("Tuple contains 'Yes' and '123'")
case ("Yes", _):
    print("Tuple contains 'Yes' and something else")
case (let string, _):
    print("Tuple contains the string '\(string)' and something else")
}
// Prints "Tuple contains 'Yes' and '123'"
```

There are a few interesting things in here. The first is the underscore, which is basically saying, "I don't care." So, the second case is saying, "I want to match all tuples that have the string 'Yes', and I don't care about their number values." The next interesting point is the variable declaration inside the third `case` statement. This captures the value of the string component of the tuple inside a variable called `string`, and as before the underscore is ignoring the number component. This is essentially saying, "I want to match all tuples regardless of their string value and store that inside this new variable called `string`, and I don't care about the number component."

 We don't have a default case for our tuple switch because the last case in the switch will catch every possible tuple that hasn't already been matched. Often when writing a tuple switch you'll require a default case, but by using _ for the number component and capturing all strings in the `string` variable in the last case we've ensured nothing will be able to get past it.

Types

Out of the box the Swift standard library comes with a plethora of common and useful types for you to use in your programs. Some of these, such as integers and strings, we've already been using:

- `Int` represents whole numbers (e.g., 1).
- `Double` represents decimal numbers (e.g., 1.3).
- `String` represents a list of characters (e.g., "Hello world").
- `Bool` represents a Boolean state (e.g., true).

These aren't the only types that Swift includes—there are more advanced types, such as sets and enumerations, that we'll also look at here—but these are the ones you will run into most often.

 Int is mapped to a specific version of integer depending on the device your code is being run on. If you need to control exactly what type of integer is used, Swift also has types for that, such as Int64 or UInt8, which represent a 64-bit signed integer and an unsigned 8-bit integer, respectively. Most of the time you won't have to worry about it and Int will be fine, but it is worth remembering this for when you need them.

Working with Strings

Strings are more complex than numbers or Boolean values. In Swift, strings are sequences of Unicode characters. This means that they're able to store pretty much any character that has ever been a part of human communication, which is great news for making your app translatable to other languages.

Creating a string in Swift is easy, as we've already seen. You can create an empty string by creating a string literal with nothing in it:

```
let emptyString = ""
```

You can also create an empty string using the String type's initializer:

```
let anotherEmptyString = String()
```

 It's worth pointing out that because both of these variables were declared using the let keyword, they can never be anything other than an empty string.

Strings can be combined in a manner similar to numbers using the + and += operators:

```
var composingString = "Hello"
composingString += " world" // "Hello world"
```

And because of their full Unicode support, there is no issue with combining different character sets together:

```
composingString += "100" // "Hello world"
```

As a string is a collection of characters, you can iterate through one as if it were a collection:

```
for character in "hello"
{
    print(character)
}
// "h"
// "e"
// "l"
// "l"
// "o"
```

Or, to see how many characters make up the string:

```
composingString.count // 13
```

 While a string looks an awful lot like an array of characters, and in many languages this is what strings are, in Swift it is a bit more complex than that. The only reason strings have been able to be treated like arrays in the past is because of assumptions made about what a character is, which resulted in non-Latin alphabet languages having limited support on computers. Under the hood a string is a collection of Unicode extended grapheme clusters, which allows you to happily combine, among other things, emoji and Latin, Arabic, and kanji characters in a single string without issue. But this power comes at a cost. Unicode characters can take up anywhere from one to four bytes, and this means that you can't make assumptions about the size of a character in a string. The upshot of this is that you can't jump straight into a point in a string using a subscript operator such as `"hello"[0]`, as this won't work the way you expect it to. If you do need to jump into the guts of a string and grab out parts, Swift strings can use *substrings*, which handle this issue. Luckily, you should rarely need to do this; if you do it is worth checking out the Apple documentation on substrings (*https://developer.apple.com/documentation/swift/substring*), as well as the documentation for Strings (*https://developer.apple.com/docu mentation/swift/string*) as there is a lot more going on than may first be apparent.

To change the case of a string you use the `uppercased` and `lowercased` methods, which return modified versions of the original string:

```
"Café".uppercased() // "CAFÉ"
"Café".lowercased() // café
```

If you need to compare strings you can just use the == operator as you would with numbers:

```
let string1 : String = "Hello"
let string2 : String = "Hel" + "lo"
if string1 == string2 {
```

```
        print("The strings are equal")
    }
```

Because Swift strings are Unicode-aware, when comparing two strings Swift will take into consideration if the individual characters match up correctly. For example:

```
    let café = "Café"
    let cafe = "Cafe\u{301}"
    if cafe == café {
        print("The strings are equal")
    }
```

In this case Swift knows that the Unicode symbol \u{301} when placed next to an e is semantically the same as é and as such considers them equal.

 Depending on your background, you might be used to the == operator checking to see if two values are equal, or if two variables refer to the same location in memory. In Swift == checks if they have the same value. If you really do want to see if two variables refer to the same object, you use the === operator (note that it's three equals signs, instead of two).

Finally, Swift has functionality for searching strings, although more often you will only need to know if a string starts or ends with a particular character or characters. For this purpose Swift can check the suffix or prefix of a string:

```
    if "Hello".hasPrefix("H") {
        print("String begins with an H")
    }
    if "Hello".hasSuffix("llo") {
        print("String ends in llo")
    }
```

 Swift has a shorthand syntax for rapidly creating strings containing the values of other variables called *string interpolation*. Using string interpolation, you can quickly create strings with minimal fuss. You do it using the \() syntax inside a string:

```
        let name = "Fred"
        let age = 21
        let line = "My name is \(name). I am \(age) years old."
        // "My name is Fred. I am 21 years old."
```

Sets

A *set* lets you store a collection of unique values of the same type. Sets are unordered and can store anything from integers and strings to classes or structs. You can think of a set as a variant on an array, and you interface with them in a similar fashion.

You can create an empty set by using the Set type's initializer. When you do this, you specify the type of values that will be stored in the set:

```
var setOfStrings = Set<String>()
```

Alternatively, you can create a set with an array literal. If you do this, Swift will figure out what type to use based on the type of values in the array:

```
var fruitSet : Set = ["apple","orange","orange","banana"]
```

Objects in a set are unique. If you add the same object twice to a set, it's only included in the set once. For example, in the preceding code, we included the string "orange" twice in the array, bringing it to a total of four items. However, if we ask the set how many objects it contains, it will report only three:

```
fruitSet.count // 3
```

 To be stored in a set, a type must be hashable. All the provided types are hashable, but you can also make your own types hashable by making them conform to the Hashable protocol. We talk more about Protocols in "Protocols" on page 70.

You can modify a set in all the usual ways, including checking if it's empty and adding and removing items:

```
if fruitSet.isEmpty {
    print("My set is empty!")
}

// Add a new item to the set
fruitSet.insert("pear")
// Remove an item from the set
fruitSet.remove("apple")
// fruitSet now contains {"banana", "pear", "orange"}
```

If you need to get an element out of a set you can use its index to do so, but because of the unordered nature of a set you can't just dive straight in like you can in an array. You need to first get the index of the element you are after:

```
// getting the index of "pear"
let index = fruitSet.index(of: "pear")
// index is now an optional Set.Index type
fruitSet[index!] // "pear"
```

You can also iterate over a set just like you would with an array or dictionary, and most of the time this will be how you use sets:

```
for fruit in fruitSet {
    let fruitPlural = fruit + "s"
    print("You know what's tasty? \(fruitPlural.uppercased()).")
}
```

You might be wondering what the purpose of a set is, as it just seems like a slightly odd array that is trickier to use. But because of the interesting properties of sets, with all elements being both unique and unordered, there are numerous interesting operations you can rapidly perform using them. These include unions, intersections, joins, checking whether sets are sub- or supersets of other sets, and so on. All of these operations are highly performant on sets when compared to arrays (which are themselves already pretty fast). So if order doesn't matter and everything can be unique, it might be worth using a set rather than an array in your code.

Enumerations

Creating an enumeration is an easy way to group a collection of related or like values and work with them in a safe, clean way. An enumeration is a first-class type that is restricted to a defined list of possible values. Defining an enumeration is easy. Use the enum keyword, name the type, and place each possible case between the braces, using the keyword `case` to differentiate each one:

```
// enumeration of top-secret future iPads that definitely
// will never exist
enum FutureiPad {
    case iPadSuperPro
    case iPadTotallyPro
    case iPadLudicrous
}
```

Once you've got your enumeration, you can use it like any other variable in Swift:

```
var nextiPad = FutureiPad.iPadTotallyPro
```

You can also change it to a different value of the same type:

```
nextiPad = .iPadSuperPro
```

 Notice how we didn't fully specify the enumeration name? In Swift you can use the shorthand form of an enumeration to refer to it as we did here. The only time you can't do this is when Swift doesn't know what enumeration you are talking about—so, we couldn't have done our first declaration using the shorthand form, but all subsequent ones work fine.

Or you use a `switch` statement to match enumeration values:

```
switch nextiPad {
case .iPadSuperPro:
    print("Too big!")
case .iPadTotallyPro:
    print("Too small!")
case .iPadLudicrous:
```

```
        print("Just right!")
    } // prints "Too big!"
```

You might be familiar with enums (or enumerations) in other programming languages. They're much the same in Swift, with the exception that they don't automatically have a corresponding integer value. The members of an enumeration are values themselves, and are of the type of that enumeration. They can, of course, have a corresponding integer number. Because Swift does it this way, enumerations are safe and explicit.

 Enumerations are a type in Swift, not a wrapper around a value. By declaring a new enumeration you are literally creating a new type that can be used in your code.

Enumerations in Swift allow you to store *associated values*. The associated values can be any type, and each member of the enumeration can have a different set of values. For example, if you wanted to represent two types of weapon that a spaceship in a video game could have, you might do this:

```
enum BasicWeapon {
    case laser
    case missiles
}
```

Using associated values, you could also allow a laser's power level, or the range of missiles, to be specified:

```
enum AdvancedWeapon {
    case laser(powerLevel: Int)
    case missiles(range: Int)
}
```

To work with these associated values, you provide them when assigning to the variable:

```
let spaceLaser = AdvancedWeapon.laser(powerLevel: 5)
```

You can use the switch statement with associated values, which allows you to pattern-match on more specific values in your enumerations:

```
switch spaceLaser {
case .laser(powerLevel: 0...10 ):
    print("It's a laser with power from 0 to 10!")
case .laser:
    print("It's a laser!")
case .missiles(let range):
    print("It's a missile with range \(range)!")
}
// Prints "It's a laser with power from 0 to 10!"
```

Enumerations with associated values aren't so much containers for those values as they are a specialization of the enumeration's value. Don't think of Laser(powerLevel: 5) as "a laser, with the number 5 inside it"; instead, think of it as "a laser of power 5."

Your enumerations can also have default values, or *raw values*, as an alternative to associated values. All raw values must be of the same type and can be provided for each of the enumeration:

```
enum Response : String {
    case hello = "Hi"
    case goodbye = "See you next time"
    case thankYou = "No worries"
}
```

You can get the raw value back out like this:

```
let hello = Response.hello
hello.rawValue // "Hi"
```

You can also create an enum from a raw value, but be wary of using this as it can fail:

```
Response(rawValue: "Hi") // is an optional Response with .hello inside
```

Finally, enumerations with raw values can use implicit values, saving you the effort of having to type them out:

```
enum Nucleobase : String {
    case cytosine, guanine, adenine, thymine
}
Nucleobase.adenine.rawValue // "adenine"

// can also give an initial value
enum Element : Int {
    case hydrogen = 1, helium, lithium, beryllium, boron, carbon, nitrogen
}
Element.lithium.rawValue // 3
```

Type Safety and Conversion

As was mentioned earlier, Swift is a statically typed language with type inference. What this really means is that most of the time Swift will work out what type your variables should be based on the values inside of them (although you can explicitly set the type yourself). Regardless of how a variable's type was determined, once it's done you can't change it.

All variables in Swift must have a type, which is determined at compile time and can never be changed.

Being statically typed has some interesting consequences for when different types need to work together. From a practical perspective this means that it is unlikely that two different types can be combined with one another. For example, say you had two numbers of type `Int`. If you were to add them together, the result would be obvious:

```
let firstInt = 3
let secondInt = 5
firstInt + secondInt // 8
```

But let's say you wanted to add the `String` `"hello"` to the first integer. How would this work? Should the result be a new `String`, with the contents `"3hello"`? Should `"hello"` instead be somehow converted into an integer and those two added together? Should the integer be used to increment the string's characters each by three places, resulting in a new value of `"khoor"`? Should something else happen? As a language designer, no matter what approach you pick there will be some confusion as to how this is meant to work. Swift resolves this by limiting what types can interact. There is no obvious way that always makes sense for a `String` and an `Int` to be added, so it isn't possible.

The advantage to this is you get type safety—you don't have to worry about the result of adding a string to a number because it can't happen. This also helps simplify testing: there is no need to test what happens when you try and store `"hello"` into an `Int` variable, as it can never happen. Finally, there are also optimizations that the compiler can make when it knows the type of a variable will never change.

Some types are given some leeway around this. For example, while an `Int` can't hold a `Double`, the inverse is true, so you are allowed to add them together as long as the resulting type is also a `Double`:

```
15.2 + 3 // 18.2
```

Sometimes, however, you need to have different types interact. In these cases, you need to look at type conversion.

To convert a value from one type to another, they need to be compatible. This means that there has to be an obvious result of explicitly changing the value into the new type. In all cases the conversion is the same; you call the initializer of the type you want the value converted into, passing in the value you want converted. For example, to convert the string `"3"` to the integer 3:

```
let three = Int("3") // 3
```

There are caveats to this, though. When converting from a type with more information than the new one can handle, there will be a loss in precision. So, for example, while it might make sense in your mind for 41.999999 to be 42 as an integer, when converting this you will instead get 41:

```
let almostMeaningOfLife = String(Int(41.999999)) // "41"
```

You also have to be careful about what you are converting, because not all possible values are convertible. If for example you have the string "lorem ipsum", there is no way for Swift to know how to convert that into a number. If you try this, however, you will notice something interesting:

```
let number = Int("lorem ipsum") // nil
```

The outcome of this is nil and not a crash, as you might have expected. If you hold down Alt and click the number variable, you'll see something interesting in the Quick Help dialog: rather than let number: Int it instead says let number: Int?. If you did the same on the earlier example of three, even though it worked fine, you would see that it is also of type Int?.

So what's going on here? We've run into a feature of Swift that is less common in other programming languages, called *optionals*.

Optionals

So far everything we've been working with has had a value of some type, either determined by us typing it manually or as the result of an expression. But in the previous example, when we tried to convert a string into an integer, we got nil as the outcome.

It's often useful to have variables that can sometimes have no value. For example, you might have a variable that stores a number to display to the user, but you don't know what that number is yet. As we've seen already, however, Swift variables need to have a value. One solution might be to use the number zero to represent "no value"; indeed, many languages, including C, C++, Java, and Objective-C, do just this. However, this creates a problem: there is no way to distinguish between the value zero and no value at all. What if the value you want to show is actually zero?

To deal with this issue, Swift makes a very clear distinction between "no value" and all other values. "No value" is referred to as nil and is a different type from all others.

 If you're coming from Objective-C, you might remember that nil is actually defined as a void pointer to zero. This makes it technically a number, which means in Objective-C you can do things like this:

```
int i = (int)(nil) + 2; // i equals 2 because nil is zero
```

This isn't allowed in Swift because Int and nil are different types.

To get around the requirement in Swift that all variables must have values, if you want a variable to be allowed to sometimes be nil, you make it an *optional* variable. This is useful in situations where you don't know if something will occur (for example, when downloading an image from the internet, you do not know if you will get back a valid image file or gibberish). You define optional variables by using a question mark (?) as part of their type:

```
// Optional integer, allowed to be nil
var anOptionalInteger : Int? = nil
anOptionalInteger = 42
```

Only optional variables are allowed to be set to nil. If a variable isn't defined as optional, it's not allowed to be set to the nil value:

```
// Nonoptional (regular), NOT allowed to be nil
var aNonOptionalInteger = 42
//aNonOptionalInteger = nil
// ERROR: only optional values can be nil
```

 If you create an optional variable and don't assign it a value it will default to nil.

You can check to see if an optional variable has a value by using an if statement:

```
if anOptionalInteger != nil {
    print("It has a value!")
}
else {
    print("It has no value!")
}
```

When you have an optional variable, you can unwrap it to get at its value. You do this using the ! character. Note that if you unwrap an optional variable and it has no value, your program will throw a runtime error and crash:

```
// Optional types must be unwrapped using !
anOptionalInteger = 2
1 + anOptionalInteger! // 3
anOptionalInteger = nil
// 1 + anOptionalInteger!
// CRASH: anOptionalInteger = nil, can't use nil data
```

If you don't want to unwrap your optional variables every time you want to use them, you can declare a variable as an implicitly unwrapped optional, like this:

```
var implicitlyUnwrappedOptionalInteger : Int!
implicitlyUnwrappedOptionalInteger = 1
1 + implicitlyUnwrappedOptionalInteger // 2
```

Implicitly unwrapped optionals are regular optionals: they can either contain nil, or not. However, whenever you access their values, the compiler unwraps them. This lets you use their values directly, but it can be unsafe because when an optional is unwrapped and has no value, your program crashes.

 Implicitly unwrapped optionals let you get away with not explicitly unwrapping optionals when you use them, which can make you forget that they can sometimes be nil. Use them with caution.

You can use an if-let statement to check to see if an optional variable has a value, and if it does, assign that value to a constant (nonoptional) variable and then run some code. This can save you quite a few lines of code, while preserving the safety of first checking to see if an optional variable actually has a value to work with.

An if-let statement looks like this:

```
var conditionalString : String? = "a string"
if let theString = conditionalString {
    print("The string is '\(theString)'")
}
else {
    print("The string is nil")
}
// Prints "The string is 'a string'"
```

There are going to be plenty of times in your code where using an if-let or even bothering to check if something is nil or not is unnecessary for your purposes, but you still need some way to use your optional values. *Optional chaining* is an alternative to unwrapping your optional variables for these situations. You use the ? operator after an optional variable to use it as if it were not optional, but should a nil be encountered, the call (whatever it may be) will fail and return nil instead of crashing. Optional chaining looks like this:

```
var optionalArray : [Int]? = [1,2,3,4]
var count = optionalArray?.count
// count is an optional Int with 4
```

If you change the array to be nil and try again, this time count is nil, but unlike if you'd done this by unwrapping the value the program does not crash on encountering the nil:

```
optionalArray = nil
count = optionalArray?.count
// count is nil
```

As the name "optional chaining" implies, you can chain multiple optionals together and if any of them are nil the statement ends:

```
let optionalDict : [String : [Int]]? = ["array":[1,2,3,4]]
count = optionalDict?["array"]?.count
// count is an optional Int with 4
```

 The ? and ! symbols are used in a few different places throughout Swift in a similar fashion as to how they are used with optionals. Generally whenever you see a ? it means "I want to try this but fail gracefully," whereas the ! generally means "I'm aware this is dangerous but I know it will work."

Swift also has a *nil-coalescing operator* to let you supply a default value when a nil is encountered. For example, say you are looking for a particular value in a dictionary, and if it doesn't exist you instead provide a default value. You could do this using if statements:

```
var values = ["name":"fred"]
var personsAge = "unspecified"

if let unwrappedValue = values["age"] {
    personsAge = unwrappedValue
}

print("They are \(personsAge) years old")
// prints "They are unspecified years old"
```

This works but is a bit clunky for such a simple operation. You can make this shorter using the nil-coalescing operator:

```
personsAge = values["age"] ?? "unspecified"
print("They are \(personsAge) years old")
// prints "They are unspecified years old"
```

Not only does this reduce the amount of code required, but it also leaves a nonoptional variable as the result, which you can use as normal.

It is worth pointing out that there is another way of doing this. Swift dictionaries (but only dictionaries) support the concept of a *default* value, which is returned instead of nil if a key can't be found. So, the following code works exactly the same as the preceding version:

```
personsAge = values["age", default: "unspecified"]
print("They are \(personsAge) years old")
// prints "They are unspecified years old"
```

Why do we demonstrate the nil-coalescing operator using dictionaries, considering that they have a built-in way of handling this situation? We did it this way because it is the easiest way to quickly create nil values in a way that isn't highly contrived. default is the best way of handling this situation for dictionaries but doesn't work in any other situation, which is why the nil-coalescing operator exists!

Type Casting

Swift is strongly typed. This means that it relies upon objects being of the type it expects when passing arguments to functions. But sometimes you need to check the type of an instance, or treat it as a different type—and that's where type casting comes in.

Using the is and as operators, you can test for types as well as downcast—that is, treat an instance as one of its subclasses. (We'll discuss subclasses in "Inheritance" on page 69.) You can also use these operators to check whether a type conforms to a protocol (more on those in "Protocols" on page 70).

One of the most common reasons you need to perform casting and type checks is when you are dealing with variables of the Any type. Any is effectively a way of saying "I don't know what type this will be" and will most often be encountered in collections of mixed type. For example, here we have a dictionary of type [String:Any]:

```
let person : [String:Any] = ["name":"Jane","Age":26,"Wears glasses":true]
```

Notice that we explicitly declared the type. As mixed-type collections are often a bad idea, Swift requires that we explicitly type them to be sure that we are aware of what we are doing.

Because Any lets you use any type inside a variable, you can do all sorts of unusual things with it:

```
var anything : Any = "hello"
anything = 3
anything = false
anything = [1,2,3,4]
```

This is all perfectly valid Swift, but it's a terrible idea. In a type-safe language trying to get around the type safety *will* lead to mistakes being made and likely cause performance issues. Don't try and trick the type system in Swift; work with it.

You can use the is operator to check if an instance is of a certain class. For example:

```
let possibleString = person["name"]
if possibleString is String {
```

```
    print("\(possibleString!) is a string!")
} // prints "Jane is a string!"
```

The `as?` operator checks the type of a variable and returns an optional value of the specified type:

```
if let name = person["name"] {
    var maybeString = name as? String
    // maybeString is an optional String containing "Jane"

    var maybeInt = name as? Int
    // maybeInt is an optional Int containing nil
}
```

The `as!` operator works in the same way as the `as?` operator, except that it returns a nonoptional value of the specified type. If the value can't be converted to the desired type, your program crashes:

```
if let name = person["name"] {
    var maybeString = name as! String
    // maybeString is a String containing "Jane"
}
```

 The `as!` operator is for when you're absolutely sure that the value you're converting is the right type, and you don't want to work with optionals. Make sure you are certain before using it, or you'll end up crashing your program!

Functions and Closures

In Swift, you define *functions* to perform tasks with data. Functions let you organize your code into small, repeatable chunks, like so:

```
func sayHello() {
    print("Hello")
}
sayHello() // prints "Hello"
```

Functions can return a value to the code that calls them. When you define a function that returns a type, you must indicate the type of the data that it returns by using the arrow (`->`) symbol:

```
func usefulNumber() -> Int {
    return 123
}

let anUsefulNumber = usefulNumber() // 123
```

When the `usefulNumber` function is called, the code between the two braces (`{` and `}`) is run.

You can pass *parameters* to a function inside the parentheses, which it's able to use to do work. When you define parameters for a function, you must also define the type of those parameters:

```
func addNumbers(firstValue: Int, secondValue: Int) -> Int {
    return firstValue + secondValue
}
let result = addNumbers(firstValue: 1, secondValue: 2) // 3
```

A function can return a single value, as we've already seen, but it can also return multiple values, in the form of a tuple. In addition, you can attach names to the values in the tuple, making it easier to work with the returned value:

```
func processNumbers(firstValue: Int,
                    secondValue: Int) -> (doubled: Int, quadrupled: Int)
{
    return (firstValue * 2, secondValue * 4)
}
```

When you call a function that returns a tuple, you can access its value by index or by name (if it has them):

```
// Accessing by number:
processNumbers(firstValue: 2, secondValue: 4).1 // = 16
// Same thing but with names:
processNumbers(firstValue: 2, secondValue: 4).quadrupled // = 16
```

> While you don't have to attach names to your returned tuples, it is good practice to do so.

By default, all parameters after the first one must have a *label* associated with them, and the label is necessary in calling the function. You can see this in action in the preceding code sample: the second parameter has secondValue: before it. Swift includes this in order to make it easier to read the code; when parameters have labels, it's a lot easier to remember what each parameter is for. However, sometimes you don't need a label before parameter names, especially when it's very obvious what the parameters are for. In these cases, you can tell Swift to not require a label before the parameters by placing an underscore before their names:

```
func subtractNumbers(_ num1 : Int, _ num2 : Int) -> Int {
    return num1 - num2
}
subtractNumbers(5, 3) // 2
```

The underscore is used throughout Swift to represent the concept "I don't care what this is." It's an idea that appears in several other languages, such as Prolog.

By default, the label for the parameter is the same as the parameter's name. However, if you prefer to, you can provide a custom label for a parameter. To override the default label for a parameter, you put the label before the parameter's name, like so:

```
func add(firstNumber num1 : Int, toSecondNumber num2: Int) -> Int {
    return num1 + num2
}
add(firstNumber: 2, toSecondNumber: 3) // 5
```

You can also create functions whose parameters have default values. This means that you can call these functions and omit certain parameters. If you do, those parameters will use the values provided in the function's definition:

```
func multiplyNumbers2(firstNumber: Int, multiplier: Int = 2) -> Int {
    return firstNumber * multiplier;
}
// Parameters with default values can be omitted
multiplyNumbers2(firstNumber: 2) // 4
```

Sometimes, you'll want to use functions with a variable number of parameters. A parameter with a variable number of values is called a *variadic* parameter. In these cases, you want a function to handle any number of parameters, ranging from 0 to an unlimited number. To do this, use three dots (...) to indicate that a parameter has a variable number of values. Inside the body of the function, the variadic parameter becomes an array, which you can use like any other:

```
func sumNumbers(numbers: Int...) -> Int {
    // in this function, 'numbers' is an array of Ints
    var total = 0
    for number in numbers {
        total += number
    }
    return total
}
sumNumbers(numbers: 1,2,3,4,5,6,7,8,9,10) // 55
```

When using variable parameters, you can have as many nonvariadic parameters as you like. However, note that you can only have a single variadic parameter, and any parameter listed after a variadic parameter must have an external parameter name.

Normally, function parameters and return values are passed by value; you are given a copy of the parameters and their return values. However, if you define a parameter with the inout keyword, you can pass the parameter by reference and directly change the value that's stored in the variable. You can use this to swap two variables using a function, like so:

```
func swapValues(firstValue: inout Int, secondValue: inout Int) {
    (firstValue, secondValue) = (secondValue, firstValue)
}
var swap1 = 2
var swap2 = 3
swapValues(firstValue: &swap1, secondValue: &swap2)
swap1 // 3
swap2 // 2
```

When you pass in a variable as an inout parameter, you must preface it with an ampersand (&). This reminds you that its value is going to change when you call the function.

Using Functions as Variables

You can store functions in variables. To do this, you first declare a variable as capable of storing a function that takes certain parameters and returns a value. Once that's done, you can store any function that takes those types of parameters and returns the same type of value in the variable:

```
var numbersFunc: (Int, Int) -> Int
// numbersFunc can now store any function that takes two Ints and returns an Int
// Using the 'addNumbers' function from before
numbersFunc = addNumbers
numbersFunc(2, 3) // 5
```

Functions can also receive and use other functions as parameters. This means that you can combine functions:

```
func timesThree(number: Int) -> Int {
    return number * 3
}
func doSomethingTo(aNumber: Int, thingToDo: (Int)->Int) -> Int {
    // We've received some function as a parameter, which we refer to as
    // 'thingToDo' inside this function.
    // Call the function 'thingToDo' using 'aNumber', and return the result
    return thingToDo(aNumber)
}
// Give the 'timesThree' function to use as 'thingToDo'
doSomethingTo(aNumber: 4, thingToDo: timesThree) // 12
```

Functions can also return other functions. This means that you can use a function that creates a new function, which you can use in your code:

```
// This function takes an Int as a parameter. It returns a new function that
// takes an Int parameter and returns an Int.
func createAdder(numberToAdd: Int) -> (Int) -> Int {
    func adder(number: Int) -> Int {
```

```
        return number + numberToAdd
    }
    return adder

}
var addTwo = createAdder(numberToAdd: 2)
// addTwo is now a function that can be called
addTwo(2) // 4
```

A function can also "capture" a value and use it multiple times. This is a tricky concept, so we'll go into it in a bit of detail. Consider the following example code:

```
func createIncrementor(incrementAmount: Int) -> () -> Int { ❶
    var amount = 0 ❷
    func incrementor() -> Int { ❸
        amount += incrementAmount ❹
        return amount
    }
    return incrementor ❺

}
var incrementByTen = createIncrementor(incrementAmount: 10) ❻
incrementByTen() // 10 ❼
incrementByTen() // 20
var incrementByFifteen = createIncrementor(incrementAmount: 15) ❽
incrementByFifteen() // 15 ❾
```

This code snippet does the following things:

❶ The `createIncrementor` function takes an `Int` parameter and returns a function that takes no parameters and returns an `Int`.

❷ Inside the function, a variable called `amount` is created and set to 0.

❸ A new function is created inside the `createIncrementor` function, which takes no parameters and returns an `Int`.

❹ Inside this new function, the `amount` variable has the `incrementAmount` parameter added to it, and then returned. Notice that the `amount` variable is outside of this function.

❺ The `incrementor` function is then returned.

❻ The `createIncrementor` function can now be used to create a new incrementor function. In the first example, one is created with the `incremementAmount` parameter set to 10.

❼ Each time this function is called, it will return a value that's 10 higher than the last time it was called. The reason it's doing this is because the function that `createIncrementor` returned *captured* the variable `amount`; every time it's called, that variable goes up by `incrementAmount`.

❽ The `amount` variable is not shared between individual functions, however. When a new incrementor is created, it has its own separate `amount` variable.

❾ The second function increments the value by 15.

This feature of Swift allows you to create functions that act as *generators*, functions that return different values each time they're called.

Closures

Another feature of Swift is that of *closures*—small, anonymous chunks of code that you can use like functions. Closures are great for passing to other functions in order to tell them how they should carry out a certain task. To give you an example of how closures work, consider the built-in `sorted` function. This function takes an array and a closure, and uses that closure to determine how two individual elements of that array should be ordered (i.e., which one should go first in the array):

```
let jumbledArray = [2, 5, 98, 2, 13]
jumbledArray.sorted() // [2, 2, 5, 13,98]
```

To sort an array so that small numbers go before large numbers, you can provide a closure that describes how to do the sort, like this:

```
let numbers = [2,1,56,32,120,13]
var numbersSorted = numbers.sorted(by: {
    (n1: Int, n2: Int) -> Bool in return n2 > n1
})
// [1, 2, 13, 32, 56, 120]
```

Closures have a special keyword, `in`. The `in` keyword lets Swift know where to break up the closure from its definition and its implementation. So, in this example, the definition was `(n1: Int, n2: Int)->Bool`, and the implementation of that closure came after the `in` keyword: `return n2 > n1`.

 If you come from Objective-C land, closures are very similar to blocks, with the `in` keyword working in a similar fashion to the ^ syntax in blocks.

A closure, like a function, takes parameters. In the preceding example, the closure specifies the name and type of the parameters that it works with. However, you don't need to be quite so verbose—the compiler can infer the type of the parameters for you, much like it can with variables. Notice the lack of types in the parameters for the following closure:

```
let numbersSortedReverse = numbers.sorted(by: {n1, n2 in return n1 > n2})
//[120, 56, 32, 13, 2, 1]
```

You can make it even more terse if you don't especially care what names the parameters have. If you omit the parameter names, you can just refer to each parameter by number (the first parameter is called $0, the second is called $1, etc.). Additionally, if your closure only contains a single line of code, you can omit the return keyword:

```
var numbersSortedAgain = numbers.sorted(by: { $1 > $0
}) // [1, 2, 13, 32, 56, 120]
```

Finally, if a closure is the last parameter in a function call, you can put it outside the parentheses. This is purely something that improves readability and doesn't change how the closure works:

```
var numbersSortedReversedAgain = numbers.sorted { $0 > $1
} // [120, 56, 32, 13, 2, 1]
```

The line breaks in this code are optional, too. You could also do this:

```
var numbersSortedReversedOneMoreTime = numbers.sorted { $0 > $1 }
// [120, 56, 32, 13, 2, 1]
```

Just like functions, closures can be stored in variables. In that case, you can call them just like a function:

```
var comparator = {(a: Int, b:Int) in a < b}
comparator(1,2) // true
```

Convenience Features

Being a modern language, Swift has a lot of different convenience functionality built in. Two features of particular interest are the guard and defer keywords.

The defer Keyword

Sometimes you'll want to run some code, but at a later date. For example, if you're writing code that opens a file and makes some changes, you'll also need to ensure that the file is closed when you're done. This is important, and it's easy to forget when you start writing your method. The defer keyword lets you write code that will run at a later time, allowing you to write your teardown code next to your setup code. Specifically, code you put in a defer block will run when the current flow of execution leaves the current scope—that is, the current function, loop body, and so on:

```
func doSomeWork() {
    print("Getting started!")
```

```
    defer {
        print("All done!")
    }
    print("Getting to work!")
}
doSomeWork()
// Prints "Getting started!", "Getting to work!", and "All done!", in that order
```

In effect, the defer block of code is run in between the end of the final print statement, but before the closing brace. This is especially helpful in cases where you need
to clean up any temporary work you did and return a value, but need the temporary
work kept around to do the return. defer gives you that capability.

 defer is a resource management and code style technique, not a
means of implementing asynchronous code!

The guard Keyword

There are often cases where your code needs to check to see if a certain condition
holds. For example, if you're writing a method to withdraw money from a bank
account, you can't go ahead with the operation if the bank account's balance is too
low. The guard keyword lets you define a test that needs to pass; alternatively, if it
doesn't pass, a different block of code is run. This might sound very similar to the if
statement, but it has a twist: the block of code that runs if the test doesn't pass is
required to exit the current flow of execution. That is, if it's inside a function, it has to
return from that function; it's a compiler error if it doesn't. This guarantees that if the
condition doesn't hold, the code following the guard statement will not be executed:

```
func doAThing(){
    guard 2+2 == 4 else {
        print("The universe makes no sense")
        return
    }
    print("We can continue with our daily lives")
}
```

This is especially helpful when dealing with optional variables that have to exist for
the code to work; you can use a guard to unwrap them, making them available to the
rest of the function. You can do this with if-let as well, but by using guard you can
avoid a potential pyramid of doom, instead having a nice, clean level of indentation:

```
func doSomeStuff(importantVariable: Int?)
{
    guard let importantVariable = importantVariable else
    {
        // we need the variable to exist to continue
```

```
        return
    }
    print("doing our important work with \(importantVariable)")
}
doSomeStuff(importantVariable: 3) // works as expected
doSomeStuff(importantVariable: nil) // exits function on the guard statement
```

Making Your Code Swifty

After the release of Swift 3, the Swift community made some guidelines to follow
when designing, creating, and naming your code and APIs. The full guidelines can be
seen on the API Design Guidelines page (*https://swift.org/documentation/api-design-
guidelines/*) and are well worth checking out, but the cornerstone of it all is clarity.
Some general rules to remember are as follow:

- When writing a function, remember that you will only write it once but will use
  it many times, so keep the name as simple and unambiguous as possible. For
  example, the remove(at:) function on arrays removes an element at the index
  passed in. Using it, like in anArray.remove(at: 2), is clear and unambiguous,
  whereas if it were just anArray.remove(2) we wouldn't know if it was removing
  the element at index 2 or removing object 2 from the array.

- Where possible, make your functions read like an English sentence. For example,
  anArray.insert(x at: y) reads better than anArray.insert(x index: y).
  Additionally, when writing mutating and nonmutating functions, make the
  mutating functions sound like verbs and name the nonmutating forms with the
  "-ed" or "-ing" suffix (so, anArray.sorted() returns a sorted copy).

- Finally, avoid abbreviations, acronyms, and obscure terms. Unless they are well
  known in the domain you're writing for, they are just going make your code
  harder to understand later on.

Conclusion

In this chapter, we've looked at the basics of programming with Swift. In the next
chapter, we'll dive into some of the more advanced components of the language, such
as classes and structs, memory management, working with data, and error handling.
After that, we'll continue our exploration of Swift through the construction of an app.

CHAPTER 3

Object-Oriented Development in Swift

The previous chapter introduced the basic building blocks of programming in Swift. In this chapter, we're going to look at some of the more advanced features, such as classes and structs, memory management, working with files and external data, and error handling. We'll also touch on interoperating with Apple's older programming language, Objective-C.

Swift is a multiparadigm language, and can work with a variety of different programming language styles. This means it can be used as an *object-oriented* programming language, where you do the majority of your work by creating and manipulating *objects*—chunks of data and code that represent a thing that can perform some useful work or store some useful data.

Classes and Objects

In Swift, as in Objective-C, Java, and C++ (and many other languages), you define templates for your objects using *classes*. Classes in Swift look like this:

```
class Vehicle {

}
```

 Each programming language (and its associated libraries) has its own particular take on object orientation. The approach that Swift and Cocoa take is that using extensions and protocols is a better idea most of the time than subclassing.

Classes contain both *properties* and *methods*. Properties are variables that are part of a class, and methods are functions that are part of a class. The Vehicle class in the following example contains two properties: an optional `String` called `color`, and an `Int` called `maxSpeed`. Property declarations look the same as variable declarations do in other code:

```
var color: String?
var maxSpeed = 80
```

Methods in a class look the same as functions anywhere else, just inside the class definition. Code that's in a method can access the properties of a class by using the `self` keyword, which refers to the object that's currently running the code:

```
func description() -> String {
    return "A \(self.color ?? "uncolored") vehicle"
}
func travel() {
    print("Traveling at \(maxSpeed) kph")
}
```

You can omit the `self` keyword if it's obvious that the property is part of the current object. In the previous example, `description` uses the `self` keyword, while `travel` doesn't.

 In your own code you should try and be consistent with how you use `self`; using it only when necessary is fine, as is always using it. Consistency is important to make it easier for you in the future when you are rereading your code, and for others who might have to use your code when you aren't around to explain how it works.

When you've defined a class, you can create instances of the class (called objects) to work with. Instances have their own copies of the class's properties and functions.

For example, to define an instance of the `Vehicle` class, you define a variable and call the class's initializer. Once that's done, you can work with the class's functions and properties:

```
let redVehicle = Vehicle()
redVehicle.color = "Red"
redVehicle.maxSpeed = 90
redVehicle.travel() // prints "Traveling at 90 kph"
redVehicle.description() // = "A Red vehicle"
```

Initialization and Deinitialization

When you create an object in Swift, a special method known as its *initializer* is called. The initializer is the method that you use to set up the initial state of an object and is always named `init`.

Swift has two types of initializers, *convenience initializers* and *designated initializers*. A designated initializer sets up everything you need to use that object, often using default settings where necessary. A convenience initializer, as its name implies, makes setting up the instance more convenient by allowing for more information to be included in the initialization. A convenience initializer must call the designated initializer as part of its setup.

In addition to initializers, you can run code when removing an object, in a method called a *deinitializer*. This method, named `deinit`, runs when the retain count of an object drops to zero (see "Memory Management" on page 87) and is called right before the object is removed from memory. This is your object's final opportunity to do any necessary cleanup before it goes away forever:

```
class InitAndDeinitExample {
    // Designated (i.e., main) initializer
    init () {
        print("I've been created!")
    }
    // Convenience initializer, required to call the
    // designated initializer (above)
    convenience init (text: String) {
        self.init() // this is mandatory
        print("I was called with the convenience initializer!")
    }
    // Deinitializer
    deinit {
        print("I'm going away!")
    }

}

var example : InitAndDeinitExample?

// using the designated initializer
example = InitAndDeinitExample() // prints "I've been created!"
example = nil // prints "I'm going away"

// using the convenience initializer
example = InitAndDeinitExample(text: "Hello")
// prints "I've been created!" and then
//   "I was called with the convenience initializer"
```

An initializer can also return `nil`. This can be useful when your initializer isn't able to usefully construct an object. For example, the URL class has an initializer that takes a string and converts it into a URL; if the string isn't a valid URL, the initializer returns `nil`. We used this earlier when we were converting one type into another:

```
let three = Int("3") // 3
```

To create an initializer that can return `nil`—also known as a *failable initializer*—put a question mark after the `init` keyword, and `return nil` if the initializer decides that it can't successfully construct the object:

```
// This is a convenience initializer that can sometimes fail, returning nil.
// Note the ? after the word 'init'.
convenience init? (value: Int) {
    self.init()

    if value > 5 {
        // We can't initialize this object; return nil to indicate failure
        return nil
    }

}
```

When you use a failable initializer, it will always return an optional, even if the initialization succeeds:

```
var failableExample = InitAndDeinitExample(value: 6) // nil
```

Properties

Classes store their data in *properties*. Properties, as previously mentioned, are variables or constants that are attached to instances of classes. Properties that you've added to a class are usually accessed like this:

```
class Counter {
    var number: Int = 0
}
let myCounter = Counter()
myCounter.number = 2
```

The most basic type of properties are *stored properties*. These are what you have when the variable is a value stored in the object, such as the `maxSpeed` property on the `Vehicle` class from earlier. You don't have to give your stored properties a value when you declare them, but all nonoptional stored properties *must* have a value at the end of the designated initializer. This is mostly useful in the case where there is no sensible default value and the correct value for the property will come from the initializer:

```
class BiggerCounter {
    var number : Int
    var optionalNumber : Int?

    init(value: Int) {
        number = value
        // self.number now has a value
        // self.optionalNumber does not
    }
}
```

```
var anotherCounter = BiggerCounter(value:3)
anotherCounter.number // 3
```

Computed properties

In the previous examples, the properties are simple values stored in the object. However, you can do more with properties, including creating properties that use code to figure out their value. These are known as *computed properties*, and you can use them to provide a simpler interface to information stored in your classes.

For example, consider a class that represents a rectangle, which has both a width and a height property. It'd be useful to have an additional property that contains the area, but you don't want that to be a third stored property. Instead, you can use a computed property, which looks like a regular property from the outside, but on the inside is really a function that figures out the value when needed.

To define a computed property, you declare a variable in the same way as you do for a stored property, but add braces ({ and }) after it. Inside these braces, you provide a get section and a set section:

```
class Rectangle {
    var width: Double = 0.0
    var height: Double = 0.0

    var area : Double {
        // computed getter
        get {
            return width * height
        }

        // computed setter
        set {
            // Assume equal dimensions (i.e., a square)
            width = sqrt(newValue)
            height = sqrt(newValue)
        }
    }

}
```

When creating setters for your computed properties, you are given the new value passed into the setter as a constant called newValue.

In the previous example, we computed the area by multiplying the width and height. The property is also settable—if you set the area of the rectangle, the code assumes that you want to create a square and updates the width and height to the square root of the area.

Working with computed properties looks identical to working with stored properties:

```
let rect = Rectangle()
rect.width = 3.0
rect.height = 4.5
rect.area // 13.5
rect.area = 9 // width & height now both 3.0
```

It doesn't make sense for many computed properties to be writable, such as count on collections. In these cases you can just create a cut-down computed property for that situation:

```
var center : (x: Double, y: Double) {
    return (width / 2, height / 2)
}
```

Which you still interact with in the exact same way as other properties, except it can't be set:

```
rect.center // (x: 1.5, y: 15)
```

Observers

When working with properties, you often may want to run some code whenever a property changes. To support this, Swift lets you add *observers* to your properties. These are small chunks of code that can run just before or after a property's value changes. To create a property observer, add braces after your property (much like you do with computed properties) and include willSet and didSet blocks. These blocks each get passed a parameter—willSet, which is called before the property's value changes, is given the value that is about to be set, and didSet is given the old value:

```
class PropertyObserverExample {
    var number : Int = 0 {
        willSet(newNumber) {
            print("About to change to \(newNumber)")
        }
        didSet(oldNumber) {
            print("Just changed from \(oldNumber) to \(self.number)!")
        }
    }
}
```

Property observers don't change anything about how you actually work with the property—they just add further behavior before and after the property changes:

```
var observer = PropertyObserverExample()
observer.number = 4
// prints "About to change to 4", then "Just changed from 0 to 4!"
```

Lazy properties

You can also make a property *lazy*. A lazy property is one that doesn't get set up until the first time it's accessed. This lets you defer some of the more time-consuming work of setting up a class to when it's actually needed. To define a property as lazy, you put the lazy keyword in front of it. *Lazy loading* is very useful for properties that are not essential to the class's operation, or those that are very resource intensive; there is no point in setting them up until they are needed, especially if they are rarely going to be used!

You can see lazy properties in action in the following example. In this code, there are two properties, both of the same type, but one of them is lazy:

```
class SomeExpensiveClass {
    init(id : Int) {
        print("Expensive class \(id) created!")
    }
}

class LazyPropertyExample {
    var expensiveClass1 = SomeExpensiveClass(id: 1)
    // Note that we're actually constructing a class,
    // but it's labeled as lazy
    lazy var expensiveClass2 = SomeExpensiveClass(id: 2)

    init() {
        print("Example class created!")
    }
}

var lazyExample = LazyPropertyExample()
// prints "Expensive class 1 created", then "Example class created!"

lazyExample.expensiveClass1 // prints nothing, it's already created
lazyExample.expensiveClass2 // prints "Expensive class 2 created!"
```

In this example, when the lazyExample variable is created, it immediately creates the first instance of SomeExpensiveClass. However, the second instance, expensive Class2, isn't created until it's actually accessed by the code.

 Lazy properties can only be declared as mutable variables; you can't have a lazy let variable in your code.

Inheritance

When you define a class, you can have it *inherit* from another one. When a class inherits from another (called the *parent* class), it incorporates all its parent's functions and properties. In Swift, classes are allowed to have only a single parent class. This is the same as Objective-C but differs from C++, which allows classes to have multiple parents (known as *multiple inheritance*).

 Because of Swift's heavy use of extensions and protocols, the lack of multiple inheritance isn't really a huge loss—and it lets you avoid some of the traps that can occur in languages with multiple inheritance.

To create a class that inherits from another, you put the name of the class you're inheriting from after the name of the class you're creating, like so:

```
class Car : Vehicle {
    var engineType = "V8"

}
```

Classes that inherit from other classes can *override* functions in their parent class. This means that you can create subclasses that inherit most of the parent's functionality, but can specialize in certain areas. For example, the Car class contains an engine Type property; only Car instances will have this property.

To override a function, you redeclare it in your subclass and add the override keyword to let the compiler know that you aren't accidentally creating a method with the same name as one in the parent class.

In an overridden function, it's often very useful to call back to the parent class's version of that function. You can do this through the super keyword, which lets you get access to the superclass's functions:

```
// Inherited classes can override functions
override func description() -> String  {
    let description = super.description()
    return description + ", which is a car"
}
```

Protocols

A *protocol* can be thought of as a list of requirements for a class. When you define a protocol, you're creating a list of properties and methods that classes can declare that they have. Failing to implement the protocol correctly is a compiler error.

Protocols are used very heavily throughout Swift and the Cocoa libraries. A great deal of the functionality of the language is built up through conformance to various protocols, and one of the more common design patterns in the language and libraries, *delegation*, is implemented through protocols.

A protocol looks very much like a class, with the exception that you don't provide any actual code—you just define what kinds of properties and functions exist and how they can be accessed.

For example, if you wanted to create a protocol that describes any object that can blink on and off, you could use this:

```
protocol Blinkable {
    // This property must be at least gettable
    var isBlinking : Bool { get }

    // This property must be gettable and settable
    var blinkSpeed: Double { get set }

    // This function must exist, but what it does is up to the implementor
    func startBlinking(blinkSpeed: Double) -> Void
}
```

Once you have a protocol, you can create classes that *conform* to that protocol. When a class conforms to a protocol, it's effectively promising to the compiler that it implements all of the properties and methods listed in that protocol. It's allowed to have more stuff besides that, and it's also allowed to conform to multiple protocols.

To continue this example, you could create a specific class called `TrafficLight` that implements the `Blinkable` protocol. Remember, all a protocol does is specify *what* a class can do—the class itself is responsible for determining *how* it does it:

```
class TrafficLight : Blinkable {
    var isBlinking: Bool = false

    var blinkSpeed: Double = 0

    func startBlinking(blinkSpeed: Double) {
        print("I am a light and I am now blinking")

        isBlinking = true

        self.blinkSpeed = blinkSpeed
    }
}
```

The advantage of using protocols is that you can use Swift's type system to refer to any object that conforms to a given protocol. This is useful because you get to specify that you only care about whether an object conforms to the protocol—the specific type of the class doesn't matter since you are using the protocol as a type:

```swift
class Lighthouse : Blinkable {
    var isBlinking: Bool = false

    var blinkSpeed : Double = 0.0

    func startBlinking(blinkSpeed : Double) {
        print("I am a lighthouse, and I am now blinking")
        isBlinking = true

        self.blinkSpeed = blinkSpeed
    }
}

var aBlinkingThing : Blinkable
// can be ANY object that has the Blinkable protocol

aBlinkingThing = TrafficLight()

aBlinkingThing.startBlinking(blinkSpeed: 4.0)
// prints "I am a light and I am now blinking"
aBlinkingThing.blinkSpeed // = 4.0

aBlinkingThing = Lighthouse()
```

 As protocols are a type they themselves can also conform to other protocols, allowing you to build up complex protocols by assembling together numerous protocols from other places. Making a protocol conform to another protocol is similar to making a class conform to a protocol:

```swift
protocol ControllableBlink : Blinkable {
    func stopBlinking()
}
```

Extensions

In Swift, you can *extend* existing types and add further methods and computed properties. This is a very heavily used feature in Swift and is the general preferred way to add new functionality to a class, rather than inheritance. Most of the standard library and Cocoa are built up using extensions in place of subclassing. This is very useful in two situations:

- You're working with a type that someone else wrote, and you want to add functionality to it but either don't have access to its source code or don't want to mess around with it.

- You're working with a type that you wrote, and you want to divide its functionality into different sections for readability.

Extensions let you do both with ease.

Even though most of the time extensions will be what you want, subclassing is still a useful thing to do. As a rule of thumb, if what you are making needs obviously different functionality that makes you interact with the class in a different way, it should be a subclass. If you are just adding some additional functionality that doesn't change the core of the class, you want an extension.

A good example of this is the UIButton class in the UIKit framework; it represents a button you can tap on and is a subclass of UIView. Adding the interactive functionality of a button to the view makes you think about it in a different way. While a button is just an interactive view, because you think about it differently here a subclass makes more sense.

In Swift, you can extend *any* type—that is, you can extend classes that you write, as well as built-in types like Int and String.

There are some rules around what can and can't be extended in Swift; we'll talk more about those in "Access Control" on page 75.

To create an extension, you use the extension keyword, followed by the name of the type you want to extend. For example, to add methods and properties to the built-in Int type, you can do this:

```
extension Int {
    var double : Int {
        return self * 2
    }
    func multiplyWith(anotherNumber: Int) -> Int {
        return self * anotherNumber
    }
}
```

Once you extend a type, the methods and properties you defined in the extension are available to *every* instance of that type:

```
2.double // 4
2.multiplyWith(anotherNumber: 5) // 10
```

You can only add computed properties in an extension. As it currently stands, you can't add your own stored properties.

You can also use extensions to make a type conform to a protocol. For example, you can make the Int type conform to the Blinkable protocol described earlier:

```
extension Int : Blinkable {
    var isBlinking : Bool {
        return false;
    }

    var blinkSpeed : Double {
        get {
            return 0.0;
        }
        set {
            // Do nothing
        }
    }

    func startBlinking(blinkSpeed : Double) {
        print("I am the integer \(self). I do not blink.")
    }
}
2.isBlinking // = false
2.startBlinking(blinkSpeed: 2.0)
// prints "I am the integer 2. I do not blink."
```

Another neat feature of extensions and protocols is they allow you to provide *default implementations* of your protocols. A default implementation lets you write a sensible implementation of parts of the protocol that will be used when classes conforming to the protocol don't provide them:

```
extension Blinkable
{
    func startBlinking(blinkSpeed: Double) {
        print("I am blinking")
    }
}
```

With this default implementation of Blinkable, if we now create a new class and don't provide the method call, it will still work:

```
class AnotherBlinker : Blinkable {
    var isBlinking: Bool = true

    var blinkSpeed: Double = 0.0
}
```

```
let anotherBlinker = AnotherBlinker()
anotherBlinker.startBlinking(blinkSpeed: 3) // prints "I am blinking"
```

 Providing a default implementation is not the same as making parts of the protocol optional. An optional part of a protocol would not require an implementation, whereas a default implementation is run when you don't provide one. Swift doesn't have support for optional protocols—you can use the `optional` keyword, but this is using Objective-C to handle the optional side of the protocol. This means if you declare parts of your protocol as `optional` you can't use it without Objective-C and its runtime.

Access Control

Swift has several different levels of access control, but before we get to those, we first need to briefly mention *modules* and *source files*. A module is a single contiguous chunk of code that is built, such as a library, or a build target such as an application. Your applications will generally each be their own modules, as will any libraries they use. Anything you import in Swift is a module. Depending on your programming background, you are probably used to using `include` statements in your code to make sure you don't accidentally import something multiple times. In Swift you don't have to worry about this. Modules are clever enough to handle potential import conflicts, letting you focus on making great apps! A source file is easy enough to understand; it is the literal file your Swift source code is being written in. Modules and source files are the two discrete chunks that access control operates on in Swift.

Swift defines five levels of access control, which determine what information is accessible to which parts of the application:

open *and* public
> `open` and `public` are very similar to one another: all classes, methods, and properties are accessible by any part of the current module and any module that imports the current module. For example, all of the classes in UIKit that you use to build iOS apps are `public`.

internal
> `internal` entities (data and methods) are only accessible to the module in which they're defined. This is why you can't access the inner workings of UIKit--they're defined as internal to the UIKit framework. `internal` is the default level of access control: if you don't specify the access control level, it's assumed to be `internal`.

fileprivate
> `fileprivate` entities are only accessible to the source file in which they're declared. This means that you can create classes that hide their inner workings

from other classes in the same module. This helps to keep the amount of surface area that those classes expose to each other to a minimum, while still allowing you to spread and use your class's implementation throughout the file.

private

private entities are only accessible to the current declaration scope (this is the most restrictive access modifier). This means you can create functions and objects that can hide their internals from everything else in the module and file. By marking something private, you create functionality you never want others to touch—the only exception to this is extensions inside the same file. This means you can declare a method or property as private inside a class, and nothing can ever access that method.

 If you are wondering what exactly the difference is between the open and public levels of access, it is down to how they work when imported into other modules.

If your classes are marked as public, they can be used by other modules but only subclassed from within their own module, whereas open classes can be both used *and* subclassed by other modules.

The kind of access control that a method or property can have depends on the access level of the class that it's contained in. You can't make a method more accessible than the class in which it's contained. For example, you can't define a private class that has a public method.

To specify the access level for a class, you add the appropriate keyword before the class keyword. To define a public class called AccessControl, for instance, you'd write the following:

```
public class AccessControl {

}
```

By default, all properties and methods are internal. You can explicitly define an entity as internal if you want, but it isn't necessary:

```
internal var internalProperty = 123
```

The exception is for classes defined as private or fileprivate—if you don't declare an access control level for a member, it's set as private or fileprivate, not internal. It is *impossible* to specify an access level for a member of an entity that is more open than that of the entity itself.

If you declare an entity as private, it's only accessible from within the scope in which it's declared:

```
private class PrivateAccess {
    func doStuff() -> String {
        return "Private Access is doing stuff"
    }
}
private let privateClass = PrivateAccess()

func doAThing()
{
    print(self.privateClass.doStuff())
}
```

If you try and use it, it all works fine as the public and internal wrappers handle the access:

```
let accessControl = AccessControl()
accessControl.doAThing() // prints "Private Access is doing stuff"
// accessControl.privateClass
// accessing this is an error, it can't be accessed
// outside of the AccessControl definition
```

The difference between private and fileprivate may not be obvious at first glance, but private is far more restrictive than fileprivate. Using private means something can only be used within the scope in which it's declared, whereas fileprivate is far more lenient. For example, suppose we create another class similar to our private one:

```
fileprivate class FileAccess {
    func doStuff() -> String {
        return "File private access is doing stuff"
    }
}
fileprivate let fileClass = FileAccess()
func doAFilePrivateThing()
{
    print(self.fileClass.doStuff())
}
```

We can use it in an identical fashion, but we can also access the internals of it as they are locked out at the source file level, not the declaration level like in the private class:

```
accessControl.doAFilePrivateThing()
accessControl.fileClass.doStuff()
```

Finally, you can render a property as read-only by declaring that its setter is private:

```
private(set) var privateSetProperty = 234
```

This means that you can freely read the property's value but nothing can change it outside of the class itself:

```
accessControl.privateSetProperty // 234
// accessControl.privateSetProperty = 4
// Trying the above is an error!
```

 If you use fileprivate instead of private as the access restriction level on your setters you can also still freely change the values inside the source file, which is handy when you're writing your code, but a lot harder to quickly demonstrate in a playground!

While not technically a form of access control, Swift also allows you to put restrictions on subclassing your classes and their methods and properties. The final keyword prevents a member or class from being overridden in a subclass:

```
final class FinalClass {}

// class FinalSubClass : FinalClass {}
// error: inheritance from a final class 'FinalClass'
```

You don't have to lock down the entire class if only some parts need to be restricted:

```
class PartiallyFinalClass {
    final func doStuff(){
        print("doing stuff")
    }
}
class PartiallyFinalSubClass : PartiallyFinalClass {
    // override func doStuff() { print("Doing different stuff") }
    // error: instance method overrides a 'final' instance method
}
```

Operator Overloading and Custom Operators

An operator is actually a function that takes one or two values and returns a value. Operators, just like other functions, can be overloaded. For example, you could change how the + function works for Int like this:

```
extension Int {
    static func + (left: Int, right: Int) -> Int {
        return left * right
    }
}
4 + 2 // 8
```

This is a horrible idea; don't do this!

Swift lets you define new operators and overload existing ones for your types, which means that if you have a new type of data, you can operate on that data using both existing operators and new ones you invent yourself.

For example, imagine you have an object called `Vector2D`, which stores two floating-point numbers:

```
class Vector2D {
    var x : Float = 0.0
    var y : Float = 0.0

    init (x : Float, y: Float) {
        self.x = x
        self.y = y
    }
}
```

If you want to allow adding instances of this type of object together using the + operator, all you need to do is provide an implementation of the + function:

```
func +(left : Vector2D, right: Vector2D) -> Vector2D {
    let result = Vector2D(x: left.x + right.x, y: left.y + right.y)

    return result
}
```

You can then use it as you'd expect:

```
let first = Vector2D(x: 2, y: 2)
let second = Vector2D(x: 4, y: 1)

let result = first + second
// (x:6, y:3)
```

You can also create new operators. You need to first define the type of operator, which can be *infix*, *postfix*, or *prefix*:

```
infix operator •
```

 An infix operator goes between two variables (such as `var1 * var2`), a postfix operator goes after a variable (such as `var1!`), and prefix operators go before a variable (such as `-var1`).

Then, as with the custom + operator, you need to write the code for the function:

```
func •(left : Vector2D, right: Vector2D) -> Vector2D {
    let result = Vector2D(x: left.x * right.x, y: left.y * right.y)

    return result
}
```

And now you can use it:

```
first • second // (x: 6, y: 2)
```

 We're only just scratching the surface of what Swift can do with operators here. For more information on some of the advanced functionality of operators, check out the "Advanced Operators" (*https://apple.co/2CDTaI0*) section of the official documentation.

Subscripts

When you work with arrays and dictionaries, you use square brackets ([and]) to indicate to Swift what part of the collection you want to work with. The term for this is *subscripting*, and it's something that your own classes and types can adopt.

You define what it means to get and set values via a subscript using the subscript keyword. For example, let's say you want to access the individual bits inside an 8-bit integer. You can do this with subscripting, like so:

```
// Extend the unsigned 8-bit integer type
extension UInt8 {
    // Allow subscripting this type using UInt8s
    subscript(bit: UInt8) -> UInt8 {
        // This is run when you do things like "value[x]"
        get {
            return (self >> bit & 0x07) & UInt8(1)
        }

        // This is run when you do things like "value[x] = y"
        set {
            let cleanBit = bit & 0x07
            let mask : UInt8 = 0xFF ^ (1 << cleanBit)
            let shiftedBit = (newValue & 1) << cleanBit
            self = self & mask | shiftedBit
        }
    }
}
```

With this in place, you can access the individual bits inside the number by reading and writing them:

```
var byte : UInt8 = 212
```

```
byte[0] // 0
byte[2] // 1
byte[5] // 0
byte[6] // 1

// Change the last bit
byte[7] = 0

// The number is now changed!
byte // 84
```

Generics

Swift is a statically typed language. This means that the Swift compiler needs to definitively know what type of information your code is dealing with.

However, this rigidity means that you lose some flexibility. Let's say you are trying to write a Tree class. It's annoying to have to write a chunk of code that does some work with strings, and then another that works with dates, and another with integers, and another with Booleans, and so on and so on.

This is where *generics* come in. Generics allow you to write code that doesn't need to know precisely *what* information it's dealing with. An example of this kind of use is in arrays: they don't actually do any work with the data they store, but instead just store it in an ordered collection. Arrays are, in fact, generics.

To create a generic type, you name your object as usual, and then specify a placeholder type name between angle brackets. T is traditionally the term used, but you can put anything you like. For example, to create a generic Tree object that contains a value and any number of child Tree objects, you'd do the following:

```
class Tree <T> {
    // 'T' can now be used as a type inside this class

    // 'value' is of type T
    var value : T

    // 'children' is an array of Tree objects that have
    // the same type as this one
    private (set) var children : [Tree <T>] = []

    // We can initialize this object with a value of type T
    init(value : T) {
        self.value = value
    }

    // And we can add a child node to our list of children
    func addChild(value : T) -> Tree <T> {
        let newChild = Tree<T>(value: value)
        children.append(newChild)
```

```
            return newChild
    }
}
```

 When working with generics it is worth naming the generic type something memorable and appropriate for what you are creating.

Once a generic type is defined, you can create a specific, nongeneric type from it. For example, the `Tree` generic type just defined can be used to create a version that works with `Int`s and one that works with `String`s:

```
// Tree of integers
let integerTree = Tree<Int>(value: 5)

// Can add children that contain Ints
integerTree.addChild(value: 10)
integerTree.addChild(value: 5)

// Tree of strings
let stringTree = Tree<String>(value: "Hello")

stringTree.addChild(value: "Yes")
stringTree.addChild(value: "Internets")
```

Structures

So far everything we've been talking about has been applied to classes. However, there is another construct in Swift: *structures*. For the most part, structures are very similar to classes: you can put properties and methods in them, they have initializers, and they generally behave in an object-like way, just like a class does. Everything we've discussed so far—generics, subscripts, initializers, protocol conformance, and extensions—applies exactly the same to structures as it does to classes. However, there are two main things that differentiate them from classes:

- Structures do not have inheritance—that is, you cannot make a structure inherit its methods and properties from another.
- When you pass a structure around in your code, the structure is always *copied*.

Arguably many of the classes we've created in this chapter would make more sense as structures instead, especially the `Vector2D` and `Rectangle` classes.

Structures are declared using the `struct` keyword as follows:

```
struct Point {
    var x: Int
    var y: Int
}
```

Additionally, if you don't provide any initializers, structures get a compiler-provided one, called the *memberwise initializer*:

```
let p = Point(x: 2, y: 3)
```

 In Swift, structures are *value types*, which are always copied when passed around. Most of the common types in Swift, including `Int`, `String`, `Array`, and `Dictionary`, are implemented as structures.

The difference between structures as value types and classes as reference types becomes apparent when there are multiple references to a single value. Say we have a structure and class that are almost the same:

```
struct NumberStruct {
    var number : Int
}
class NumberClass {
    var number : Int

    init(_ number: Int) {
        self.number = number
    }
}
```

If we have two instances of both of them, initially they are both what we expect:

```
var numberClass1 = NumberClass(3)
var numberClass2 = numberClass1
numberClass1.number // 3
numberClass2.number // 3

var numberStruct1 = NumberStruct(number: 3)
var numberStruct2 = numberStruct1
numberStruct1.number // 3
numberStruct2.number // 3
```

However, when we change them we can see the difference between the struct and class forms:

```
numberStruct2.number = 4
numberStruct1.number // 3

numberClass2.number = 4
numberClass1.number // 4
```

Error Handling

It's normal for computer programs to generate errors. When that happens, you need to be ready to handle them, and Swift makes this particularly easy and robust.

If you've programmed using Objective-C or Swift 1.0, you might be familiar with a different error-handling system. Previously, an NSError object would be passed as a pointer; when something could fail, you'd pass in an NSError object as a parameter, and if there was an error you could fill the object with information.

This pattern still exists in some of the Cocoa libraries, and you'll encounter it every now and then.

This was powerful, as it allowed the return value of a method to be separated from any potential error information. But it was easy to forget to look inside the NSError object. Swift 2.0 replaced this system, and while the new mechanism expects a little more from programmers, it is much clearer to read, gives you greater safety by making sure all errors are caught, and requires less messing around with pointers (that is to say, *no* messing around with pointers).

In Swift, errors can be any type that conforms to the Error protocol. The Error protocol doesn't have any required functions or properties, which means that any class, enum, or structure can be an error. When your code encounters an error, you *throw* an error.

For compatibility in Swift, the Objective-C error type NSError is an Error, which means it can be thrown like every other Error.

For example, let's define an enumeration for problems that can relate to a bank account. By making the enumeration an Error, we can throw it as an error:

```
enum BankError : Error {
    // Not enough money in the account
    case notEnoughFunds

    // Can't create an account with negative money
    case cannotBeginWithNegativeFunds

    // Can't make a negative deposit or withdrawal
    case cannotMakeNegativeTransaction(amount:Float)
}
```

Functions that can throw errors must be marked with the throws keyword, which goes after the function's return type:

```
// A simple bank account class
class BankAccount {

    // The amount of money in the account
    private (set) var balance : Float = 0.0

    // Initializes the account with an amount of money.
    // Throws an error if you try to create the account
    // with negative funds.
    init(amount:Float) throws {

        // Ensure that we have a non-negative amount of money
        guard amount > 0 else {
            throw BankError.cannotBeginWithNegativeFunds
        }
        balance = amount
    }

    // Adds some money to the account
    func deposit(amount: Float) throws {

        // Ensure that we're trying to deposit a non-negative amount
        guard amount > 0 else {
            throw BankError.cannotMakeNegativeTransaction(amount: amount)
        }
        balance += amount
    }

    // Withdraws money from the bank account
    func withdraw(amount : Float) throws {

        // Ensure that we're trying to deposit a non-negative amount
        guard amount > 0 else {
            throw BankError.cannotMakeNegativeTransaction(amount: amount)
        }

        // Ensure that we have enough to withdraw this amount
        guard balance >= amount else {
            throw BankError.notEnoughFunds
```

```
        }

        balance -= amount
    }
}
```

When you call any function, method, or initializer that `throws`, you are required to wrap it in a do-catch block. In the do block, you call the methods that may potentially throw errors; each time you do this, you preface the potentially throwing call with `try`. If the method call throws an error, the do block stops executing and the `catch` clause runs:

```
do {
    let vacationFund = try BankAccount(amount: 5)

    try vacationFund.deposit(amount: 5)

    try vacationFund.withdraw(amount: 11)

} catch let error as BankError {

    // Catch any BankError that was thrown
    switch (error) {
    case .notEnoughFunds:
        print("Not enough funds in account!")
    case .cannotBeginWithNegativeFunds:
        print("Tried to start an account with negative money!")
    case .cannotMakeNegativeTransaction(let amount):
        print("Tried to do a transaction with a negative amount of \(amount)!")
    }

} catch let error {
    // (Optional:) Catch other types of errors
}
```

However, it can sometimes be cumbersome to wrap calls to methods that can throw errors in a do-catch block. Sometimes you may not care about the specifics of the error; you just care if there was an error or not. This is where the `try?` statement comes in. If you preface a call to something that can throw an error with `try?`, and it *does* throw an error, the result will be `nil`:

```
let secretBankAccountOrNot = try? BankAccount(amount: -50) // nil
```

 This means that the return type of any call that you `try?` will be an optional.

Finally, there are sometimes cases where your program *needs* the method call to succeed and guarantee a returned value. If you call a method with `try!`, and it throws an error, your program will simply crash. This has the same effect as using `try?` to receive an optional and then using the force-unwrap operator (`!`) on that optional:

```
let secretBankAccount = try! BankAccount(amount: 50)
// this call will exit or crash if we put in an invalid amount
```

 The `try?` and `try!` statements do *not* need to be in a do-catch block. If you do put them in one, any errors won't be caught by the `catch` block; they'll still just either evaluate to `nil` or cause a crash.

Memory Management

Objects in Swift are *memory managed*. When an object is being used, Swift keeps it in memory; when it's no longer being used, it's removed from memory.

The technique that Swift uses to keep track of which objects are being used and which are not is called *reference counting*. When an object is assigned to a variable, a counter called the *retain count* goes up by one. When the object is no longer assigned to that variable, the retain count goes down. If the retain count ever reaches zero, that means that no variables are referring to that object, and the object is then removed from memory.

The nice thing about Swift is that this all happens at the compiler level. As the compiler reads your code, it keeps track of when objects get assigned to variables and adds code that increments and decrements the retain count. Rarely do you ever have to think about this; that's the job of the compiler.

 You shouldn't focus too much on the specifics of reference counting. Doing so encourages you to think things like "I have three objects referencing `var1` and two referencing `var2`," which gets you trapped into trying to keep track of all the tiny specific numeric details going on under the hood. You can easily get lost this way. Instead, think of it in terms of *ownership*. When you are using an object, you own it. When you are done you relinquish this ownership, and when no objects own another object, it goes away. You are only responsible for those objects you currently own; when you finish owning them they are no longer your problem. This is a much simpler way of thinking about it.

However, this memory management system has one potential snag that you need to keep an eye out for: *retain cycles*.

A retain cycle is where you have two (or more) objects that refer to each other, but are otherwise not referred to by any other part of the application. Because those objects refer to each other, their retain count is not zero, which means they stay in memory; however, because no variable in the rest of the application refers to them, they're inaccessible (and consequently useless).

Swift solves this using the concept of *weak references*. A weak reference is a variable that refers to an object, but doesn't change the retain count of that object. You use weak references when you don't particularly care whether an object stays in memory or not (i.e., your code isn't the owner of that object).

This becomes more obvious with an example. Say we have two classes, one that represents a person and another that represents a dog:

```
class Human {
    var bestFriend : Dog?

    var name : String

    init(name:String){
        self.name = name
    }

    deinit {
        print("\(name) is being removed")
    }
}
class Dog {
    var friendBeast : Human?

    var name : String

    init(name:String){
        self.name = name
    }
    deinit {
        print("\(name) is being removed")
    }
}
```

 We are using the deinit call here so that we can see when they get removed from memory.

Each human can have a dog, and each dog can have a human. So we can create a new human and a dog, and if we set them to nil we will get the deinit method being run:

```
var turner : Human? = Human(name:"Turner")
var hooch : Dog? = Dog(name:"Hooch")
turner = nil // prints "Turner is being removed"
hooch = nil // prints "Hooch is being removed"
```

 Both of our variables are optional, so we can set them to nil, which is the easiest way of releasing ownership on a variable.

Now let's delete those calls to set turner and hooch to nil, and instead set it up so that our person and our dog refer to one another:

```
turner?.bestFriend = hooch
hooch?.friendBeast = turner
```

If we add our calls to set our variables to nil again, something interesting will happen:

```
turner = nil // does nothing
hooch = nil // does nothing
```

We never get our printed messages—this is because the deinit is never run. In our case turner has a *strong reference* to hooch and hooch has a strong reference to turner; they are both owners of each other. This means when we set the variables to nil, even though the variables no longer own the instances of those classes, they are still owned by each other. We have created a retain cycle.

To fix this, we can use the weak keyword. If we change both the classes to use weak they will no longer have a strong hold on each other:

```
class Human {
    weak var bestFriend : Dog?

    var name : String

    init(name:String){
        self.name = name
    }

    deinit {
        print("\(name) is being removed")
    }
}
class Dog {
    weak var friendBeast : Human?
```

```
    var name : String

    init(name:String){
        self.name = name
    }
    deinit {
        print("\(name) is being removed")
    }
}
```

And the objects will go away when set to `nil` as we expect:

```
turner = nil // prints "Turner is being removed"
hooch = nil // prints "Hooch is being removed"
```

A side effect of using a weak reference is that it has to be an optional type—there is no way around this. What if, however, you have a setup where you have two objects that need to refer to each other, but where one of the objects will exist only for as long as the other object with a shorter lifespan? An example of this is a person and a passport. A person can have a passport (so this would be an optional property), and a passport needs a person (so should be a nonoptional property), and a passport only exists for, at most, the same amount of time as the person (and often less time). Because of this, the passport knows its person will never become `nil` as long as passport exists, so making it optional doesn't really make sense. This is where *unowned references* come into play.

 We aren't continuing with our `Human` and `Dog` analogy here because that would imply a dog can only exist for as long as its human does and can't exist without a human, and we don't want to live in that kind of world.

Now, we could create this using the same pattern as before, but it really wouldn't make sense. A passport *has* to have a person; otherwise, it isn't a passport. Instead, we can declare the `person` property in the `passport` class as `unowned`:

```
class Person {
    var name : String
    var passport : Passport?

    init(name: String) {
        self.name = name
    }

    deinit { print("\(name) is being removed") }
}
class Passport {
    var number : Int
    unowned let person : Person
```

```
init(number: Int, person: Person) {
    self.number = number
    self.person = person
}

deinit { print("Passport \(number) is being removed") }
}
```

This is only an example—don't *ever* store passport numbers in your app like this. Not only are passport numbers not just numbers, but this is not secure in the slightest! When dealing with something as personal and identifying as a passport number in your app, seriously think about how to do this and ask yourself if it is necessary.

Now if we make a new person and give this person a passport, we have a structure that looks very much like it has a retain cycle inside:

```
var viktor : Person? = Person(name: "Viktor Navorski")
viktor!.passport = Passport(number: 1234567890, person: viktor!)

viktor?.passport?.number // 1234567890
```

But if we remove our ownership over viktor we will see both deinit calls occur:

```
viktor = nil
// prints "Viktor Navorski is being removed"
// prints "Passport 1234567890 is being removed"
```

This is because our passort's reference to its human is unowned. There is only one owner of the passport—the human—and when the human goes away, so does the passport.

If you are wrong about the relationship between an unowned object and its owner, and it does get deallocated before your code has finished using it, your code will crash!

When to use unowned versus weak is both a personal preference and a design decision. The only restriction is an unowned reference can only be used when the object is guaranteed to exist for the same amount of time or less than the other object it needs to reference.

Design Patterns in Swift

Cocoa is built around a number of design patterns whose purpose is to make your life as a developer more consistent and (one hopes) more productive. Three key patterns are the *model–view–controller* (MVC) pattern, upon which most of Cocoa and Cocoa

Touch are built; the *delegation* pattern, which allows both your code and Cocoa to be highly flexible in determining what code gets run by whom; and *notifications*, which allow your code to watch for important events that happen within your app. We'll be working with notifications in a very hands-on way later in the book (in Chapter 11); at the moment, let's dive in to MVC and delegation!

Model–View–Controller

The model–view–controller design pattern is one of the fundamental design patterns in Cocoa. Let's take a look at the three components:

Models
> Objects that contain data or otherwise coordinate the storing, management, and delivery of data to other objects. Models can be as simple as a string or as complicated as an entire database—their purpose is to store data and provide it to other objects. They don't care what happens to the data once they give it to something else; their only concern is managing how the data is stored.

Views
> Objects that work directly with the user, providing information to them and receiving input back. Views do not manage the data that they display—they only show it to the user. Views are also responsible for informing other objects when the user interacts with them. Like data and models, views do not care what happens next—their responsibility ends with informing the rest of the application.

Controllers
> Objects that mediate between models and views and contain the bulk of what some call the "business logic" of an application—the actual logic that defines what the application is and how it responds to user input.

> At a minimum, the controller is responsible for retrieving information from the model and providing it to the view; it is also responsible for providing information to the model when it is informed by the view that the user has interacted with it.

For an illustration of the model–view–controller design pattern in action, imagine a simple text editor. In this example, the application loads a text file from disk and presents its contents to the user in a text field. The user makes changes in the text field and saves those changes back to disk.

We can break this application down into model, view, and controller objects:

- The model is an object that is responsible for loading the text file from disk and writing it back out to disk. It is also responsible for providing the text as a string to any object that asks for it.

- The view is the text field, which asks another object for a string to display and then displays the text. It also accepts keyboard input from the user; whenever the user types, it informs another object that the text has changed. It is also able to tell another object when the user has told it to save changes.

- The controller is the object responsible for instructing the model object to load a file from disk, and it passes the text to the view. It receives updates from the view object when the text has changed and passes those changes to the model. Finally, it can be told by the view that the user has asked to save the changes; when that happens, it instructs the model to do the work of actually writing the file out to disk.

Breaking the application into these areas of responsibility enables us to more easily make changes to it.

For example, if the developer decides that the next version of the application should add the ability to upload the text file to the internet whenever the file is saved, the only thing that must be changed is the model class—the controller can stay the same, and the view never changes.

Likewise, clearly defining which objects are responsible for which features makes it easier to make changes to an application while maintaining a clear structure in the project. If the developer decides to add a spell-checking feature to the application, that code should clearly be added to the controller, as it has nothing to do with how the text is presented to the user or stored on disk. You could, of course, add some features to the view that would allow it to indicate which words are misspelled, but the bulk of the code would still need to be added in the controller.

The majority of the classes described in this chapter, such as the `Data`, `Array`, and `Dictionary` classes, are model classes; all they do is store and present information to other classes. `NSKeyedArchiver` is a controller class; it takes information and performs logical operations on it. `NSButton` and `UITextField` are examples of view objects; they present information to the user and do not care about how the data is managed.

The model–view–controller paradigm becomes very important when you start looking at the more advanced Cocoa features, like the document architecture and bindings.

Delegation

Delegation is Cocoa's term for passing off some responsibilities of an object to another. An example of this is the `UIApplication` object, which represents an application on iOS. This object needs to know what should happen when the application moves to the background. Many other languages handle this problem by subclassing

—for example, in other programming languages, the `UIApplication` class would define an empty placeholder method for `applicationDidEnterBackground`, and then you as a developer would subclass `UIApplication` and override that method.

 Don't worry about what those specific classes do; we'll talk more about them in "Structuring an App" on page 97.

However, this is a particularly heavy-handed solution and causes additional problems; it increases the complexity of your code, and also means that if you want to override the behavior of two classes, you need separate subclasses for each one.[1] Cocoa's answer to this problem is built around the fact that an object can determine, at runtime, whether another object is capable of responding to a method.

Let's say Object A wants to let Object B know that something is going to happen or has happened, and stores a reference to Object B as an instance variable. This reference to Object B is known as the *delegate*. When the event happens, Object A checks to see if the delegate object (Object B) implements a method that suits the event—for delegates of the `UIApplication` class, for example, the application delegate is asked if it implements the `applicationDidEnterBackground` method. If it does, that method is called.

Because of this loose coupling, it's possible for an object to be the delegate for multiple objects. For example, an object could become the delegate of both an audio playback object and an image picker, and be notified both when audio playback completes and when an image has been captured by the camera.

Because the model–view–controller pattern is built around a very loose coupling of objects, it helps to have a more rigidly defined interface between objects so that your application can know with more certainty how one object expects others to behave.

The specific messages used by delegates are often listed in protocols. For example, if your object wants to be the delegate of an `AVAudioPlayer` object, it should conform to the `AVAudioPlayerDelegate` protocol.

Working with delegates in Swift is easy. Imagine you have two classes, and you want one of them to act as the delegate for another:

```
// Define a protocol that has a function called handleIntruder
protocol HouseSecurityDelegate {
```

---

1 C++'s answer to this problem is multiple inheritance, which has its own problems.

```
        // We don't define the function here, but rather
        // indicate that any class that is a HouseSecurityDelegate
        // is required to have a handleIntruder() function
        func handleIntruder()
    }

    class House {
        // The delegate can be any object that conforms
        // to the HouseSecurityDelegate protocol
        var delegate : HouseSecurityDelegate?

        func burglarDetected() {
            // Check to see if the delegate is there, then call it
            delegate?.handleIntruder()
        }
    }

    class GuardDog : HouseSecurityDelegate {
        func handleIntruder() {
            print("Releasing the hounds!")
        }
    }

    let myHouse = House()
    myHouse.burglarDetected() // does nothing

    let theHounds = GuardDog()
    myHouse.delegate = theHounds
    myHouse.burglarDetected() // prints "Releasing the hounds!"
```

The burglarDetected method needs to check that a security delegate exists for the house before calling its handleIntruder method. It does this using a Swift feature called *optional chaining*, which lets you access something that depends on an optional having a value, without specifically testing the optional first. If the optional has a value, in this case a houseSecurityDelegate, its handleIntruder method is called. If the optional is nil, nothing happens. You can use optional chaining to access the properties, methods, or subscripts of your classes, structures, and enumerations in this way. One of the best parts about the delegation model is that there is a loose coupling between the objects. As all the house cares about is that the delegate conforms to the security protocol, we can change from a dog-based security system to a robot-based one and nothing needs to change from the house's perspective:

```
    class KillerRobot : HouseSecurityDelegate {
        func handleIntruder() {
            print("Deploying T-800 battle chassis")
        }
    }

    let killerRobot = KillerRobot()
```

```
myHouse.delegate = killerRobot
myHouse.burglarDetected() // prints "Deploying T-800 battle chassis"
```

Swift Libraries

The different features you work with in Swift come from different places, or *libraries*, depending on how platform-specific they are. These are the four main libraries you'll access:

The Swift standard library
> Contains all of the lowest-level types and functions that you'll be working with, including `Int`, `String`, mathematics functions, arrays, and dictionaries. You don't need to do anything special to access the standard library; all Swift programs have access to it.

Foundation
> A slightly higher-level library that provides more tools and types, such as `NSNotificationCenter`, which is used to broadcast application-wide notifications, and `JSONSerialization`, which allows you to read and write JSON data. Many of the classes in Foundation start with the prefix "NS" for historical reasons. Parts of Foundation are written in Objective-C and parts in Swift; however, there has been a big push to port all of Foundation to Swift and that work is now done to the degree where you can safely assume Foundation objects are available anywhere that Swift exists. You import the Foundation library with the `import Foundation` statement at the top of your file.

Cocoa
> Specific to macOS, this library includes features like buttons, windows, image views, and menus. All of the Cocoa classes are also prefixed with "NS" (e.g., `NSButton`). You import Cocoa with the `import Cocoa` statement, and Cocoa includes Foundation.

Cocoa Touch
> Also known as UIKit, this library provides equivalent tools and functionality to Cocoa on iOS: views, touch input, sensor capabilities, and so on. All of the Cocoa Touch classes are prefixed with "UI" (e.g., `UIButton`). You import Cocoa Touch with the `import UIKit` statement, and it includes Foundation.

 There are also equivalent libraries for tvOS, watchOS, and Linux as well as many third-party tools and libraries for Swift, but these are well beyond the scope of this book.

There are a great deal of other libraries for Swift built into the various operating systems, such as `CoreLocation`, which gives you functionality for determining and manipulating location data (including accessing the GPS hardware built into iOS devices), `AVFoundation`, which has functionality for the playback and creation of movies and audio files. And much like Cocoa and Cocoa Touch, many of these built-in libraries follow the pattern of prefixing their objects with an abbreviation of the name of the library; for example, `CLLocation` is the object that represents a location in the `CoreLocation` library. This is just a tiny look at the available libraries; for more information, check out Apple's library and API documentation (*https://devel oper.apple.com/documentation*).

 Throughout this book we will often be using the term "Cocoa" generically to refer to the different operating system–specific libraries (Cocoa on macOS, Cocoa Touch/UIKit on iOS, watchKit on watchOS, and so on), which are remarkably similar to each other by design. This is just a convenient shorthand.

As most of this book will be focusing on using Cocoa Touch, it is worth talking in a little more detail about some of the core components of this library and the design patterns they use. We do that in the next section.

Structuring an App

iOS and macOS are built on the idea of *event-driven programming*. Anything that your app does is in response to an event of some kind. On macOS, events include the mouse moving or clicking, keyboard input, and the window resizing; on iOS, they include touch input and sensor input. On both iOS and macOS, events can also include timers firing or the screen refreshing.

At their core, apps are about the *run loop*, an infinite loop that waits for an event to fire and then takes appropriate actions. Most of those actions are handled by the built-in parts of your app; for example, swiping your finger on a list will cause the list to adjust its position. However, there are several events that your code handles. For example, when a button is clicked, as part of handling this event, the code calls a method that you write.

Applications and delegates

From a code perspective, the center of any iOS application is the `UIApplication` class. An instance of this class represents the app itself. Rarely will you be interacting with the application object itself, however, as this is managed by the operating system. Most of the time you will be using the `UIApplicationDelegate` class.

This class is a delegate for the application. In the case of an iOS app, the delegate is what gets told about important events such as when the application has launched, is about to be closed, or has lost the primary focus. By default, when using the Xcode templates you will be given a new `UIApplicationDelegate` subclass with stubbed-out method calls for the important app delegate events. You provide code in these methods to run when the events occur.

Views

When it comes time to actually present something on the screen, you need a way to do so. This is where `UIView` and `UIWindow` come into play. `UIWindow` is the *window* for the application and is where the contents of the various *views* will be drawn. In iOS development there will only be a single window in your application and there isn't much you'll ever have to worry about with it; most of the time you will be playing around with views.

In some circumstances in iOS you can have multiple windows, such as when you have external displays connected.

`UIView` is the object that represents a view that is presented in the window. A view is just a rectangle (often with a heavily customized appearance) that gets drawn into the window.

Under the hood a `UIView` is a wrapper around various `CGRect` objects, which are rectangles designed to be shown on a screen. `CGRect` comes from the Core Graphics library.

It has a *frame* that represents its (*x*, *y*) position on the screen, as well as its width and height relative to the window. It also has a *bounds*, another rectangle, that describes the view inside its own coordinate system.

In iOS position (0,0) in the window represents the top-left corner of the screen. Positive increases in *x* and *y* move it further toward the bottom-righthand corner. This is different from macOS and most graphics programs, where (0,0) is the bottom-left corner, but otherwise the iOS screen points work like a normal Cartesian plane.

In iOS most of the time your views will be positioned by *constraints*, which describe in a formal language how one view is associated with another. By using constraints you are able to describe how your view will be positioned and sized. Assuming they were written in English, your constraints might look something like: "I want my view positioned 16 points away from the left edge of the screen, and 8 points down from the top. It will be 44 points long, and 80 points wide. It will also be at least 8 points away from the next view." The constraint solver then sets about the task of positioning the various views in a way that matches these constraints. The reason for this system is that it allows for flexible layouts regardless of the size of the device the application is running upon.

The UIView class itself is only occasionally used; more often you will be using one of the premade subclasses. Everything shown on a screen in an iOS application—from buttons to text fields to switches, scroll views, and image container views—is going to be a UIView or UIView subclass of some kind.

Technically you can draw directly to the window if you want, bypassing the UIView for drawing, but this is a pretty rare thing.

Views are designed to be built up in a hierarchy. At the top level there is a single view; it will have multiple subviews inside it, each of which may then have further subviews inside it. Any event that changes a parent view, such as moving its position or hiding it, will have follow-on effects for its child views, resulting in them also changing. This allows you to break up your UI into logical chunks.

UIViewController

View controllers manage a view's contents on both iOS and macOS. View controllers are a specialization of the controller part of the model–view–controller paradigm and are designed for managing a single view of your app. Every view controller has a single property called view, which is the main view it is responsible for, and that view may have its own views as well. On iOS a view controller is usually full-screen, but on macOS that may not be the case (although the view that the controller manages is usually the full size of the window containing it).

Much like application delegates, view controllers get informed of relevant events that occur to the views they are responsible for managing, such as the view being loaded into memory or appearing or disappearing.

The default view controller class, UIViewController, is designed to be subclassed, providing the specific functionality that is necessary for that part of the application. There are also several premade subclasses of view controllers, such as the

`UITableViewController` subclass, designed to show lists of data. View controllers can manage other view controllers; for example, navigation controllers are a type of view controller that manages multiple child view controllers.

View controllers are one of the fundamental components of iOS and macOS development; a great deal of the work we will be doing in the rest of this book will be using view controllers and view controller subclasses.

 Because of the design of view controllers and the model–view–controller structure it can be tempting to fill them full of code, a lot of which doesn't need to be placed there. This has led to a joke about MVC standing instead for "massive view controller." As with anything in programming, you should always try and ensure your code is broken up into logical chunks. Stuffing a single class full of all sorts of functionality is generally going to be a bad idea.

Storyboards and nibs

When an application starts, it needs to load its interface. The interface is stored inside one of two types of files: *nib files* and *storyboard files*. Both are used in the interface builder inside of Xcode to design and lay out an interface.

Nib files contain collections of objects, and are generally used to represent a single window or view; they also contain nonvisible objects, such as controller objects, when needed.

 Any nibs you have will be called something like *<filename>.xib*— but despite the *.xib* extension, they are still called nibs. The reason for this is that originally a *.nib* custom file format was used, but Apple transitioned to an XML-based one. To differentiate between the two in your code, they changed the file extension.

Storyboards take this idea and extend it by storing multiple interfaces—that is, views and windows—and letting you describe how you get from one interface to another, using connections called *segues*. Each interface in the storyboard is called a *scene* and nearly always represents a single view controller in your application.

Storyboards are the newer and now default way of building up your interface. Nibs are still used sparingly in most apps, but gone are the days when you would have had many different nib files, each for a different view controller.

You can do all your UI construction in code if you like, and we will do some of it in code, but it's better to use storyboards for at the very least the high-level structure of the app. We highly recommend that you get used to using storyboards for your UI. The vast majority of the time it is faster, even if initially it feels slow compared to writing your UI in code.

Swift Package Manager

There's an old adage that says "don't reinvent the wheel," and in software development there are loads of highly performant and excellent third-party wheels out there just waiting to be used. Whenever you have an issue, it is quite likely that someone else has already solved it, and all you need to do is integrate their solution into your project.

If you are using someone else's code, you have to follow the terms they have set out in the code's license. There are many different licenses out there that give various options for how you as a developer want others to use your code. For example, Swift is released under the Apache license, and by using Swift you agree to the terms in this license (*https://github.com/apple/swift/blob/master/ LICENSE.txt*).

Whenever you download someone else's code you are agreeing to follow the terms they have chosen. If you don't agree with the terms the developer has chosen to license their code under, you can't use it—it's that simple.

If you are after a starting point for choosing a license for your own code, GitHub made *https://choosealicense.com* for this very reason.

When you need to get access to other people's code and libraries, you can just manually download the Swift files and add them to your codebase. This is error prone, however, and requires you to handle downloading not only the code you want but all the code it needs to run, and to resolve any dependency issues that might arise when doing this. A better option is to use a tool to handle all this. For Cocoa development, there are two popular tools for this purpose: Carthage and CocoaPods. But Apple wanted something that everyone can use, which is why they made the Swift Package Manager.

You might be wondering why you should bother with a package manager at all; the slight inconvenience of downloading and building files surely doesn't justify such a complex tool. You might even be thinking, "I could do this in an hour with cURL and a shell script"—and you'd be partially correct. Downloading and building third-party software is the easy part. The real problem that a package manager solves is dependency resolution, which is a much bigger problem than it might first seem.

If all you are doing is grabbing a single library and it has no dependencies, than you could recreate the package manager's functionality yourself easily, but as soon as you have to worry about how different libraries interact with different requirements it becomes a nastier problem. The Swift Package Manager takes care of this; it works out what is needed and what isn't, it figures out which versions can interact with each other, and finally it handles the downloading and building. If the package manager can't resolve the dependencies it will throw up an error letting you know that what you've asked for can't be done.

The Swift Package Manager is simple enough to use: you create a package file that describes what you want to include, you tell the package manager to resolve the dependencies and download the code, and the package manager then downloads and builds the code into a library you can use in your project. Let's take a look at using the Swift Package Manager to download some code we can then use. For this, we will use the example package manager project Apple created and made available, under the Apache license, for people to experiment with on GitHub (*https://github.com/apple/example-package-dealer*).

At the time of writing this book, the Swift Package Manager isn't integrated into Xcode. However, this is something that's likely to change in future releases.

We will be recreating the project from scratch instead of using the completed one; our goal will be to create a Swift program that can create a standard deck of playing cards, shuffle the deck, and then deal out some cards, displaying what is on each card. Most of the work is done for us; we just need to write some code to hook all the bits together. The library we will be downloading is called DeckOfPlayingCards; this is our only dependency. DeckOfPlayingCards, however, has two dependencies, PlayingCard and FisherYates. PlayingCard represents a single card and Fisher Yates is a little function to shuffle an array into a random order.

The Swift Package Manager is designed to run through the command line. We will still be using Xcode for our editing, but controlling the package manager is easier inside the Terminal app.

If you aren't super comfortable using the command line, don't worry, we'll be describing each step fully. You don't have to know *bash* to do any of this, although it's worth getting a handle on it for your own projects.

Follow these steps to create and then build and run the sample program:

1. Make a new folder and call it *Dealer*. This folder will be where we store our code, the code the package manager downloads, and the built project we will run.

2. Open the folder inside the Terminal app. The easiest way to do this is to drag the folder from the Finder onto the Terminal icon. You can also navigate to the folder through the Terminal by typing:

   ```
   cd path/to/where/you/saved/the/dealer/folder
   ```

   Replace `path/to/where/you/saved/the/dealer/folder` with the path of the *Dealer* folder you made earlier and press Return to run the command.

3. Initialize the folder as a new package. In the Terminal, type the following and press Return:

   ```
   swift package init --type executable
   ```

This will run the Swift commands to generate the folders and files necessary for a Swift package.

Notice the `--type executable` part of the preceding command—this is the flag you set if you want to make a program using the package manager (which we do). By default, the Swift Package Manager assumes you are making a library to be used by another project. If you are making a library, you can just drop this part.

Of these folders, the most interesting is *Sources*. This is where any source code will go, including our own. Of the different files created, the most relevant is the *Package.swift* file. This file is the package manifest; the package manager will read it in a moment to determine what code it needs to download.

You have to name your package file *Package.swift* and it has to be in the root folder of your project. Otherwise, the Swift Package Manager won't be able to find it!

4. Open *Package.swift* and replace its contents with the following:

```swift
import PackageDescription

let repo = https://github.com/apple/example-package-
    deckofplayingcards.git

let package = Package(
    name: "Dealer",
    dependencies: [
        // Dependencies declare other packages
        // that this package depends on.
        // .package(url: /* package url */, from: "1.0.0"),
        .package(url: repo,from: "3.0.0")
    ],
    targets: [
        // Targets are the basic building blocks of a package.
        // A target can define a module or a test suite.
        // Targets can depend on other targets in this package,
        // and on products in packages that this package
        // depends on.
        .target(
            name: "Dealer",
            dependencies: ["DeckOfPlayingCards"])
    ]
)
```

 Whenever you are inside the Terminal, if you type open <file name> and press Return it will open up the file you requested as if you'd double-clicked it in the Finder.

Let's take a look at what this is doing. First, we import the `PackageDescription` module; this module allows us to define a `Package` that will tell the package manager what to download. Then we create a new `Package`, which has two parameters: a name for the package (`Dealer`), and an array of the dependencies our package will need. In this case we only need the `DeckOfPlayingCards` dependency, so we provide the URL where we can get this package and then a version number.

All Swift packages use the semver (*http://semver.org*) semantic versioning system, so we can specify major, minor, and patch versions, but in this case we'll just require version 3 or later. It is worth noting that the dependencies are a set; we can have as many packages as we want, and we can also have greater control over the modules being downloaded, including excluding certain modules, setting ranges for the versions, or even making multiple build targets that chain into one another. For this example, though, we want to keep it simple.

 Our goal here is to explain how you will most likely be using the package manager for grabbing third-party libraries. We're only showing the basics, but it is a very complex tool. If you are interested in seeing what flexibility it possesses or need to do something more than what we are doing here, the specification is fully detailed on the GitHub page for the package manager (*http://bit.ly/2HDw6MV*).

Next, we need to write a small program to make use of all the modules we're about to download.

5. Open *main.swift* from inside the *Sources/Dealer* folder and replace its contents with the following:

```
import DeckOfPlayingCards

var deck = Deck.standard52CardDeck()
deck.shuffle()

for _ in 0...4
{
    guard let card = deck.deal() else
    {
        print("No More Cards!")
        break
    }
    print(card)
}
```

This program is pretty straightforward: first we import the DeckOfPlayingCards module, then we create a new deck of cards and shuffle them. Then we enter a for loop that runs five times, printing out cards after doing a quick check that the deck hasn't run out of cards.

With our package ready and our program to use it complete, it is time to build the project. We are going to be building and running the project through the command line.

6. Reopen the Terminal window you had open before.

7. Type `swift build` and press Return.

The Swift Package Manager will download any necessary files and build them, and with that done we can run our program.

In this case we are asking the package manager to both download any required packages and build them into a program we can run. If you just need to download the package files and you plan on building them yourself, use the `swift package resolve` command instead.

8. Run the program by typing `swift run Dealer` (recall that `Dealer` is the name we set for our program back in the *Package.swift* file). The output will look something like:

```
♠8
♣7
♠9
♣2
♢5
```

You can also run the executables built manually if you like. The *.build/* folder is a hidden folder inside the project folder that is where the build tool places executables and libraries as it compiles them.

Inside this are two more folders, one called *debug* (for the debug builds) and the other *release*. So, if you prefer, you can type `./.build/debug/Dealer`, and this will do the same thing as the preceding command.

We just used the Swift Package Manager and a teensy bit of our own code to write a small program. This is only scraping the surface of what the Swift Package Manager can do; it is a very powerful tool with hundreds of options, and it is well worth taking a full look at the official site on GitHub (*https://github.com/apple/swift-package-manager*).

In its current form, the package manager is not very well integrated with Xcode. You can, however, ask the package manager to generate an Xcode project for your package if you like. The command is `swift package generate-xcodeproj`. Bear in mind, though, that if you update the dependencies you will need to regenerate this project file.

Conclusion

In this chapter, you've learned about object-oriented programming in Swift and how to get some more real-world tasks done using the functionality provided by Swift and its supporting libraries. In the next part of the book, we'll start putting everything covered so far to use in building a real app.

Building Selfiegram

CHAPTER 4

Setting Up Our App

In Part I we looked at the tools you use to build applications on Apple platforms: Xcode, the Apple Developer Program, and the Swift language. Now we're actually going to build an app using them!

In this chapter we will start building *Selfiegram*, an iOS app that lets us take new selfies and view old ones. It's not a new idea for an app, but it lets us explore a great number of the different features of Swift and the various frameworks Apple has provided to build apps. By the end of this part of the book we'll have a basic application that uses the images, location, filesystem, notifications, and map frameworks of iOS; then, in Part III, we will extend and polish it even further.

 Our goal isn't that by the end of the book you'll have an app capable of replacing an app like Instagram; we are simply aiming to show off how you'd actually go about building up an app such as this, while at the same time demonstrating just how much of the work of building apps is already done for you. So, even though Selfiegram might not be an original idea, there is a lot you can learn from it.

The application will be built up in small stages, with a little bit of code and UI work to do in each. We have tagged our repo on GitHub (*https://github.com/thesecretlab/learning-swift-3rd-ed*) at each stage so you can look at how it progresses if you wish.

Throughout this book, we need to call some methods with rather long names—`func tableView(_ tableView: UITableView, cell ForRowAt indexPath: IndexPath) -> UITableViewCell` comes to mind—and paper and its electronic friends, like PDFs, are width-limited. This means in a few places in the book we will be breaking up our code over multiple lines just so it can be displayed neatly on the page. You don't have to write your code this way if you don't want to; writing the method calls on one line will work just as well as breaking them up across multiple lines.

We'll begin by building up the skeleton of Selfiegram, which will give us a launching point for the later sections.

Designing Selfiegram

When we started to think about how this app should work, the only idea we had was "let's make a selfie app," which is a very broad goal. To lock this down to something a bit more concrete, we started drawing up some wireframes.

A wireframe is a very rough drawing of the app that you're about to make. It's much faster to get your ideas down on paper (digital or physical) than it is to actually implement the app itself, and the act of drawing your ideas helps you think as well.

You can see the original wireframe for Selfiegram in Figure 4-1.

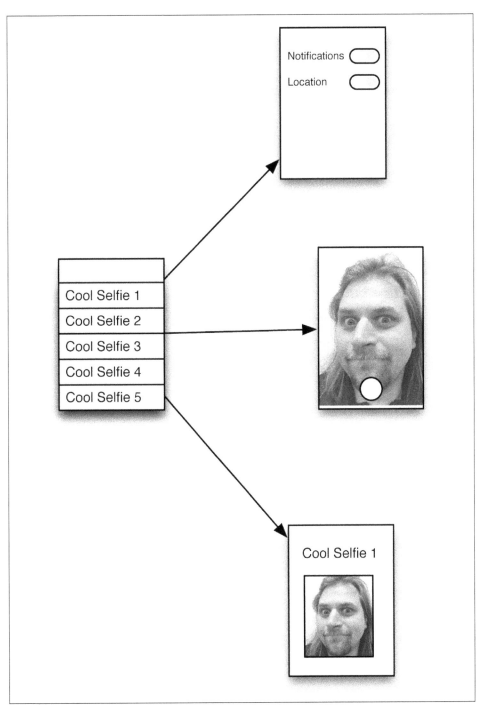

Figure 4-1. Selfiegram's wireframe

There is no one correct way to do a wireframe. Ours were done in a drawing tool called OmniGraffle, which has an array of stencils for this sort of work. They're quite high-fidelity in comparison to the initial wireframes you might find yourself making, but we did our first pass by hand on a whiteboard. We then moved them into Omni-Graffle, as we needed something that we could use in a book. At each stage of redrawing the wireframes, things changed slightly, and this is a good thing, as you tend to discover things you missed on the first pass. You don't need to do wireframes as high-fidelity as the ones we've done for this book; there is nothing wrong with using hand-drawn wireframes as long as everyone in the team knows how they are meant to work.

The main focus of the app is around the list of selfies you have taken, and that is going to be the hub for all the actions of the app. The selfies will be presented as a list shown in reverse order of when you took them, so most recent at the top. Tapping a selfie will let you edit its name as well as see it and its metadata in detail. From the list of selfies you'll be able to take a new selfie or open up the settings to configure the app.

By the end of Part II we'll have finished the app outlined in the wireframes in Figure 4-2.

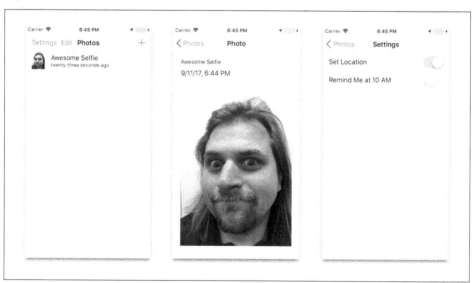

Figure 4-2. Initial version

Creating the Project

The first thing we need to do is create the Xcode project for Selfiegram. We'll be using this for the majority of the book. If you need a refresher on Xcode and the development tools, check out "Xcode" on page 3. When you're ready, let's get started:

1. Launch Xcode. You'll see the Welcome to Xcode screen as shown in Figure 4-3.

Figure 4-3. The "Welcome to Xcode" screen

2. Click the "Create a new Xcode project" button. The list of project templates will appear. Select iOS in the top row (which includes categories for Apple's other platforms, such as macOS, tvOS, and watchOS), and choose the Master-Detail App template (Figure 4-4). Click Next.

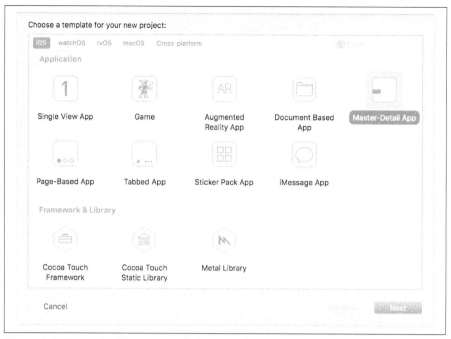

Figure 4-4. Select the Master-Detail App template

The templates provide default setups for different types of applications. You can do everything provided by each template manually, if you want; they're just collections of provided files and code. The templates shown in our screenshot are those provided by Apple, and ship with Xcode.

3. You'll be prompted to give the project a name and provide some additional information. Use the following settings:

- **Product Name**: Selfiegram.

- **Organization Name**: Your company's name. Enter your own name if you're not making this app for a company.

- **Organization Identifier**: Your domain name, reversed; for example, if you own *mycompany.com*, enter com.mycompany (customize this based on your domain name; if you don't have one, enter com.example).

The organization name and the product name are used to create the app's *bundle identifier*. A bundle identifier is a period-separated string that uniquely identifies a bundle of code and resources. For example, if you use `com.example` as your organization identifier, the bundle ID will be `com.example.Selfiegram`.

Bundle identifiers are used everywhere in the macOS and iOS ecosystem. A bundle identifier forms the basis of your *app ID*, which is the unique string that identifies your app on the App Store. Your app's bundle ID is also used as the basis of other IDs, such as the document uniform type identifier for document-based apps. The upshot of all this is that it's worth keeping this ID in the back of your mind.

- **Language**: Swift.
- **Devices**: Universal.
- **Use Core Data**: Off.

Core Data is a framework provided by Apple that lets you store data in a manner similar to a database, but local to your app. We're not using Core Data in this book, as it's a topic that befits a book all on its own. Additionally, the limits of Core Data are quite easy to hit, and it's often more useful, as well as more of a learning experience, to build storage infrastructure for your app from scratch. If you turn this on, stubs for Core Data, as well as a data model, will be added to the project that Xcode will generate for you. If you're a masochist, you can learn more about Core Data in the documentation (*https://apple.co/2GEID1B*). Don't say we didn't warn you!

- **Include Unit Tests**: On.
- **Include UI Tests**: On.

Leaving these two on creates stubs for unit tests and UI tests, respectively. We'll touch on these subjects in "Testing the SelfieStore" on page 130.

4. Click the Next button, and Xcode will ask you where you'd like to save the project (which will be a folder with the same name you put in the Product Name field).

Xcode will ask you if you want to create a Git repository for your project. We recommend that you store this project (and, indeed, anything else that you might work on) in Git, or a similar version control system. It's out of the scope of this book to explore Git, but we strongly recommend you take some time to do so if you're not already using it. As an added bonus, Xcode has support for Git built in.

Then it will create a project for you to work with (see Figure 4-5).

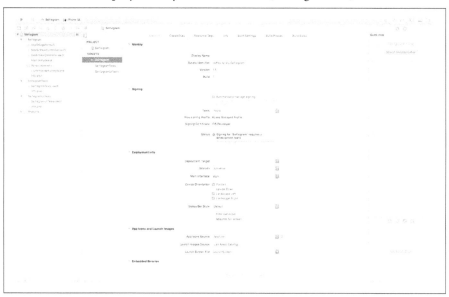

Figure 4-5. Our project

The Structure

The Master-Detail template is one of the most common templates you'll use when doing iOS development. It gives you a basic, ready-to-use UI, comprised of multiple view controllers. The top-level view controller is the split view controller, designed for presenting Master-Detail style information; it has two children, a master and a detail view controller. This view controller doesn't have an appearance of its own; it instead takes its appearance from the two view controllers it is attached to, and it can be configured to present them in any number of ways. By default on small devices the master and detail view controllers will each take up the whole screen when presented, while on larger devices the master will be overlaid on top of the detail view controller.

Below the split view controller are its two navigation controllers. There are two because of the nature of the split view controller; one points to the master and the other to the detail view controller (see Figure 4-6). A navigation controller provides a few nice features: by default it gives us a navigation bar, and it gives us a navigation hierarchy we can manipulate. The master view controller contains a *table view*, which is a common way to show lists of data; this will be where our list of selfies will go. The detail view controller contains just a label—this will be where we put our detailed selfie information. Tapping on an item in the master view controller will segue into the detail view controller, showing the details for that item.

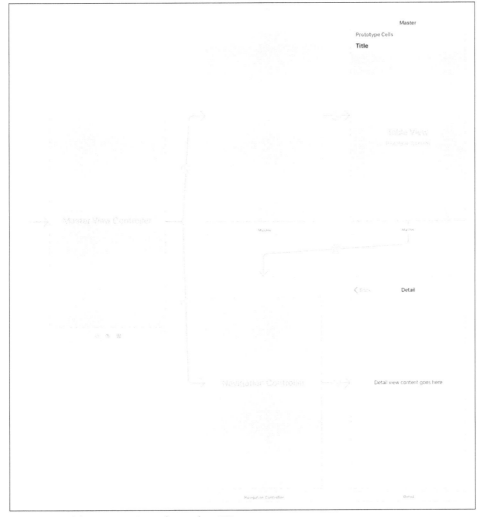

Figure 4-6. The Master-Detail template UI

Renaming the Views

Despite the UI that the template provided being pretty close to what we want, it does use some terminology that isn't really applicable to our app. So, let's do some renaming:

1. Open *Main.storyboard*.
2. Select the master view controller from the Document Outline. There will be two of these; you want the one with the table view inside of it.
3. In the Attributes inspector, select the Title attribute and change it to `Selfies List`.
4. Select the navigation item inside the view controller.
5. Using the Attributes inspector, change its title to `Selfies`. Figure 4-7 shows the result.

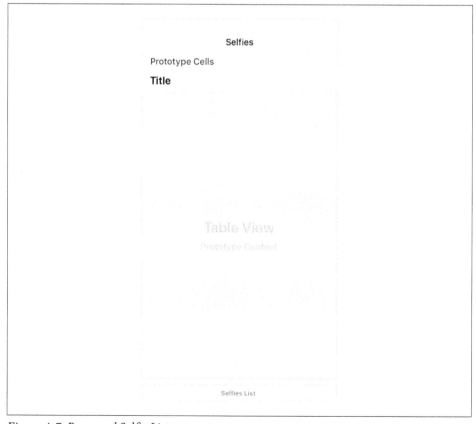

Figure 4-7. Renamed Selfie List

Changing these two properties means that when we're in the document outline we can easily see our selfies list, and when we run the app the navigation bar will show the word "Selfies" instead of "Master," which makes a lot more sense. Now we need to do the same to the detail view controller:

1. Select the detail view controller from the document outline.

2. In the Attributes inspector, select the Title attribute and change it to `Selfie Detail`.

3. Select the navigation item inside the view controller.

4. Using the Attributes inspector, change its title to `Selfie`.

With that done, our basic project is set up and ready to go. Most of the work was done for us by the Master-Detail template, which gave us our basic UI and some unit and UI tests that we will build up later on (for now, these are empty).

If you run the application right now, you'll be able to create a new entry in the list and view previous entries by selecting them, but otherwise it does very little. In the next chapter, we'll add some new functionality.

CHAPTER 5

Building the Model Object

Although we don't yet have any functionality in the app beyond what the template gave us, we will need some sort of model object and storage for those objects when we get around to using them. For this reason, we'll be creating the model part of our app first. We'll create two classes for this: our model will be called `Selfie`, and our manager `SelfieStore`. Making the model first gives us a platform on which to build up the rest of the app without having to stub out functionality when it needs the model to be working.

The Selfie Object

The first object we need to create will be a new class to represent an individual selfie in the application:

1. Create a new Swift file by going to File → New File.

2. In the iOS category, under the Source heading, select the Swift File option.

3. Name the file *SelfieStore.swift*.

4. Save it into the *Selfiegram* folder and make it target the Selfiegram target (see Figure 5-1).

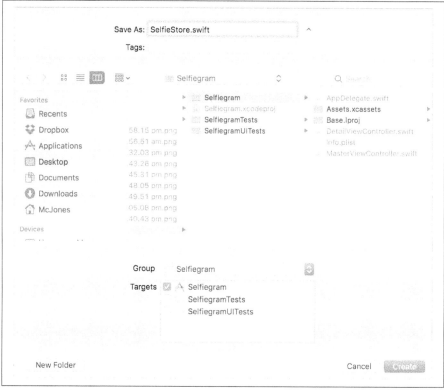

Figure 5-1. The model file

5. Near the top of the file, underneath the import line, import the `UIKit.UIImage` library:

```
import UIKit.UIImage
```

We are only importing the `UIImage` part of `UIKit` because the `UIKit` framework is quite large, and we only need this one small piece of it. This will give us access to the `UIImage` class, which will hold the image data we need for our selfies. In our case we will be using it to store JPGs, but the class itself supports many different image formats.

6. Create a new class and call it `Selfie`:

```
class Selfie : Codable
{

}
```

This class will represent a single selfie and all its associated selfie metadata. We are making it conform to the `Codable` protocol, which is a new protocol in Swift 4 that combines two different ones, `Encodable` and `Decodable`. This gives us the ability to serialize and deserialize our model into JSON format, which we will use to save our selfies to and load them from disk. The really nice thing about using Codable is that if we make our class out of objects that already conform to this protocol, such as String objects, we don't have to write any code to conform to Codable.

 If you do need specific control over the encoding and decoding, the methods to override are init(from decoder: Decoder) and encode(to encoder: Encoder). We don't need to do this because everything that makes up our Selfie class already conforms to Codable, and as a general rule for programming, one should never do more work than is necessary.

7. Implement the created and id constant properties:

```
// When it was created
let created : Date

// A unique ID, used to link this selfie to its image on disk
let id : UUID
```

These two properties are the core metadata of the selfie. The created property will be set on creation of a new selfie and will be used later to sort the selfies in the list. id will be a unique identifier that we will use throughout the project to uniquely identify each selfie regardless of any other metadata.

8. Implement the title property:

```
// The name of this selfie
var title = "New Selfie!"
```

The title of the selfie will be a user-configurable setting. By default it will say "New Selfie!" but later on users will be able to change it to whatever they want.

9. Implement the image computed property:

```
// The image on disk for this selfie
var image : UIImage?
{
    get
    {
        return SelfieStore.shared.getImage(id: self.id)
    }
    set
    {
        try? SelfieStore.shared.setImage(id: self.id, image: newValue)
    }
}
```

This property returns a `UIImage` from the disk that is the actual image component of the selfie—after all, it isn't much of a selfie without an image! The property uses information from a class we haven't written yet to load the selfie image, but don't worry about that; we'll write it in a moment.

10. Finally, we need to implement an intializer for the selfie:

```
init(title: String)
{
    self.title = title

    // the current time
    self.created = Date()
    // a new UUID
    self.id = UUID()
}
```

The initializer is fairly simple: it creates a new selfie with a specific title and sets the two constant properties. The `created` property will have as its value the moment in time when the selfie was initialized and `id` will be set to a new UUID. The UUID will be used to uniquely identify the selfie when we save it to and load it from disk.

UUID stands for *universally unique identifier*. Under the hood it's a 128-bit number, so there are approximately 340 undecillion (we had to look that word up, but trust us, it's big) of them possible. Because this number is so mind-bogglingly huge, we don't have to be concerned about accidentally generating one that is already in use. UUIDs are designed for this very purpose, so don't worry too much about generating billions of them; you won't make a dent. The UUID struct has a property called `uuidString` that returns a `String` form of the UUID, which we'll be using numerous times in the code. If you are curious, a UUID is broken up into a specific pattern, so if you print one out, it will look something like `093A58F9-CC55-4EB6-B898-B576C29CB734`.

With this done, our `Selfie` class is complete. We have a model object ready to use, but now we need something to handle all the interaction with the selfies and the rest of the app. We'll make that next.

The SelfieStore

While our `Selfie` class represents a single selfie, it doesn't have any capability to interact with the rest of the app or to be saved to and loaded from disk. We need a manager to handle this for us, so let's create one now.

 Throughout this book we refer a lot to "the disk." This is because we all hail from a time back when computers had actual spinning hard disk drives as their storage. iPhones and even most computers these days have very fancy hardware and nothing as old-fashioned as a hard drive would be welcome, but old habits die hard. Any time you see the word *disk*, feel free to replace it in your mind with *drive*, *storage*, or any other word that means "place where things are saved."

Our manager is going to need to handle events that can fail. When this happens, we want to throw errors. Our first step is then to make a new error that we can throw when needed.

Add the following to the *SelfieStore.swift* file, just below the `Selfie` class:

```
enum SelfieStoreError : Error
{
    case cannotSaveImage(UIImage?)
}
```

The new error is an enum that uses `Error` as its base class, so we can throw it like an error any time we need to, with no extra code required. Using an enum means is it trivially easy to add new subtypes of errors simply by adding new cases to the enum itself. Our only error case so far, `cannotSaveImage`, takes in an optional `UIImage` and will be used for when we fail to save a selfie to the disk.

Now that we are set up to throw errors when necessary, it is time to start building up the `SelfieStore`. For this app we are going to be building our `SelfieStore` as a singleton—that is, an object of which there can only ever be one copy. This means we can refer to it from anywhere in our code without having to pass it around between different views in the app, simplifying our design.

 Overuse of singletons in your apps (or any program, really) can lead to hard-to-follow code. This singleton is a very useful and powerful design pattern, but like with any pattern you have to keep your overall program structure in mind. Don't just make singletons willy-nilly solely because they are easy!

We'll be building up our singleton in a few parts. First we will create the basic structure of the class with method stubs. We will then write unit tests to test the functionality, and then fill in our stubs. This way we can test our code as we write it. Let's get started:

1. Create a new class called `SelfieStore`:

```
final class SelfieStore
{

}
```

   We are making the class `final` as we want it to be locked down—because there can only be one of these at a time, it makes no sense to allow subclassing.

2. Create a `static` property for other parts of the app to use to access the functionality of this class. By making it `static` we are letting Swift do all the heavy lifting, ensuring there is only one version of the singleton:

```
static let shared = SelfieStore()
```

   The design of our singleton means that it will be accessed through this variable, so to use it we'll write code similar to `SelfieStore.shared.someFunction()` instead of instantiating a copy of the class.

3. Create the following method stubs:

```
/// Gets an image by ID. Will be cached in memory for future lookups.
/// - parameter id: the id of the selfie whose image you are after
/// - returns: the image for that selfie or nil if it doesn't exist
func getImage(id:UUID) -> UIImage?
{
    return nil
}

/// Saves an image to disk.
/// - parameter id: the id of the selfie you want this image
/// associated with
/// - parameter image: the image you want saved
/// - Throws: `SelfieStoreObject` if it fails to save to disk
func setImage(id:UUID, image : UIImage?) throws
{
    throw SelfieStoreError.cannotSaveImage(image)
}

/// Returns a list of Selfie objects loaded from disk.
/// - returns: an array of all selfies previously saved
/// - Throws: `SelfieStoreError` if it fails to load a selfie correctly
/// from disk
func listSelfies() throws -> [Selfie]
{
```

```
        return []
    }

    /// Deletes a selfie, and its corresponding image, from disk.
    /// This function simply takes the ID from the Selfie you pass in,
    /// and gives it to the other version of the delete function.
    /// - parameter selfie: the selfie you want deleted
    /// - Throws: `SelfieStoreError` if it fails to delete the selfie
    /// from disk
    func delete(selfie: Selfie) throws
    {
        throw SelfieStoreError.cannotSaveImage(nil)
    }

    /// Deletes a selfie, and its corresponding image, from disk.
    /// - parameter id: the id property of the Selfie you want deleted
    /// - Throws: `SelfieStoreError` if it fails to delete the selfie
    /// from disk
    func delete(id: UUID) throws
    {
        throw SelfieStoreError.cannotSaveImage(nil)
    }

    /// Attempts to load a selfie from disk.
    /// - parameter id: the id property of the Selfie object you want loaded
    /// from disk
    /// - returns: the selfie with the matching id, or nil if it
    /// doesn't exist
    func load(id: UUID) -> Selfie?
    {
        return nil
    }

    /// Attempts to save a selfie to disk.
    /// - parameter selfie: the selfie to save to disk
    /// - Throws: `SelfieStoreError` if it fails to write the data
    func save(selfie: Selfie) throws
    {
        throw SelfieStoreError.cannotSaveImage(nil)
    }
```

There are various method stubs in here. We don't need to worry about what they do currently, as we are going to change it, but we do need to know what they *will* be doing:

- getImage(id:) will return the image associated with a particular selfie's id, or nil if it can't find one.

- setImage(id: image:) will save the image to disk using the id passed in to associate it back with a selfie.

- `listSelfies` will return an array of every selfie in the store.
- `delete(selfie:)` will delete the selfie and its associated image. It does this by calling the other `delete` function and using the selfie's `id`.
- `delete(id:)` will delete the selfie (and its associated image) that matches the `id` parameter.
- `load(id:)` will load the selfie that matches the `id` from disk.
- `save(selfie:)` will save the passed-in selfie to disk.

With our `SelfieStore` fully stubbed out, we can start writing our unit tests.

Testing the SelfieStore

Unit tests have been around for a while now, and while they may not be the only way to test code, they certainly are one of the more popular options. Luckily for us, Xcode has unit testing capability built directly into the editor. One of the nice things about Swift is its very strongly typed nature. This means a great deal of unit tests focusing on trying to store invalid data types can be skipped; the compiler has taken care of all that for us already, letting us focus on testing the functionality. So, with our `SelfieStore` stubbed out, let's write some tests we can use to verify it is working correctly:

1. Create a new unit test. Go to File → New File, and from the list select Unit Test Case Class (see Figure 5-2).

Figure 5-2. Creating a new unit test file

2. Call it *SelfieStoreTests.swift* and make sure it is a subclass of `XCTestCase`. Save the new file into the *SelfiegramTests* folder and make sure it targets SelfiegramTests (Figure 5-3).

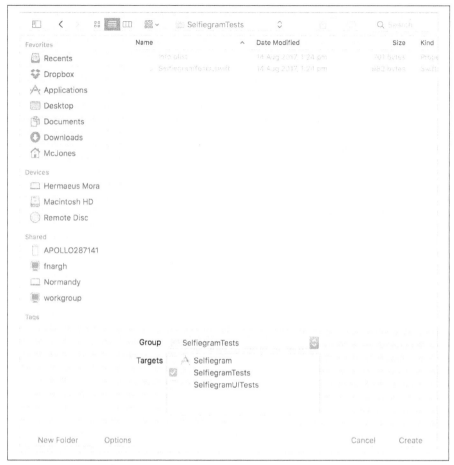

Figure 5-3. Saving the unit test

3. Open *SelfieStoreTests.swift*. Inside there is a new class, `SelfieStoreTests`, which is a subclass of `XCTestCase`. This is the base test class used by Xcode and includes everything we might need to do tests. We will be writing all our tests inside this class as functions.

4. Import the `Selfiegram` module as testable:

    ```
    @testable import Selfiegram
    ```

    This is just a normal `import` statement, although instead of a built-in or third-party library, the module we are importing is our own. By including the `@test able` flag we are telling the importer to bring it in in a form that is designed for testing, so internal functionality (such as internal functions and variables) that would normally be hidden is made available.

5. Import the `UIKit` framework:

```
import UIKit
```

This will give us access to `UIImage` and other associated classes and functions we'll need as part of our testing.

6. Create a helper function to generate some sample images. Because we want to test our model object's ability to store and load selfies (including their images), we need some images to test with. We don't want to bother testing the camera frameworks or `UIKit` itself, as Apple wrote them and not us, so we instead write a little function that will take in a string and return an image with that text rendered into it:

```
/// A helper function to create images with text being used as the
/// image content.
/// - returns: an image containing a representation of the text
/// - parameter text: the string you want rendered into the image
func createImage(text: String) -> UIImage
{
    // Start a drawing canvas
    UIGraphicsBeginImageContext(CGSize(width: 100, height: 100))

    // Close the canvas after we return from this function
    defer
    {
        UIGraphicsEndImageContext()
    }

    // Create a label
    let label = UILabel
        (frame: CGRect(x: 0, y: 0, width: 100, height: 100))
    label.font = UIFont.systemFont(ofSize: 50)
    label.text = text

    // Draw the label in the current drawing context
    label.drawHierarchy(in: label.frame, afterScreenUpdates: true)

    // Return the image
    // (the ! means we either successfully get an image, or we crash)
    return UIGraphicsGetImageFromCurrentImageContext()!
}
```

There is a lot going on in this function. First, we begin a new image context and pass in a size. Essentially this is saying we want a new image of 100 by 100 pixels. Next, we use `defer` to close the image context when we return. We do this because we *have* to close an image context we have begun, but we need the context when we are returning—we use `defer` to close the context after we return the image out of the context. Then we create a label with the text inside of it, and draw that label into the context we set up. Finally, we get an image of this label from the graphics context we created.

7. Delete the placeholder functions. By default we are given a setUp and tearDown functions as well as two test cases; we don't need any of these for our tests, so we can just remove them.

8. Create a new function called testCreatingSelfie:

```
func testCreatingSelfie()
{
    // Arrange
    let selfieTitle = "Creation Test Selfie"
    let newSelfie = Selfie(title: selfieTitle)

    // Act
    try? SelfieStore.shared.save(selfie: newSelfie)

    // Assert
    let allSelfies = try! SelfieStore.shared.listSelfies()

    guard let theSelfie =
        allSelfies.first(where: {$0.id == newSelfie.id}) else
    {
        XCTFail("Selfies list should contain the one we just created.")
        return
    }

    XCTAssertEqual(selfieTitle, newSelfie.title)
}
```

This test is as simple as we can make it. We create a new selfie and ask the Self ieStore to save it. We then load the list of selfies back from the store and check to see if our selfie is in there.

9. Create a testSavingImage test case:

```
func testSavingImage() throws
{
    // Arrange
    let newSelfie = Selfie(title: "Selfie with image test")

    // Act
    newSelfie.image = createImage(text: "100")
    try SelfieStore.shared.save(selfie: newSelfie)

    // Assert
    let loadedImage = SelfieStore.shared.getImage(id: newSelfie.id)

    XCTAssertNotNil(loadedImage,"The image should be loaded.")
}
```

This tests whether or not our `SelfieStore` can save an image and then load it back from disk. In this test case we are using our helper function we set up earlier to create the image. We're also using emoji as the input, because who doesn't love emoji?

10. Create a `testLoadingSelfie` test case:

```
func testLoadingSelfie() throws
{
    // Arrange
    let selfieTitle = "Test loading selfie"
    let newSelfie = Selfie(title: selfieTitle)
    try SelfieStore.shared.save(selfie: newSelfie)
    let id = newSelfie.id

    // Act
    let loadedSelfie = SelfieStore.shared.load(id: id)

    // Assert
    XCTAssertNotNil(loadedSelfie, "The selfie should be loaded")
    XCTAssertEqual(loadedSelfie?.id, newSelfie.id,
                "The loaded selfie should have the same ID")
    XCTAssertEqual(loadedSelfie?.created, newSelfie.created,
                "The loaded selfie should have the same creation date")
    XCTAssertEqual(loadedSelfie?.title, selfieTitle,
                "The loaded selfie should have the same title")
}
```

This tests the `SelfieStore`'s ability to save and load a specific selfie. A selfie is created, saved, loaded, and then compared to the original selfie. If they differ, the test fails.

11. Create a `testDeletingSelfie` test case:

```
func testDeletingSelfie() throws
{
    // Arrange
    let newSelfie = Selfie(title: "Test deleting a selfie")
    try SelfieStore.shared.save(selfie: newSelfie)
    let id = newSelfie.id

    // Act
    let allSelfies = try SelfieStore.shared.listSelfies()
    try SelfieStore.shared.delete(id: id)
    let selfieList = try SelfieStore.shared.listSelfies()
    let loadedSelfie = SelfieStore.shared.load(id: id)

    // Assert
    XCTAssertEqual(allSelfies.count - 1, selfieList.count,
                "There should be one less selfie after deletion")
    XCTAssertNil(loadedSelfie, "deleted selfie should be nil")
```

```
        }
```

This test creates a selfie, saves it, deletes it, and checks to make sure it is no longer available. This will verify that the `SelfieStore` is correctly deleting selfies.

 You might notice that as you create test functions a small diamond appears in the line gutter. This allows you to run just this test by clicking it. Once the test completes the diamond will show the result, allowing you to quickly look down the gutter to see which tests are failing and which are passing. The testing diamond on the class will also reflect the overall state of the tests; if any test inside fails, it marks itself as failing.

With these written out, we can now run our tests. There are a couple of different ways we can do this. One option is to press and hold the Run button in Xcode and select Test from the drop-down that appears. This, however, will run all the tests, including the UI tests we aren't currently using. As we only want to run our newly written tests, we can instead click the testing diamond next to the `SelfieStoreTests` class definition; this will run all the tests inside it.

If you run the tests now you'll see they all fail, which is exactly what we want at this stage.

Filling Out the Method Stubs

Now that our tests are nicely failing it is time to go back to our `SelfieStore` class and implement the stubbed-out methods so that we can start using it properly. Let's get started:

1. Add a new `imageCache` property to the class. This will be a dictionary indexed by `String` and returns a `UIImage`:

   ```
   private var imageCache : [UUID:UIImage] = [:]
   ```

   This property will be used later on to save the number of times we have to load from the disk. Whenever a selfie's image is requested the store will use the `id` property as the key and look for the image in the cache. If it isn't in there it will load it from the disk and store it into the cache to speed up retrieval the next time it is needed. The idea behind the cache is that we'll need a selfie's image quite a lot, so we might as well keep it around instead of loading it from disk each and every time.

2. Add a new `documentsFolder` computed property. This will return the file URL for the application's *Documents* folder:

```
var documentsFolder : URL
{
    return FileManager.default.urls(for: .documentDirectory,
                                    in: .allDomainsMask).first!
}
```

 A file URL is pretty much exactly the same as other URLs; the only difference is the protocol of a file URL starts with *file://* instead of something you're more used to, such as *https://*. File URLs are used in many iOS frameworks as ways to target files and folders on disk.

Each app in iOS is given a private folder called *Documents* for storing any important user-created content that needs to persist across launches of the app. The *Documents* folder is where we will be storing our selfies and their associated images. We use the FileManager class to access this folder.

 iOS is a managed environment. If you try to access folders and files by means other than those provided by Apple, your app will be blocked or killed by the operating system to prevent users' privacy from being invaded. Being able to program is a great skill, but don't wield it for evil!

FileManager is a class designed to handle file operations in a nice, clean way, freeing you up as a developer to work on making your program. It works by accessing the singleton FileManager default and telling it what operations you want to perform, such as save and delete, on a particular path. The path is generally passed in as a URL, but you can also use strings. In the case of this computed property, we are asking it for the path to the *Documents* folder. This is because in iOS we don't have direct control over the filesystem and where our apps will be installed, so we can't just assume this folder will be in a fixed spot like *~/Documents/*, as it is on a Mac. This function returns an array, as even though we know there will be only a single folder the FileManager APIs can't make assumptions like that—after all, we could be asking for any number of arbitrary folders.

With the release of iOS 11, there is an app installed on all iOS devices called Files. Files is a *Documents* folder browser for every app that enables support for it. From here you can see all the various apps' *Documents* folders and browse their contents.

In our case we are not adding in support for Files, as a single selfie is composed of multiple files and we don't want our users to accidentally delete part of a selfie. If you are curious as to how you can support document browsing in your apps, Apple has a full guide with multiple articles. (*https://apple.co/2HGvWo9*)

3. Replace the `getImage(id:)` method with the following:

```
/// Gets an image by ID. Will be cached in memory for future lookups.
/// - parameter id: the id of the selfie whose image you are after
/// - returns: the image for that selfie or nil if it doesn't exist
func getImage(id:UUID) -> UIImage?
{
    // If this image is already in the cache, return it
    if let image = imageCache[id]
    {
        return image
    }

    // Figure out where this image should live
    let imageURL =
    documentsFolder.appendingPathComponent("\(id.uuidString)-image.jpg")

    // Get the data from this file; exit if we fail
    guard let imageData = try? Data(contentsOf: imageURL) else
    {
        return nil
    }

    // Get the image from this data; exit if we fail
    guard let image = UIImage(data: imageData) else
    {
        return nil
    }

    // Store the loaded image in the cache for next time
    imageCache[id] = image

    // Return the loaded image
    return image
}
```

This first checks to see if the image is in the cache; if it is, we just return that. Otherwise, we build up a URL to where the image is saved. We know its name, as it will be the `id` property passed into the method. We then try and load that file in as a generic `Data` object. If that succeeds, we transform it into a `UIImage`. Then that gets saved into the cache for next time, and we return the image.

 `Data` is another one of those structs you'll see pop up all over the place in iOS. It is able to hold pretty much any arbitrary data (as a byte buffer) you want to push into it. We're barely scratching the surface of what these objects can do, but you can think of them as containing any binary data, which you can then transform into a more useful form or send and save elsewhere. The `Data` struct is designed for arbitrary loading and saving from various sources, such as from a URL or from disk, and is a common intermediate format that you will be using all over the place in iOS.

4. Replace the `setImage(id:)` method with the following:

```
/// Saves an image to disk.
/// - parameter id: the id of the selfie you want this image
/// associated with
/// - parameter image: the image you want saved
/// - Throws: `SelfieStoreObject` if it fails to save to disk
func setImage(id:UUID, image : UIImage?) throws
{
    // Figure out where the file would end up
    let fileName = "\(id.uuidString)-image.jpg"
    let destinationURL =
        self.documentsFolder.appendingPathComponent(fileName)

    if let image = image
    {
        // We have an image to work with, so save it out.
        // Attempt to convert the image into JPEG data.
        guard let data = UIImageJPEGRepresentation(image, 0.9) else
        {
            // Throw an error if this failed
            throw SelfieStoreError.cannotSaveImage(image)
        }

        // Attempt to write the data out
        try data.write(to: destinationURL)
    }
    else
    {
        // The image is nil, indicating that we want to remove the image.
```

```
        // Attempt to perform the deletion.
        try FileManager.default.removeItem(at: destinationURL)
    }

    // Cache this image in memory. (If image is nil, this has the
    // effect of
    // removing the entry from the cache dictionary.)
    imageCache[id] = image
}
```

This method works in a similar fashion. First it works out what the image should be called when it's saved. If the image passed in isn't optional, we convert it into a Data object holding a JPEG representation of the image. Then we save that data to disk. If the image passed in is nil, however, we instead delete the image file associated with that image.

5. Replace the listSelfies method with the following:

```
/// Returns a list of Selfie objects loaded from disk.
/// - returns: an array of all selfies previously saved
/// - Throws: `SelfieStoreError` if it fails to load a selfie correctly
/// from disk
func listSelfies() throws -> [Selfie]
{
    // Get the list of files in the Documents directory
    let contents = try FileManager.default
        .contentsOfDirectory(at: self.documentsFolder,
        includingPropertiesForKeys: nil)

    // Get all files whose path extension is 'json',
    // load them as data, and decode them from JSON
    return try contents.filter { $0.pathExtension == "json" }
        .map { try Data(contentsOf: $0) }
        .map { try JSONDecoder().decode(Selfie.self, from: $0) }
}
```

We're using a lot of closures here, but the basic functionality of what the method is doing is fairly straightforward. First we ask for all files inside the *Documents* folder. We then filter this to only be the files that end in *.json*, which is the format we'll save our selfies as in a later method. Then we convert them into Data objects, loading them into memory. Finally, we turn them all into Selfie objects using JSONDecoder and return all the selfies.

6. Replace the delete(selfie:) and delete(id:) methods with the following:

```
/// Deletes a selfie, and its corresponding image, from disk.
/// This function simply takes the ID from the Selfie you pass in,
/// and gives it to the other version of the delete function.
/// - parameter selfie: the selfie you want deleted
/// - Throws: `SelfieStoreError` if it fails to delete the selfie
/// from disk
```

```
func delete(selfie: Selfie) throws
{
    try delete(id: selfie.id)
}

/// Deletes a selfie, and its corresponding image, from disk.
/// - parameter id: the id property of the Selfie you want deleted
/// - Throws: `SelfieStoreError` if it fails to delete the selfie
/// from disk
func delete(id: UUID) throws
{
    let selfieDataFileName = "\(id.uuidString).json"
    let imageFileName = "\(id.uuidString)-image.jpg"

    let selfieDataURL =
    self.documentsFolder.appendingPathComponent(selfieDataFileName)
    let imageURL =
      self.documentsFolder.appendingPathComponent(imageFileName)

    // Remove the two files if they exist
    if FileManager.default.fileExists(atPath: selfieDataURL.path)
    {
        try FileManager.default.removeItem(at: selfieDataURL)
    }

    if FileManager.default.fileExists(atPath: imageURL.path)
    {
        try FileManager.default.removeItem(at: imageURL)
    }

    // Wipe the image from the cache if it's there
    imageCache[id] = nil
}
```

The first of these is pretty easy to understand: it just calls the other `delete`
method, which does all the work. The other `delete` method first builds up the
filenames of the selfie and its image. It then asks the `FileManager` to delete them
if they exist. Finally, it wipes the image from the `imageCache`—there is no need to
leave that image in the cache seeing as it will never be referenced again.

7. Replace the `load` and `save` methods with the following:

```
/// Attempts to load a selfie from disk.
/// - parameter id: the id property of the Selfie object
/// you want loaded
/// from disk
/// - returns: the selfie with the matching id, or nil if it
/// doesn't exist
func load(id: UUID) -> Selfie?
{
```

```
        let dataFileName = "\(id.uuidString).json"

        let dataURL =
          self.documentsFolder.appendingPathComponent(dataFileName)

        // Attempt to load the data in this file,
        // and then attempt to convert the data into a Photo,
        // and then return it.
        // Return nil if any of these steps fail.
        if let data = try? Data(contentsOf: dataURL),
           let selfie = try? JSONDecoder().decode(Selfie.self,
             from: data)
        {
            return selfie
        }
        else
        {
            return nil
        }
    }

    /// Attempts to save a selfie to disk.
    /// - parameter selfie: the selfie to save to disk
    /// - Throws: `SelfieStoreError` if it fails to write the data
    func save(selfie: Selfie) throws
    {
        let selfieData = try JSONEncoder().encode(selfie)

        let fileName = "\(selfie.id.uuidString).json"
        let destinationURL =
        self.documentsFolder.appendingPathComponent(fileName)

        try selfieData.write(to: destinationURL)
    }
}
```

The load method builds up a URL to the selfie's location on disk, then tries to load this in as Data. If that succeeds, it uses JSONDecoder to convert the loaded JSON into a valid Selfie object. The save method takes in a selfie and uses the JSONEncoder class to turn the selfie into a JSON representation of it. It then tries to write this to disk.

JSONDecoder can take any type and appropriate JSON data and return an object of that type with the JSON data inside. Anything that conforms to the Decodable protocol can use JSONDecoder to get easy deserialization of custom objects. The JSONEncoder class works in the opposite direction: anything that conforms to the Encodable protocol can be passed to it, and it returns a JSON representation of it. Both the Decodable and Encodable protocols are designed to work with one another, which is why they are available together as one in the Codable protocol.

If you look at the JSON used in the case of our Selfie objects, it will look similar to the following:

```
{
  "created":524643733.54513001,
  "id":"B1B02912-EAD7-4C7E-AD14-A11275FDF693",
   "title":"New Selfie"
}
```

Now that we have all our methods stubs replaced with working code, if we run our tests again they'll all pass! While a working model is essential, ours isn't exactly easy to use, so it's time to build up some UI for our app.

CHAPTER 6

Building the Selfie List UI

With a model object tested and working, it is time to start building up the UI for the app. To start with, we'll make the UI for showing the list of previously taken selfies.

Creating the Selfie List

As we are using a Master-Detail template, the basic UI has been set up already in the storyboard; we just need to bash it into the shape that we need. The bulk of what we are going to be doing is using the UITableView and UITableViewController classes to make our selfie list.

The UITableView class is a specialized subclass of UIView designed to show lists of information. A table view is comprised of one or more sections, and each section has zero or more table view cells. A table view cell can be thought of as just a normal view —it can present anything you want it to.

The data for the table view cells and sections comes from the table view's UITable ViewDataSource property. Whenever a table view needs to present information, such as how many cells are there in a section or what a single cell should show, it asks its data source for the answer. This means a table view itself has no knowledge of what it is showing or how it is to be structured—that is all handled for it by the data source. A table view also has a delegate that gets told when non–data related events are occurring, such as when a row has been selected.

Index paths are an important part of table views that get used a great deal by both the data source and the delegate. An index path is a simple object that represents the path of a single cell in the table view. It does this through its two properties, section and row. Both of these are Ints and allow you to pinpoint a specific cell in the table view without the need to pass an entire cell around between methods.

The `UITableViewController` is the other object we'll be using a lot to make our UI. It is a subclass of `UITableViewController` and is designed to control a table view. It is essentially a convenience class that, instead of managing a view, manages only a table view. There's nothing that a table view controller does that you can't do yourself by conforming to the relevant protocols; it's just easier to use the prebuilt code than to reinvent the wheel. To help with this, a `UITableViewController` is already set up as its table view's delegate and data source.

 You might be wondering why it is call a *table* view if it only shows lists of data. This is because `UITableView` and all its associated objects are based on `NSTableView` from macOS development, which could present data in both rows and columns. If you are after something similar to a table view but with a bit more multidimensionality, take a look at `UICollectionView`, which you interact with and control in an almost identical fashion to a table view but which can support any layout appearance you desire.

Let's turn our template master view controller into a view controller that can show a list of selfies:

1. Open the *MasterViewController.swift* file and refactor its name. Select the class name in the definition, then go to Editor → Refactor → Rename (or right-click the class name and select Refactor → Rename). Once you've done this, the Refactor window will appear. This will show you what changes will take effect.

2. Rename the class to `SelfieListViewController`. This will change the name of the file, the class name in comments, the class definition, and the class in the storyboard—four changes in total (see Figure 6-1).

Figure 6-1. Refactoring the MasterViewController class

 We don't *need* to refactor the class—nothing we are doing is dependent on it being named `SelfieListViewController`. It's just nicer-looking for our app's development than `MasterView Controller`, and as it only takes a few seconds to do, we think it is worth doing.

3. Delete the `objects` variable and replace it with the list of selfies:

```
// The list of Photo objects we're going to display
var selfies : [Selfie] = []
```

This is what we want the table view to show. We are instantiating it as an empty array initially, but we will get the list of selfies from the `SelfieStore` in a moment. Xcode will warn you about some errors at this point, because we deleted the old property; don't worry about these, as we are about to replace those sections of the code.

4. Replace `viewDidLoad` with the following:

```
override func viewDidLoad()
{
    super.viewDidLoad()

    // Load the list of selfies from the selfie store
    do
    {
```

```
        // Get the list of photos, sorted by date (newer first)
        selfies = try SelfieStore.shared.listSelfies()
            .sorted(by: { $0.created > $1.created })
    }
    catch let error
    {
        showError(message:
            "Failed to load selfies: \(error.localizedDescription)")
    }

    if let split = splitViewController
    {
        let controllers = split.viewControllers
        detailViewController = (controllers[controllers.count-1]
            as? UINavigationController)?.topViewController
            as? DetailViewController
    }
}
```

This method does a few things. First, it tries to load the list of selfies from the
SelfieStore. If it fails it calls a method called showError, which we are about to
write, to handle the error. If it succeeds it loads the list of selfies, sorted by date.
The last part of the method comes from the template, and is some necessary
boilerplate code to ensure that SplitViewController is correctly configured to
use the DetailViewController class as the detail part of the Master-Detail template.

5. Create the showError method now:

```
func showError(message : String)
{
    // Create an alert controller, with the message we received
    let alert = UIAlertController(title: "Error",
                                  message: message,
                                  preferredStyle: .alert)

    // Add an action to it - it won't do anything, but
    // doing this means that it will have a button to dismiss it
    let action = UIAlertAction(title: "OK",
        style: .default, handler: nil)
    alert.addAction(action)

    // Show the alert and its message
    self.present(alert, animated: true, completion: nil)
}
```

This method will be used whenever we encounter an issue we can't resolve, and is
designed to just let the user know that something has gone wrong. This isn't the
best means of handling errors, but it will do for now. We first create an instance
of the UIAlertController class, which is used for those pop-up–style views that

appear from time to time in apps. They can be configured to appear in two different ways, but we want them to look like alerts to signal that something has gone wrong. The style is set using the `preferredStyle` parameter of the alerts initializer. Then we add an action to the alert. Actions can be configured to do almost anything you need—in this case we only want it to dismiss our alert when the button is pressed, so we aren't giving it a handler, but if you do want more control the `handler` property can receive a closure. Finally, we present the alert.

6. Update the table view methods now:

```
override func tableView(_ tableView: UITableView,
                        numberOfRowsInSection section: Int) -> Int {
    return selfies.count
}
override func tableView(_ tableView: UITableView,
                        cellForRowAt indexPath: IndexPath
                        ) -> UITableViewCell
{
    let cell = tableView.dequeueReusableCell(withIdentifier: "Cell",
                                             for: indexPath)

    let selfie = selfies[indexPath.row]
    cell.textLabel?.text = selfie.title

    return cell
}
```

The first of these, `numberOfRowsInSection`, is the `UITableViewDataSource` call for configuring how many cells there are to be in each section of the table view. As we only have one section in our table view we can just return the number of selfies in our selfies array. The other method is a bit more complex. `cellForRowAt indexPath:` is called by the table view, when it needs to know what to display at each row in each section. The `indexPath` parameter is an object that has two components, a section and a row. Together these allow us to uniquely identify which cell we are trying to configure and send back to the table view to display. First we dequeue a reusable cell with an identifier. The identifier (in this case "Cell") was configured in the storyboard as part of the template. We are dequeuing a cell instead of creating a new one because creating a table view cell isn't an instantaneous operation. As we might be rapidly scrolling, those few milliseconds where we create the next cell we need to show will make the table view look laggy. Instead, the table view creates a bunch of cells and queues them up ready to be used. So, by calling `dequeueReusableCell` we are saying to the table view, "Hey, you know those cells you already made. Please give me one to configure." This can save quite a lot of time in something as important as scrolling a table view. We then configure it by setting the `textLabel` inside the cell to show the title of our selfie.

7. Finally, now we can delete the unnecessary methods `insertNewObject`, `pre pare(for segue: sender:)`, `tableview(commit editingStyle: forRowAt indexPath:)`, and `tableview(canEditRowAt indexPath:)`, and run the app. Once it has launched it will show a list of selfies, with all the selfies we created and saved while we were testing the `SelfieStore` (see Figure 6-2).

Figure 6-2. Showing our list of selfies from the tests

Improving the Selfie List

While our code works, the result isn't exactly the best looking. After all, a selfie really should show the actual image that is the core of the selfie (or will be when we add in camera support). Let's update the table view so that we not only show the image that is a part of the selfie but also have a small sublabel inside the table view cell that shows how old the selfie is:

1. Add a new property to the `SelfieListViewController` class:

```
// The formatter for creating the "1 minute ago"-style label
let timeIntervalFormatter : DateComponentsFormatter = {
    let formatter = DateComponentsFormatter()
    formatter.unitsStyle = .spellOut
    formatter.maximumUnitCount = 1
    return formatter
}()
```

This will be used to print out a human-readable string indicating how recent the selfie is, which will look similar to "1 minute ago." We are using a `DateCompo nentsFormatter` to do this—this is a class specifically created to handle formatting dates into a form that is pleasant to look at as a human. As a date is stored as a number of seconds since a fixed point in time, if we directly print it will we just have a long list of numbers. We could work out what this should look like in human-readable form, but dates are tricky and Apple has kindly already done the work for us here. We can control how the date appears using the `unitsStyle` and `maximumUnitCount` properties. Here we only want a single unit and we want it fully spelled out (i.e., "1 minute" as opposed to "1m").

2. Update `cellForRowAt indexPath:` to show the time and image:

```
override func tableView(_ tableView: UITableView,
            cellForRowAt indexPath: IndexPath) -> UITableViewCell
{
    // Get a cell from the table view
    let cell = tableView.dequeueReusableCell(withIdentifier: "Cell",
                                            for: indexPath)

    // Get a selfie and use it to configure the cell
    let selfie = selfies[indexPath.row]

    // Set up the main label
    cell.textLabel?.text = selfie.title

    // Set up its time ago sublabel
    if let interval =
        timeIntervalFormatter.string(from: selfie.created, to: Date())
    {
        cell.detailTextLabel?.text = "\(interval) ago"
```

```
    }
    else
    {
        cell.detailTextLabel?.text = nil
    }

    // Show the selfie image to the left of the cell
    cell.imageView?.image = selfie.image

    return cell
}
```

This isn't hugely different from how it was before; all we are doing now is using two more elements of the table view cell, subtitle and imageView, and giving them appropriate values to show.

If we were to try to run this now it wouldn't work, as the properties (or at least some of them) we are using on the table view cell don't exist. But if they don't exist, how was Xcode able to offer us autocomplete options when typing them in and highlight them correctly?

This is because table view cells have a few different possible appearance styles. The default and simplest is called "Basic"; it has a label called textLabel and is what we've been using so far. There are various different styles out there, including "Custom," which is where you fully control the appearance. To account for the different styles possible inside a UITableViewCell, there are two options: use optional properties for all the possibilities or use subclasses and make people typecast the cell before configuring it. There are strengths and weaknesses to both approaches. Apple chose the former, as optionals are easy enough to handle in Swift already and forcing a type check doesn't fit as well with the language's philosophy. We now need to change the cell to use the correct appearance style so we can make use of the code we wrote:

1. Open *Main.storyboard* and select the SelfieListViewController.

2. Select the prototype cell inside the table view.

3. Using the Attributes inspector, change the style from Basic to Subtitle.

 In the Attributes inspector, you might notice the Identifier property of the cell is set to "Cell". This is the identifier we use in cellForRowAt indexPath: when we are dequeuing a cell for reuse. You can use this identifier to have multiple different types of prototype cells inside a single table view.

The Subtitle cell style has a main label, like the Basic style, but underneath this it has a subtitle label. This is where we will be showing the date. There is also a UIImageView over to the left side of the cell in both cases; this is where we will be showing our selfie preview.

If we run the app once more we will get a similar result as before, but now the cells will display how long ago the selfies were created, and for the selfies that have an image, such as the one we created using emoji in our testing, that image will appear over to the side (see Figure 6-3).

Figure 6-3. Our improved list of selfies

At this point we have a useful list of selfies being shown, but we have no way to delete the selfies we created as part of our testing or add new ones. So, our next step is to make it so we can add new selfies and delete existing ones.

CHAPTER 7

Adding and Deleting Selfies

We now have a workable UI for viewing all the selfies, but we don't have any way to add new selfies or to delete existing ones. Selfiegram won't really be much of an app if the only selfies inside it are those we created as part of the tests—it's time to change that.

Deleting Selfies

First we will make the changes necessary to delete selfies. We are doing this first because it is easier. We will be writing some code that allows us to use the standard iOS swipe-to-delete behavior, which you may have seen in the mail app. To do this we will need to use two different table view data source methods, `tableView(_ canEditRowAt indexPath:)` and `tableView(_ commit editingStyle: forRowAt indexPath:)`. The first of these returns a `Bool`; if the `Bool` is `true` the table view allows deletion of that row, and if it's `false` it blocks it. The second is called once an edit has been made. In our case the edit will always be a deletion, but this is the same method that gets called for any edit, including cell rearrangement:

1. Implement the `canEditRowAt indexPath:` method:

    ```
    override func tableView(_ tableView: UITableView,
                        canEditRowAt indexPath: IndexPath) -> Bool
    {
        return true
    }
    ```

    As we allow for every selfie to be deleted all we are doing in here is returning `true`, but if you do need to control this the `indexPath` parameter is included for this purpose.

2. Implement the `commit editingStyle: forRowAt indexPath:` method:

```
override func tableView(_ tableView: UITableView,
                        commit editingStyle: UITableViewCellEditingStyle,
                        forRowAt indexPath: IndexPath) {
    // If this was a deletion, we have deleting to do
    if editingStyle == .delete
    {
        // Get the object from the content array
        let selfieToRemove = selfies[indexPath.row]

        // Attempt to delete the selfie
        do
        {
            try SelfieStore.shared.delete(selfie: selfieToRemove)

            // Remove it from that array
            selfies.remove(at: indexPath.row)

            // Remove the entry from the table view
            tableView.deleteRows(at: [indexPath], with: .fade)
        }
        catch
        {
            let title = selfieToRemove.title
            showError(message: "Failed to delete \(title).")
        }
    }
}
```

Here, the first thing we do is determine if it was a deletion operation that caused this method to trigger. Then we work out which selfie we want to delete by using the indexPath—once we have that information, we can attempt to delete it. We then try and delete the selfie from the SelfieStore, but as this is an operation that can fail we have to mark it as such using the try keyword. If it fails, we create a new alert to let the user know the deletion failed. If it doesn't fail, however, we delete the selfie from the local list of selfies, and finally we let the table view itself know that a row inside it has been deleted using the deleteRows(at: with:) method. We tell the table view to delete the row with a simple fade animation to make it look a bit nicer than just having it pop out of existence.

 A great deal of table views are designed around remaining as performant as possible, so many of the methods are designed to run as a batch operation. This is why the deleteRows(at: with:) call takes in an array of indexPaths to delete instead of just one. In our case we don't have UI support for deleting multiple selfies, nor would it make a lot of sense in our app, but where possible you should try and batch your calls when dealing with table views.

If we run the app once again, we can now swipe from right to left on a cell to delete it (Figure 7-1).

Figure 7-1. Deleting a selfie from the list

Taking New Selfies

For quite a while we've had no ability to add any new selfies to the list, and the only ones in there are holdovers from our unit tests. It's time now to add in support for taking new selfies. We will need to do a few different things to make this work—we'll need to access the device's camera, and we'll need to create a new selfie, save it into the selfie store, and finally add it to the selfie list.

A great deal of what we are going to be doing is using the `UIImagePickerController` and its delegate class `UIImagePickerControllerDelegate`. The image picker is a pre-configured class designed to handle interactions with the camera; you can use it to verify if you are allowed to access the camera and configure it to use a particular camera or photo library. Once it is configured how you want, you give it a delegate to talk to and then present the image picker. The delegate callbacks will then be used to get the image back out to save.

The advantage of using the image picker is that it is very fast to set up and handles all the UI for managing the camera and selecting and editing photos. The disadvantage is we can't configure how it looks or works—for Selfiegram that isn't an issue, but it might be in your own apps.

Follow these steps to enable adding new selfies to the list:

1. Add the following to the `viewDidLoad` method inside `SelfieListViewControl ler` class:

```
let addSelfieButton = UIBarButtonItem(barButtonSystemItem: .add,
                                      target: self,
                                      action: #selector(createNewSelfie))
navigationItem.rightBarButtonItem = addSelfieButton
```

This piece of code will create a new `UIBarButtonItem` (a button class designed to go inside a navigation or tab bar), and add it to the right side of the navigation bar. The only slightly odd parts about this code are the `target` and `action` properties. The target-action mechanism is used in many different Cocoa and Cocoa Touch frameworks as a way for objects to talk to one another. The basic idea is that the target (in our case, `self`) gets sent an action (`createNewSelfie`) for it to perform. You can think of the `action` part of the call as saying, "What method do you want to call on the target?" Unfortunately, the target-action mechanism was developed quite a long time ago in Objective-C and doesn't work in a Swifty-looking fashion, which would most likely use a closure instead. So, because of all this we have to wrap our action inside the `#selector` macro to bundle it up into a form that the Objective-C Cocoa libraries can understand.

2. Implement the `createNewSelfie` method:

```
@objc func createNewSelfie()
{
    // Create a new image picker
    let imagePicker = UIImagePickerController()

    // If a camera is available, use it; otherwise, use the photo library
    if UIImagePickerController.isSourceTypeAvailable(.camera)
    {
        imagePicker.sourceType = .camera

        // If the front-facing camera is available, use that
        if UIImagePickerController.isCameraDeviceAvailable(.front)
        {
            imagePicker.cameraDevice = .front
        }
```

```
    }
    else
    {
        imagePicker.sourceType = .photoLibrary
    }

    // We want this object to be notified when the user takes a photo
    imagePicker.delegate = self

    // Present the image picker
    self.present(imagePicker, animated: true, completion: nil)
}
```

The first thing you might notice about this code is the @objc call at the front of the function definition. This tells Swift that we need this code to interop with Objective-C, and this is necessary if we want to use it as a selector (which we do). The rest of the function is configuring the UIImagePickerController. First we do some checks to see if the camera is available and we've been given permission to use it. The most likely reason for this check failing is if the user has rejected access or if the camera is already being used by something else. If we don't have camera access we fall back to using the photo library. Once the image picker is configured we set ourselves up to be the delegate so we will be told when a selfie has been taken, and then present the image picker to the user.

 As the simulator doesn't have a camera, the check for the camera will *always* fail. Luckily the fallback to the photo library will still work, and Apple has preinstalled some photos in the simulator's photo library specifically for situations like these. This means, however, that any code that is meant to run when you have camera access can't be tested in the simulator. Remember to always test on real devices to make sure the behavior is what you expect.

3. Add an extension to make our SelfieListViewController conform to both the UIImagePickerControllerDelegate and UINavigationControllerDelegate protocols:

```
extension SelfieListViewController : UIImagePickerControllerDelegate,
    UINavigationControllerDelegate
{
}
```

4. We are only going to be using calls from the image picker delegate class, but to conform to the UIImagePickerControllerDelegate protocol correctly we also need to be a navigation controller delegate.

5. Implement the `imagePickerControllerDidCancel` and `imagePickerControl ler(didFinishPickingMediaWithInfo)` image picker delegate calls:

```
// called when the user cancels selecting an image
func imagePickerControllerDidCancel(_ picker: UIImagePickerController)
{
    self.dismiss(animated: true, completion: nil)
}
// called when the user has finished selecting an image
func imagePickerController(_ picker: UIImagePickerController,
                    didFinishPickingMediaWithInfo info: [String : Any])
{
    guard let image =
        info[UIImagePickerControllerEditedImage] as? UIImage
        ?? info[UIImagePickerControllerOriginalImage] as? UIImage else
    {
        let message = "Couldn't get a picture from the image picker!"
        showError(message: message)
        return
    }

    self.newSelfieTaken(image:image)

    // Get rid of the view controller
    self.dismiss(animated: true, completion: nil)
}
```

There are two image picker delegate calls we are interested in. The first occurs should the user cancel creating or selecting an image. In this case all we do is dismiss the image picker from the view. The second is called when the user selects an image using the picker. Here, we attempt to get either the edited image (should it exist) or the original image. If neither of those actions are possible, we send out an error message. Once we have the image we call a new method, which we are about to write, to handle it from here, and dismiss the image picker.

 We are using the `info` parameter from the `imagePickerCon troller(didFinishPickingMediaWithInfo)` call here. This is a dictionary that contains all manner of useful information about the user's selection. To get information from it, we use predetermined strings (in our case `UIImagePickerController EditedImage` and `UIImagePickerControllerOriginalImage`) to access the relevant parts. This is another holdover from the Objective-C libraries; if you were writing a similar function fully in Swift, using an enum would not only look nicer but would mean there was less chance of someone else using your code making a mistake.

6. Implement the newSelfieTaken(image:) method:

```swift
// called after the user has selected a photo
func newSelfieTaken(image : UIImage)
{
    // Create a new image
    let newSelfie = Selfie(title: "New Selfie")

    // Store the image
    newSelfie.image = image

    // Attempt to save the photo
    do
    {
        try SelfieStore.shared.save(selfie: newSelfie)
    }
    catch let error
    {
        showError(message: "Can't save photo: \(error)")
        return
    }

    // Insert this photo into this view controller's list
    selfies.insert(newSelfie, at: 0)

    // Update the table view to show the new photo
    tableView.insertRows(at: [IndexPath(row: 0, section:0)],
        with: .automatic)
}
```

Here, we create a new selfie and give it the image the user selected from the image picker. We then try and save the selfie. If that works, we insert that selfie into the top of the table view and as the first element of the local array of selfies.

There is one final step before our image picker is complete: we need to ask for permission to use the camera. Cameras and photos are considered private, and our app needs to be given explicit permission by the user before we are allowed to use them. So, we need to make sure we have permission before continuing.

 If you were to run the app in its current form it would work fine on the simulator, as there is no camera. However, on a real device the app will crash with an error about attempting to "access privacy-sensitive data without a usage description." This is basically saying we haven't configured our project correctly to support camera access.

This isn't something we need to do in code—all our code is correct. The changes we have to make are in the project itself:

1. Open the project's *info.plist* file.

   This will open up a nested table structure inside the Xcode editor, and it is in here that we will add the appropriate permissions.

   info.plist is a property list file that shows all the relevant information about your application. This will be used by iOS and the App Store at various stages to ensure your project is correctly configured and determine what functionality it supports. The file contains various settings, such what storyboard to load initially and what orientations are supported. Essentially, this is where application-relevant information goes.

2. Add a new row into the plist.

3. Change the name of the key to "Privacy - Camera Usage Description".

4. Set the type to be String.

5. Set the value to be "We use the camera to take those sweet, sweet selfies."

6. Add a new row into the plist.

7. Change the name of the key to "Privacy - Photo Library Additions Usage Description".

8. Set the type to be String.

9. Set the value to be "We use the library to save your sweet, sweet selfies."

We're essentially doing two things here. First, we're telling iOS that our application is configured to access the camera. Second, we're setting a string that will be displayed to the user when Selfiegram first tries to access the camera. We then do the same thing, but for permission to save photos into the library.

This isn't a feature we are going to be using immediately, but will be necessary later down the track when we want to save and share selfies outside of the app, so we might as well configure it now. Based on this string a user will determine if your app can use the camera and photo library, so make sure you put a bit of thought into it!

Under the hood, a plist is an XML file. Xcode presents it in this manner because editing XML by hand is fraught with danger, but if you want to see the raw version you can. If you right-click the plist inside in the Xcode navigator and select Open As → Source Code you will see the XML form.

With all of that done, we can now run our app and add new selfies! Figure 7-2 shows this in action.

Figure 7-2. Adding a new selfie

CHAPTER 8

Viewing and Editing Selfies

So far all the work we've done has been centered around the list of selfies, which makes sense because it is the jumping-off point for Selfiegram—but now it's time to add the ability to look at past selfies. After all, there isn't any point in taking all those selfies if we can't later look at how great they are! We'll also add the ability to edit the selfie titles, so they don't all have the same boring label.

The Selfie Viewer

Let's get started on creating our selfie viewer:

1. Open *Main.storyboard* and select the selfie detail view controller.

2. Delete the template text label in the middle of the main view.

3. Drag in a `UITextField` and place it near the top left of the main view.

4. Use the Add New Constraints menu to position the text field as follows:

   - 16 points away from the left edge of the view
   - 16 points away from the right edge of the view
   - 16 points away from the top edge of the navigation bar
   - Height: 30 points

5. Inside the Attributes inspector, set the placeholder of the text field to "Selfie Name".

6. Set the border style to be None (the dotted line option in the list).

   This is the first part of our selfie viewer. We are using a text field because later we are going to make it so users can rename selfies from here. The constraints we've set up on it ensure that no matter how large or small the device may be it will always be pinned to the top of the view, stretching across the width of the device.

7. Drag in a `UILabel` and place it underneath the text field.

8. Use the Add New Constraints menu to position the label as follows:

   - 16 points away from the left edge of the view
   - 16 points away from the right edge of the view
   - 8 points down from the text field
   - Height: 21 points

   This label will show the date the selfie was taken, similar to the subtitle in the table view cells. The constraints we've applied to it mean it will always be below the text field, and equally wide.

   There are multiple ways of setting up constraints to get the same desired effect. For example, we could have horizontally centered the label and set a constraint on it to share the width of the text field. This would have given us the exact same appearance. There is a lot of flexibility in the constraints system, and it is worth experimenting to see what approach works best for your workflow and desired look.

9. Drag in a `UIImageView` and place it underneath the label.

10. Use the Add New Constraints menu to position the label as follows:

    - 16 points away from the left edge of the view
    - 16 points away from the right edge of the view
    - 16 points away from the bottom edge of the view
    - 8 points down from the label

11. Inside the Attributes inspector, set the content mode to Aspect Fit.

    The image view will show the image (good name for the class, really) of the selfie. We've set constraints that tell it to take up all the remaining space of the view, and using Aspect Fit ensures that the image view will make the selfie's photo fill up the available space without distorting the image.

    `UIImageView`s can have a number of different content modes that control how the image inside is to be displayed. We're using Aspect Fit because it maintains the aspect ratio of the image while also not cutting off any of the image. This does mean that if the aspect ratios of the image and the image view are different, there will be some empty space; if you want the image to fill the view entirely use Aspect Fill instead. This does mean parts of the image may get trimmed off the top and bottom to make it fit, but it won't be distorted.

Connecting the Code and the UI

Now that our UI for viewing individual selfies is set up, we need to hook up the UI to some code to give it something to present:

1. Open DetailViewController and, using the Refactor → Rename menu option, rename the class SelfieDetailViewController. This will affect numerous different uses of the old name in the project.

2. Open *Main.storyboard* and select the selfie detail view controller.

3. Open the assistant editor to show the SelfieDetailViewController class next to the storyboard version of the view controller (see Figure 8-1).

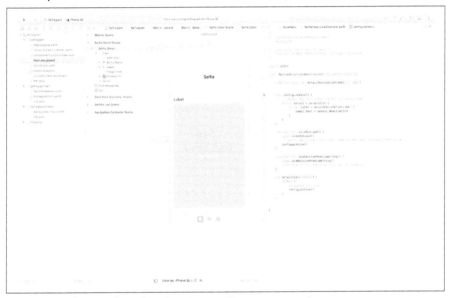

Figure 8-1. The storyboard and assistant editor open together

 By default the assistant editor will be set to use Automatic mode, so it will open whatever it thinks is needed. In our case it will open the *SelfieDetailViewController.swift* file, which is what we want. If you don't want the Automatic mode or if it isn't opening the item you want, you can control it using the jump bar at the top of the assistant editor window.

4. Create an outlet for the text field:

   a. Select the UITextField inside the storyboard view.

   b. Holding down Control, drag from the text field into the code.

c. Release the drag and, inside the Connections inspector, make the connection an Outlet and name it `selfieNameField` (Figure 8-2).

Connection	Outlet
Object	Selfie Detail
Name	selfieNameField
Type	UITextField
Storage	Weak
Cancel	Connect

Figure 8-2. The Connections inspector for the text field

5. Create an outlet for the label:

   a. Select the `UILabel` inside the storyboard view.

   b. Holding down Control, drag from the label into the code.

   c. Release the drag and inside the Connections inspector, make the connection an Outlet and name it `dateCreatedLabel`.

6. Create an outlet for the image view:

   a. Select the `UIImageView` inside the storyboard view.

   b. Holding down Control, drag from the image view into the code.

   c. Release the drag and inside the Connections inspector, make the connection an Outlet and name it `selfieImageView`.

   The three new properties on the class should now be set up as follows:

   ```
   @IBOutlet weak var selfieNameField: UITextField!
   @IBOutlet weak var dateCreatedLabel: UILabel!
   @IBOutlet weak var selfieImageView: UIImageView!
   ```

 There are many different ways to create outlets and actions. We prefer Control-dragging from the UI element into the code as this way you can make sure you've got the right item, but you can also Control-drag from the outline in the storyboard or use the Connections inspector. If you prefer, you can write the actions and outlets first and then drag from the well (the small circle) in the line gutter onto the UI to make connections. There isn't a *right* way of doing this, so whichever feels best to you is the one you should use.

At this point, we are finished with the UI and can close the assistant editor. The rest of what we will be doing will all be in code:

1. Open *SelfieDetailViewController.swift* and delete the `detailDescriptionLabel` property, as we do not need it any longer.

2. Using the refactoring tools, rename the `detailItem` property to `selfie` and change its type from an optional `Date` to an optional `Selfie`:

   ```
   var selfie: Selfie? {
       didSet {
           // Update the view
           configureView()
       }
   }
   ```

   This will be the individual selfie we want to show and will be passed to this class by the selfie list.

3. Add in a date formatter property:

   ```
   // The date formatter used to format the time and date of the photo.
   // It's created in a closure like this so that when it's used, it's
   // already configured the way we need it.
   let dateFormatter = { () -> DateFormatter in
       let d = DateFormatter()
       d.dateStyle = .short
       d.timeStyle = .short
       return d
   }()
   ```

   This will work in a different manner to the formatter from the list of selfies, and will be used to show when the selfie was taken as opposed to how recent it is.

4. Replace the `configureView` method with the following:

   ```
   func configureView()
   {
       guard let selfie = selfie else
       {
           return
       }
       // Ensure that we have references to the controls we need
       guard let selfieNameField = selfieNameField,
             let selfieImageView = selfieImageView,
             let dateCreatedLabel = dateCreatedLabel
           else
       {
           return
       }

       selfieNameField.text = selfie.title
   ```

```
        dateCreatedLabel.text = dateFormatter.string(from: selfie.created)
        selfieImageView.image = selfie.image
    }
```

Inside here we configure all the different UI elements to show their respective parts of the selfie. This method will be called anytime the selfie itself is changed; in our case this will happen only once, when the `selfie` property is set by the selfie list.

5. Open *SelfieListViewController.swift* and add in the `prepare(for` `segue:` `sender:)` method:

```
// Called when we tap on a row.
// The SelfieDetailViewController is given the photo.
override func prepare(for segue: UIStoryboardSegue, sender: Any?)
{
    if segue.identifier == "showDetail"
    {
        if let indexPath = tableView.indexPathForSelectedRow
        {
            let selfie = selfies[indexPath.row]
            if let controller =
                (segue.destination as? UINavigationController)?
                    .topViewController as? SelfieDetailViewController
            {
                controller.selfie = selfie
                controller.navigationItem.leftBarButtonItem =
                    splitViewController?.displayModeButtonItem
                controller.navigationItem
                    .leftItemsSupplementBackButton = true
            }
        }
    }
}
```

This method is called by one view controller when it is about to segue into another one. It has two important parameters: `segue`, which contains all the relevant information about the segue itself, including its identifier and what it is going to segue into; and `sender`, which represents what caused the segue to occur. We use the segue's `identifier` property to work out if this segue is a segue into a selfie detail controller. We then determine which selfie in the list of selfies was selected. After that, we get the destination view controller out of the segue. We have to tweak it a little bit because of the extra navigation controller in between the master and detail view controllers, but once we have the new view controller, we set its selfie object to the selfie that we worked out was the one the user wanted to view in detail.

You might be wondering how the string "showDetail" for the identifier means "the segue that means I want to see an individual selfie in detail." This is the identifier set for this segue by default in the Master-Detail template. You can see this if you open the storyboard, select the segue between the selfie list and selfie detail view controllers (the little arrow with a circle in the middle showing one view controller sliding over the top of another), and look at the Identifier attribute in the Attributes inspector. You could change it here if you like—perhaps "viewSelfie" is more to your liking—but if you do, remember to also update the check for it inside the `prepare(for segue: sender:)` method.

Now if you run the app you can select a selfie from the selfie list and see it in full detail (Figure 8-3).

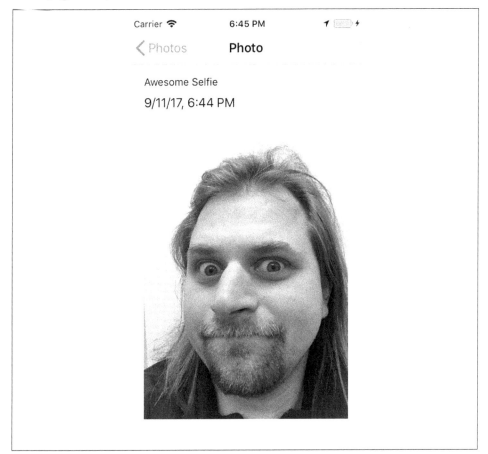

Figure 8-3. A selfie in full glorious detail

Editing a Selfie

So far every selfie we've added (outside of the ones we created during our testing) has had the same title, "New Selfie." While this has worked fine as a placeholder title, it's time to make it so we can we can edit a selfie's title:

1. Open *Main.storyboard* and select the selfie detail view controller text field.

2. In the Attributes inspector, set the Return Key to Done. This doesn't affect the operation of the editing, but it looks better than Return.

3. Open the assistant editor and ensure the *SwiftDetailViewController.swift* file is open.

4. Create an action for the text field:

   a. Holding down Control, drag from the text field into the code.

   b. Release the drag inside the `SelfieDetailViewController` class.

   c. Inside the Connections inspector, make sure the connection type is Action.

   d. Name the action `doneButtonTapped`.

   e. For the event, select Primary Action Triggered.

   This will create a new connection between the text field and the function that was just created for us called `doneButtonTapped`. Now when we tap the text field a keyboard will be brought up; tapping the Done button on the keyboard will trigger this connection to be fired and call the method.

5. Implement the `doneButtonTapped` method:

   ```swift
   @IBAction func doneButtonTapped(_ sender: Any)
   {
       self.selfieNameField.resignFirstResponder()

       // Ensure that we have a selfie to work with
       guard let selfie = selfie else
       {
           return
       }

       // Ensure that we have text in the field
       guard let text = selfieNameField?.text else
       {
           return
       }

       // Update the selfie and save it
       selfie.title = text
   ```

```
        try? SelfieStore.shared.save(selfie: selfie)
    }
```

This method is quite straightforward: it collects the new title from the text field, modifies the selfie, and then asks the `SelfieStore` to save this new selfie. The call to `resignFirstResponder` tells the text field to dismiss the keyboard.

 When we make the call to `resignFirstResponder`, there is a lot more going on under the hood than *just* dismissing the keyboard. iOS has a very complex chain made up of various `UIResponder` objects (most UIKit objects, including `UIView` and `UIButton`, are `UIResponder` objects). Whenever an event is generated, such as by tapping a button or making a gesture, UIKit works out which responder in the chain is the one that should be told about it and become the *first responder*. In our case the obvious first responder is the text field, as it is what was tapped, but if necessary UIKit will pass the event down the chain until a responder that is capable of handling the event is found. When we are telling the text field to `resignFir stResponder` we are actually telling it that it is no longer responsible for handling this event, which in the case of a text field means that the keyboard is dismissed.

If you'd like more information about the responder chain, Apple has written an article on it that is worth checking out (*https://apple.co/2GKON0a*).

At this point if we were to run the app again we would be able to update selfie titles, but it wouldn't quite work properly. The selfie list won't show the updated titles. This is because even though we've changed the selfie title, we haven't told the table view's data source about it. Let's change that now:

1. Open the *SelfieListViewController.swift*.
2. Add the following to the `viewWillAppear` method:

```
// Reload all data in the table view
tableView.reloadData()
```

All we are doing here is telling the table view to reload all its data.

With this done, now we can run the app and edit a selfie's title. In the next chapter, we'll move on to adding location data to the selfies.

CHAPTER 9

Adding Location Info to the Selfies

While we have our selfie app's basic functionality working like a charm, it isn't exactly very featureful. As our selfies are each meant to represent a single moment in time, it would be nice to not only know when we took them but also *where* we took them. So with that in mind, in this chapter we are going to be adding in location support for the selfies, allowing us to save the locations where they were taken.

Visually, we are going to make it so that the map is a small square off to the side of the selfie detail view controller, and when we tap it, it will launch the main Maps application. By the end of this chapter we will have a new feature in our app that will show a small map on each selfie that when tapped will take us to the exact place where the selfie was taken.

To do this we are going to have to add support for locations to our model, add new tests for the updated model, update the UI to support showing a location, and finally configure our project to be able to access the device's location hardware so we can generate locations.

Updating the Model

The first step is to add location support to the `Selfie` class and associated methods in the manager, `SelfieStore`:

1. Open *SelfieStore.swift*.

2. Import the `CLLocation` class from the Core Location module:

    ```
    import CoreLocation.CLLocation
    ```

Core Location is a large and powerful framework that provides various services for generating and manipulating location-related data. A CLLocation object represents a single location on Earth and has amongst other parts a latitude and longitude. We'll be using more of Core Location a bit later, especially when it comes time to get a location from the device's location hardware, but from the model's perspective all we need is the representation of a location.

3. Create the `Coordinate` struct inside the `Selfie` class:

```
struct Coordinate : Codable, Equatable
{
    var latitude : Double
    var longitude : Double

    // required equality method to conform to the Equatable protocol
    public static func == (lhs: Selfie.Coordinate,
                           rhs: Selfie.Coordinate) -> Bool
    {
        return lhs.latitude == rhs.latitude &&
            lhs.longitude == rhs.longitude
    }

    var location : CLLocation
    {
        get
        {
            return CLLocation(latitude: self.latitude,
                longitude: self.longitude)
        }
        set
        {
            self.latitude = newValue.coordinate.latitude
            self.longitude = newValue.coordinate.longitude
        }
    }

    init (location : CLLocation)
    {
        self.latitude = location.coordinate.latitude
        self.longitude = location.coordinate.longitude
    }
}
```

This is a simple struct that will represent a single location for the selfie. There are two properties inside the struct, `longitude` and `latitude`; both are doubles and they will represent the precise position on the Earth that the selfie was taken. We are using doubles as this type maps (pun intended) to how the Core Location framework represents location, with the Equator representing 0 degrees latitude and the Prime Meridian (running through Greenwich in the UK) representing 0 degrees longitude. Rarely will you ever be looking directly at the coordinates; instead, we will be using the various methods inside of Core Location to turn the numbers into something a bit more user friendly and understandable.

The Coordinate type conforms to two different protocols, Codable (which we spoke about in Chapter 5) and Equatable. Equatable is one of the most common protocols you will encounter in Swift and iOS development. By conforming to Equatable, you promise to implement an ==(lhs: rhs:) method. This allows you to use the != and == operators in your types. You only need to implement the == method, as Swift can work out the != automatically by returning the negation of the equality method. This method needs to take in two Coordinates and returns a Bool. Notice that the method is static—this is because we need it to be available to the entire type and not just on an instance of that type. All of this means we are able to use the Coordinate struct in assertions and expressions no differently than we can use a Double, which is why we are conforming to that protocol in the first place.

 Swift 4 is adding in support for the autosynthesis of protocol conformance where possible. Codable was the first protocol to get support for this functionality, but Equatable is likely to soon also be autosynthesized. This means in the future you won't have to implement the == method yourself, but until we reach that future we have to do the work ourselves. If you are already in the future, feel free to skip writing that method while you enjoy flying around on your jetpack.

The struct has one computed property, location; this will be the main way that the location will be extracted from our struct. The reason we are doing it this way is because a CLLocation is really what we need—it's what all the various frameworks out there will expect—but unfortunately CLLocation is quite a large class and doesn't conform to the Codable protocol. So, we are instead making a lightweight struct that will be used for saving, loading, and presenting a CLLocation from it.

Finally, the initializer takes in a CLLocation, which is what we'll be getting from the device's hardware, and extracts the coordinate information from within that.

There is already a very similar type inside Core Location called `CLLocationCoordinate2D`, which looks remarkably similar but doesn't conform to the `Codable` protocol. We could have extended `CLLocationCoordinate2D` to make it conform to `Cod able` instead, and this might be something you might want to consider for your own apps. For Selfiegram, though, we felt it best to create a new type to demonstrate building up all the required functionality as a learning exercise.

4. Add a new optional `Coordinate` property to the `Selfie` class:

```
// the location where the selfie was taken
var position : Coordinate?
```

This is where we will save our locations once we start getting some from the location hardware.

Testing Our New Model

Now that we've added support for locations into the model, we need to write a test to make sure it can correctly store and load a selfie that has a location as part of it. This test will create a new selfie, give it a location, save the selfie, and finally load it back from the store and see if the location persisted:

1. Open *SelfieStoreTests.swift*.

2. Import the Core Location framework:

```
import CoreLocation
```

3. Implement `testLocationSelfie`:

```
func testLocationSelfie()
{
    // a location for Hobart
    let location = CLLocation(latitude: -42.8819, longitude: 147.3238)

    // a new selfie with an image
    let newSelfie = Selfie(title: "Location Selfie")
    let newImage = createImage(text: "🤳
    newSelfie.image = newImage

    // storing a location into the selfie
    newSelfie.position = Selfie.Coordinate(location: location)

    // saving the selfie with a location
    do
    {
        try SelfieStore.shared.save(selfie: newSelfie)
```

```
    }
    catch
    {
        XCTFail("failed to save the location selfie")
    }

    // loading the selfie back from the store
    let loadedSelfie = SelfieStore.shared.load(id: newSelfie.id)

    XCTAssertNotNil(loadedSelfie?.position)
    XCTAssertEqual(newSelfie.position, loadedSelfie?.position)
}
```

The first thing we do in this test is create a new location. We are manually creating a location that maps to Hobart, Australia (which is where we are from, and as the authors we get to pick the test locations). We then create a new selfie with an image and then create a new `Coordinate` from the `CLLocation` object. In the normal operation of our app we will be getting `CLLocation` objects from the location hardware, but for now a fake location will suffice.

 We are creating a location manually here because we want to test our model's ability to save and load locations, not test how our app handles interfacing with the location hardware libraries. This means we will later have to handle dealing with the location hardware and its quirks. Essentially we are testing the model, not the app, here, but in your apps you will have to do more than just test if the model works.

Next we try to save the selfie, and if that succeeds we load it back and check if it has changed after being reloaded.

Now we can run this test, and it will pass—our model has been updated and tested to work with locations!

Showing a Selfie's Location

Much like back in Chapter 6, when we had all those selfies saved but no way to view them, we currently have a new feature being supported in our model but we have no way to show it. Now it is time to modify the UI of the selfie detail view controller to show the location:

1. Open *Main.storyboard* and select the selfie detail view controller.

2. Select the constraint that pins the text field to the right side of the view controller.

3. Delete this constraint.

4. Select the constraint that pins the label to the right side of the view controller.

5. Delete this constraint.

6. Select the constraint that pins the image view below the label.

7. Delete this constraint.

After you do this you might see some warnings that things aren't alright with the constraint solver—don't worry, we will fix that soon. Now we are going to be adding a map view (of type `MKMapView`) into the view controller. This will be used to show the location attached to this selfie. Follow these steps:

1. Search for a map view in the object library, and drag it into the view.

2. Resize the map view so that it is 67 points high and wide.

3. Place the map view near the top-right corner of the view controller.

4. Use the Add New Constraints menu to position the map view as follows:

   - 16 points away from the right edge of the view
   - 16 points away from the top edge of navigation bar
   - 8 points away from the top edge of the image view
   - Width: 67 points
   - Height: 67 points

 67 points is an arbitrary choice. It's the same as the distance between the top of the text field and the top of the image view, but was just what we felt looked about the right size for the UI.

Our map view and image view are both constrained correctly, but our label and text field are not. Let's fix this now:

1. Select the text field.

2. Use the Add New Constraints menu to position the text field 8 points away from the left edge of the map view.

3. Select the label.

4. Use the Add New Constraints menu to position the label 8 points away from the left edge of the map view.

All of our UI elements are correctly constrained now, and we can start to use them:

1. Select the map view and open the Attributes inspector.

2. Change the map view type to Muted Standard.

   This is a low-color but otherwise normal-looking street map. We are using this type simply because we don't want a highly colored map detracting from our lovely selfies!

3. Untick all the Allows toggles on the map.

4. Untick all the Shows toggles on the map.

   This means our map will be just that, a map. There won't be any clutter overlaid on top of it.

5. Under the View section of the Attributes inspector, tick the Hidden property.

   This means our map view will be hidden from the view by default—it will still be there for the purposes of the constraints system, and we can talk to it in the code, it just won't be visible on the screen. We are working on the assumption that most people won't be willing to save their location, so turning this off by default makes the most sense.

Now it is time to hook up the UI to our code so we can start configuring it:

1. Select the map view.

2. Open the assistant editor and ensure the *SelfieDetailViewController.swift* file is open.

3. Control-drag from the map view into the `SelfieDetailViewController` class.

4. Release the drag and make a new outlet for the map view called `mapview`.

We are now finished with the UI. You can close the assistant and open the *SelfieDetailViewController.swift* file in the main editor. There will be an error on the new outlet we just created, because even though we correctly created the outlet we haven't included the library that includes the `MKMapView` class. Let's fix that now:

1. Import the `MapKit` library:

   ```
   import MapKit
   ```

MapKit is the library for showing, controlling, and manipulating maps. It is designed to work well with Core Location and has imported that framework internally, meaning we don't have to bother doing so in this class (although we could if we so desired). The importer in Swift is quite clever and automatically knows whether an import statement is redundant or not. Depending on your programming experience, you might be used to writing header guards to prevent including already imported files and modules; this is unnecessary in Swift.

2. Add the following to the end of the configureView method:

```
if let position = selfie.position
{
    self.mapview.setCenter(position.location.coordinate, animated: false)
    mapview.isHidden = false
}
```

All we are doing here is a quick check to see if our selfie has a location. If it does, we set the center of the map to be the selfie's location and set it to be visible.

With that done we can run the app once again, and if we select the selfie we created as part of our location testing we'll see the map (Figure 9-1).

Figure 9-1. Our location test selfie, showing the map

Expanding the Map

While our map looks very nice up there in the corner, its lack of functionality doesn't really make it worth leaving in the app—it's time to make it do a bit more than just sit there. We are going to modify our map so that when the user taps it, it will launch the main Maps app of the device and put a pin on the map where the selfie was taken:

1. Open *Main.storyboard* and select the selfie detail view controller scene.
2. Inside the object library, search for a tap gesture recognizer.
3. Drag the recognizer from the library onto the map view.

It is very important that you don't drag the recognizer onto anything other than the map view. Otherwise, the recognizer will respond to taps on whatever you added it to instead of the map.

A tap gesture recognizer is a special subclass of the more generic gesture recognizer class UIGestureRecognizer. It is configured to respond to a single tap on a UIView, and we will be using it to determine when the user taps the map.

The gesture recognizer class is highly configurable: it can be made to respond to different numbers of taps, swipes, multiple fingers, panning, and so on. If you need a complex interaction pattern and aren't sure how to do it, take a look at the UIGestureRecognizer class. We are only scratching the surface of what it can do.

4. Open the SelfieDetailViewController inside the assistant editor.

5. Control-drag from the tap gesture recognizer into the assistant.

6. Using the Connections inspector, create a new action called expandMap.

The easiest way to select the recognizer (or most UI elements) so you can drag from it to make a connection is via the document outline sidebar.

Now whenever the user taps on the map, the expandMap function will be run, and in here we can write our code to open up the main Maps app.

7. Implement the expandMap function:

```
@IBAction func expandMap(_ sender: Any)
{
    if let coordinate = self.selfie?.position?.location
    {
        let options = [
            MKLaunchOptionsMapCenterKey:
                NSValue(mkCoordinate: coordinate.coordinate),
            MKLaunchOptionsMapTypeKey:
                NSNumber(value: MKMapType.mutedStandard.rawValue)]

        let placemark = MKPlacemark(coordinate: coordinate.coordinate,
                                    addressDictionary: nil)
        let item = MKMapItem(placemark: placemark)
        item.name = selfie?.title
```

```
              item.openInMaps(launchOptions: options)
        }
    }
```

Inside this method we are creating a dictionary of [String:NSValue] with some configurations for how we want the map to launch. We give it a center and a type, much like what we did with our smaller map. The reason we need to wrap everything up as an NSValue is because the communication to MapKit and the Maps app is all handled by Objective-C, and it doesn't understand some of the newer Swift features like enumerations; so, we bundle them all up as NSValues before passing them on.

 Unlike Swift, where types like Int and Bool are valid objects, Objective-C draws a clear distinction between objects and scalar types. An NSValue is sort of a catch all container class for holding different types when a call expects only objects. The Cocoa developers needed a way for these nonobject types to be bundled so they can be treated as if they are objects, and NSValue is how they did it. This is a holdover from Objective-C, and as the APIs are modernized it will very likely go away.

Then we create a new placemark. This is a user-friendly description of a point on a map and is designed to be shown on a map as a pin. Finally, we create an item, which will be what is sent to the map. The item is configured to hold our placemark; we name it after our selfie, and then we tell the item to open itself in the Maps application.

If we run the app once more, select the test selfie that had a location, and tap the map, we will be taken out of Selfiegram and into the Maps app, where we now have a pin showing the location of our selfie as well as the selfie's name! You can see this in action in Figure 9-2.

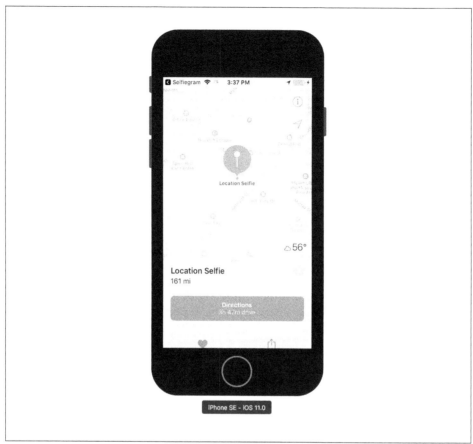

Figure 9-2. Our location test selfie, showing the map

Determining Locations

While it is good to know our code will handle locations correctly, it isn't exactly very exciting without some actual locations to show. All we've been doing so far is using the location we generated manually as part of our tests. It is time to change that now. We are going to be adding in support for determining locations from the location hardware on the device, using the Core Location framework.

Configuring the App to Support Location

Before we can begin we need to make sure our app supports accessing the location hardware of the device. As the users' location often will be something they want to keep private, Apple has made it so that we need to get explicit permission before we can access the location hardware. We'll set up our project so that it has support for location in the app's *info.plist* file:

---

1. Open *info.plist* and add a new row into the list of entries. You can do this in a variety of ways, but the easiest is to right-click in the empty space below the already existing entries and select Add Row from the menu that pops up.

2. In the Key column, enter "Privacy - Location When In Use Usage Description".

3. Set the Type to String, if it isn't already.

4. Set the Value to "We'll use your location to add location info to your selfies".

What this is doing is telling the app that we will be wanting to use the location hardware at some point. In particular, we are saying we want to use the location capabilities only when the app is in use. This is different than if we wanted to use the location in the background—there is a different key for that, as well as a key for when you need both. Now when we go to use the location capabilities of the device the message we put in the Value column will appear in an alert view requesting the user's permission. As we chose to use the "when in use" key our app will *only* support generating locations when the app is currently being used; there is no way to make our app access locations when it's put in the background.

It is a good general practice to only ask for the capabilities you truly need. It doesn't make sense for a selfie app to know about the users' location when they aren't taking a selfie. We could have asked for permission to access locations in the background, but we don't need that functionality. You should always treat your users with respect; they know when they want to take a selfie and as the developer that is the only time you should ask for their location.

This is all we need to do to tell our project that we want to use the location hardware —we still need to write a bunch of code to actually access it, but we are set up from a privacy and capability point of view. We are now ready to start writing some code.

If you are ever discovered to *not* be respecting users' privacy, Apple may well pull your application from the App Store. Location is just one of many different areas that is considered private; others include the Contacts database, health data, and the microphone. You will have to ask the user's permission before you can access any private areas. If you ever find yourself thinking "Hmm, how can I get around asking the user for this data?" stop and ask for permission—your app is *never* more important than your user's right to privacy.

Talking to the Location Hardware

When it comes time to get a location from the location hardware on a device, there are a variety of different ways this can be done: you can do cellular tower triangulation, use a geo-table of WiFi hotspots, listen in to GPS satellites, wait for beacons to transmit, or a combination of all of these. Luckily for us as developers we don't have to worry about the exact technique being used, as we will be using Core Location to handle all this for us. Core Location will handle the actual communication with the various location hardware and does so very cleverly. The framework will independently merge data sources and techniques together to return the best possible location match based on how you've configured it to do so.

To use Core Location you create a location manager to control how the framework works, such as how accurate it should be, and once it's configured and told to start looking for locations the manager will handle it from there. Whenever the manager determines a new location, or encounters an error, it will tell its delegate about this happening, and the delegate will be responsible for dealing with this. In our case our `SelfieListViewController` will be the location manager delegate and we will be doing all our work inside there. We will create a manager, configure it to determine the location with a high degree of accuracy, and store this into a new optional property that will then be used when it comes time to create a new selfie. So, let's do that now:

1. Open *SelfieListViewController.swift*.

2. Import the Core Location framework:

   ```
   import CoreLocation
   ```

3. Add a new optional property of type `CLLocation` called `lastLocation`:

   ```
   // stores the last location that Core Location was able to determine
   var lastLocation : CLLocation?
   ```

   This is the property where we will save the most recent location that Core Location has determined for us.

4. Add a new property to be the manager for Core Location:

   ```
   let locationManager = CLLocationManager()
   ```

5. At the end of the `viewDidLoad` method, set `self` to be the delegate for the new location manager property and configure the desired accuracy:

   ```
   self.locationManager.delegate = self
   locationManager.desiredAccuracy = kCLLocationAccuracyNearestTenMeters
   ```

   We have chosen an accuracy of within 10 meters as our setting. We don't need better accuracy for selfies—after all, people won't be navigating using them—but it will be good enough that it won't be confusing looking on a map. At this point you might get Xcode showing an error about how the class doesn't conform correctly to the protocol—we'll fix that next.

 The accuracy setting of kCLLocationAccuracyNearestTenMeters is another one of those weird holdovers from Objective-C where it would be better in Swift to use an enum.

6. Create a new extension for the SelfieListViewController to make it conform to the CLLocationManagerDelegate protocol:

```
extension SelfieListViewController : CLLocationManagerDelegate
{
}
```

To conform correctly to the protocol there are two methods we need to implement, locationManager(didUpdateLocations locations:) and locationManager(didFailWithError error:). The first will be called should the location manager determine a location, the second will be called if there is an error doing so.

7. Implement the locationManager(didUpdateLocations locations:) method:

```
func locationManager(_ manager: CLLocationManager,
                    didUpdateLocations locations: [CLLocation])
{
    self.lastLocation = locations.last
}
```

This is very straightforward. The method returns an array of locations, which may contain one or several items. We want the last location in the array, because the locations are sorted oldest to newest and we want our selfies to have only the freshest location.

 You might be wondering why you would get multiple locations back from the manager. This is because determining location is not an instantaneous event. There are a great number of different pieces that have to fall into place, and because of this the hardware might work out several locations almost all at once. Therefore, it makes sense to return all of these to you as the developer in case you might need them.

8. Implement the locationManager(didFailWithError error:) method:

```
func locationManager(_ manager: CLLocationManager,
                    didFailWithError error: Error)
{
```

```
        showError(message: error.localizedDescription)
    }
```

Whenever we encounter an error, we are going to tell the user about that error.
As location isn't a core component of a selfie we don't have to worry too much
about doing anything advanced with our error handling; just throwing out an
error message will be enough. If location is a bigger part of your app you might
need to examine what went wrong and tell your location manager to try again.

Now that we are correctly conforming to the delegate protocol, we need to tell our
location manager to start determining a location:

1. At the top of the `createNewSelfie` method add the following:

    ```
    // Clear the last location, so that this next image doesn't
    // end up with an out-of-date location
    lastLocation = nil

    // Handle our authorization status
    switch CLLocationManager.authorizationStatus()
    {
    case .denied, .restricted:
        // We either don't have permission, or the user is
        // not permitted to use location services at all.
        // Give up at this point.
        return
    case .notDetermined:
        // We don't know if we have permission or not. Ask for it.
        locationManager.requestWhenInUseAuthorization()
    default:
        // We have permission; nothing to do here
        break
    }

    // Request a one-time location update
    locationManager.requestLocation()
    ```

There is a fair bit going on here, so let's break it down. First we are setting the
`lastLocation` property to `nil`—this is to prevent a new selfie being created with
the location of an old one. Then we have a `switch` statement, switching over
`CLLocationManager.authorizationStatus`, which will return an enum with the
current authorization status of our app (indicating whether or not it can use the
location hardware).

The first two cases are for if the user has denied us access or if access is restricted
for a different reason, such as the device being in parental mode. In either of
these cases, we just give up. If the status is indeterminate, we ask for permission
to access the location hardware. On the first launch this will cause an alert to pop

up asking the user if he wishes to allow access. If neither of these cases are true, it means we have permission to use the location hardware.

 If you fail to check for authorization and just try and use the location manager to get locations, it will not work. Always ask for the authorization status first!

Then we tell our location manager that we would like it to determine a single location by calling the requestLocation method. This method will instantly return, but the delegate callback to say the manager has determined a location could take several seconds. We set this up now, before the image picker has been presented to the user, so that hopefully by the time the user has finished taking their selfie the location manager will have determined a location.

 If you need more than just a single location there are method calls to make the location manager begin determining location (startUpdatingLocation), and continue determining location until told to stop (stopUpdatingLocation). In our case a single location is good enough, so that is what we are using.

2. Finally, add the following to the newSelfieTaken method, after the creation of the selfie but before the do-catch block that attempts to save the selfie:

```
if let location = self.lastLocation
{
    newSelfie.position = Selfie.Coordinate(location: location)
}
```

In here we first check if we have a location, and if we do we turn it into a Coordinate and attach that to our new selfie. This will mean the location will be saved with our selfie and can be retrieved later by the code we wrote earlier.

With that done we can run the app once again, and when we go to create a new selfie we will be asked if we want to allow location access (Figure 9-3). If we do allow it, that selfie will have a location stored with it that we can then view.

Figure 9-3. The location access dialog

CHAPTER 10

Building a Settings View

At this point Selfiegram is working pretty darn well—we have an entire working app for taking, editing, and deleting selfies that have a variety of different information saved as a part of them. What we are going to be adding in now is a settings view where we will let users configure what features of the app they wish to make use of.

For the Selfiegram settings we're going to use another table view controller, with each row containing a toggle switch letting our users turn on and off particular features. Initially it will only contain two rows, one for enabling location support and another for setting a reminder in the app to take a selfie each day. This is intentionally limited because at the moment our app is nice and simple; as we expand the app we can easily add in more settings if necessary. In this chapter we will be doing the main chunk of work required for the settings to work and enabling users to configure location support. In the next chapter we will add in support for optional reminders.

Building the Settings UI

Our first step is to get the new UI for our settings up and running. As mentioned previously, we will be using table views again—but this time, instead of a dynamic table view we will be using static cells, where the content is locked in based on what we will be drawing into the storyboard. This will minimize the amount of code we need to write but will also mean any time we want to add in more settings we will have to do so manually. For settings this is a perfectly acceptable trade-off to be making, as the number of settings should always be small and manageable. So, let's get started:

1. Open *Main.storyboard*.

2. Drag a new `UITableViewController` into the scene and place it near the selfie list.

3. In the Attributes inspector, change the title to "Settings".

4. Select the table view inside the settings view controller.

5. In the Attributes inspector, change the content type from Dynamic Prototypes to Static Cells.

   This will cause the dynamic cell that was originally there to disappear and be replaced with several empty static table view cells.

6. Delete all but one of the static cells.

7. Drag a `UILabel` into the table cell and place it near the lefthand side of the cell.

8. Change the label text to say "Store Location".

9. Set up constraints on the label:

   a. Control-drag from the label up into the empty space of the cell and select "Center Vertically in Container" from the menu that appears.

   b. Using the Add New Constraints menu, select "Constrain to margin."

   c. Position the left edge of the label 0 points away from the cell's margin.

   This has now pinned the label in the vertical center of the cell and up against the left margin, or 8 points away from the left edge of the cell. Now it is time to add in the toggle and constrain it as well.

10. Drag a `UISwitch` into the cell and place it near the right edge of the cell.

11. Set up constraints on the switch:

    a. Control-drag from the switch to the label and select Center Vertically from the menu that appears.

    b. Using the Add New Constraints menu, select "Constrain to margin."

    c. Pin the right edge of the switch 2 points away from the cell's margin.

    d. Control-drag from the label to the switch and select Horizontal Spacing from the menu that appears.

    e. Select the new Horizontal Spacing constraint.

    f. In the Attributes inspector, change the relation to "Greater Than or Equal."

    g. Change the constant value to 8.

12. In the Attributes inspector, set the state of the switch to Off.

Because of the size of the label and switch, you might be wondering why we bothered to create a constraint saying they must always be greater than 7 points away from each other. This is because even though we, as clever humans, *know* they will never meet, iOS can't work that out without being told. So, to prevent a warning popping up telling us we don't have proper constraints set up, we need to add in a constraint for the horizontal spacing.

With our switch vertically centered and pinned to the right edge of the table view cell and our label similarly set up on the left side, we are done with settings for now. Our UI for this is simple because the last thing we want is for our settings to be confusing!

Your apps can register a *settings bundle* to have their settings appear inside the Settings application. Whether it's preferable to do this or, as we've done, create your own settings UI depends on your app and your users' needs. We haven't done it as we are focusing mostly on Swift in this book, and the settings bundle is all done through property lists. If you are interested in using settings bundles, Apple has written a guide on them (*https://apple.co/2GHDSUT*).

Connecting the Settings into Our Hierarchy

Currently our settings view controller is just off to the side, unconnected to the existing view controller hierarchy, which means there is no way to get to it. So, let's connect it up now. We will be making it so that we can launch the settings from the selfie list view controller by adding another button into the navigation bar:

1. Drag a button into the left side of the navigation bar of the selfie list view controller.

2. Change the button's text to "Settings".

3. Control-drag from the button to the settings view controller.

4. From the menu that appears, select the "Show" segue option.

5. Inside the Attributes inspector, change the style of the bar button item that contains our button from Plain to Done. This has no impact on the button itself but removes a warning in Xcode telling us that Plain is an unsupported style in navigation buttons.

Our settings view controller is now able to be interfaced with—all we need to do is hook it up (see Figure 10-1).

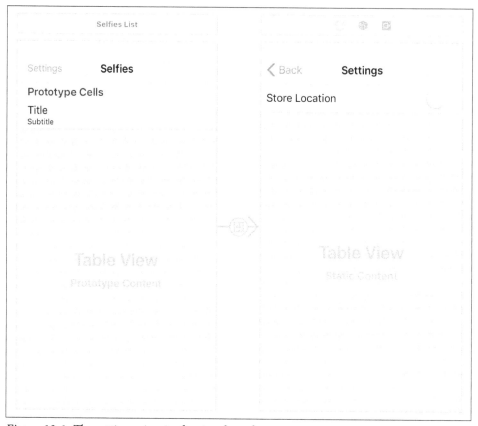

Figure 10-1. The settings view in the storyboard

Hooking Up the Settings

With our UI done, we need to associate it with a controller class so that we can actually start using it in our code:

1. Create a new Swift file by going to File → New File.

2. In the iOS category, under the Source section, select Cocoa Touch Class.

3. Make it a subclass of `UITableViewController`.

4. Name it *SettingsTableViewController.swift*.

5. Save it into the *Selfiegram* folder and make it target the Selfiegram target.

6. Open *Main.storyboard* and select the settings view controller scene we made earlier.

7. In the Identity inspector, change the class to be the `SettingsTableViewController` we just created.

8. Open the assistant editor.

9. Create a new outlet for the switch, and name it `locationSwitch`.

10. Create a new action for the switch. Name it `locationSwitchToggled`, and ensure the event type is Value Changed.

11. Open *SettingsTableViewController.swift* and delete all the table view controller data source method stubs. We don't need the empty commented-out methods because we're using a static table view; all of the work normally done by the data source has been drawn up in the storyboard.

With that done our UI is hooked up and we can begin to write code to actually work with, and respect, users' settings.

Implementing the Settings

For any settings to be of use we need some way to make them persist across multiple launches of the app, and to be accessible from anywhere in the app that might need them. Now, we could create our own custom settings model object that works in a similar fashion to our `Selfie` and `SelfieStore` objects, but luckily for us Apple decided that storing and loading settings was such a common task that it made a class to do that for us. We will be using the `UserDefaults` class to store our preferences. It works very much like a persistent dictionary (with a few quirks), and is designed to store, as its name implies, user defaults and the preferences they have set. The user defaults are interfaced with through a singleton in an almost identical fashion to how we talk to our selfie store. The singleton object is named `standard`.

 You are not meant to store your entire model inside `UserDefaults` —it is built around the assumption that it will contain small amounts of user-created preferences and is perfect for settings that need to persist. There is little stopping you from storing your entire model for your app here, but it might not work as well as expected and would be rather silly, especially as we've already gone to the effort of making a proper file store using the *Documents* folder.

With all of this in mind, let's start saving our users' preferences:

1. Outside of the `SettingsTableViewController` class, create a new enumeration called `SettingsKey`:

```
enum SettingsKey : String
{
    case saveLocation
}
```

This will be used for storing all of the different keys we will be saving in the user defaults store. For now we have only a single case for whether or not we should be saving location information, but we can easily expand the enum later as needed. We could just use strings for this, but by using an enum we get autocompletion in Xcode, which will help prevent any typos.

2. Implement the `locationSwitchToggled` `IBAction` method:

```
@IBAction func locationSwitchToggled(_ sender: Any)
{
    // Update the setting in UserDefaults
    UserDefaults.standard.set(locationSwitch.isOn,
                    forKey: SettingsKey.saveLocation.rawValue)
}
```

This method will get called whenever the location switch is toggled. All we do then is get the current state of the switch through its `onOff` property, which returns a `Bool`, and ask `UserDefaults` to store that value using the raw value of the enum we just created.

3. Add the following to the end of the `viewDidLoad` method:

```
// Make sure that the location switch is set correctly.
locationSwitch.isOn =
    UserDefaults.standard.bool(forKey: SettingsKey.saveLocation.rawValue)
```

Whereas in the `locationSwitchToggled` method we save the switch state into the user defaults, now we are getting the state of that default and using it to set the appearance of the switch (essentially, doing the opposite of what we did previously). On the first run there won't be a value inside the user defaults store for this key, but when requesting a `Bool`, if one does not exist it will default to `false`. This is why we don't have to bother to do any `nil` checking before we can use it.

 At no point are we telling `UserDefaults` to *save* the preferences. This is because iOS will periodically write them to disk, when it feels it is time to do so. If for some reason you *absolutely must save them now* there is a method you can call, `synchronize()`, which will save the preferences to disk when called, but rarely is this necessary.

At this point we are correctly saving and loading the user's preference regarding storing location information as part of their selfies. However, we aren't actually using it for anything outside of the settings view controller itself. While we are saving the preference correctly, it does nothing from the user's perspective. So, it's time to make the selfie creation code respect the user's settings:

1. Open *SelfieListViewController.swift*.

2. Replace the code that checks for permission and requests the user's location with the following:

```
let shouldGetLocation =
    UserDefaults.standard.bool(forKey: SettingsKey.saveLocation.rawValue)

if shouldGetLocation
{
    // Handle our authorization status
    switch CLLocationManager.authorizationStatus()
    {
    case .denied, .restricted:
        // We either don't have permission, or the user is
        // not permitted to use location services at all.
        // Give up at this point.
        return
    case .notDetermined:
        // We don't know if we have permission or not. Ask for it.
        locationManager.requestWhenInUseAuthorization()
    default:
        // We have permission; nothing to do here
        break
    }
    // Set us as the location manager delegate
    locationManager.delegate = self
    // Request a one-time location update
    locationManager.requestLocation()
}
```

This works in an identical fashion as before, except we perform a simple check on the state of the user's preferences before asking for their location.

Now you might be wondering, "Won't this mean that on first launch the app won't support location gathering until the user sets it up to do so?" And you'd be absolutely correct. Because location information is both private and a secondary feature of a selfie, we feel it is fine to have this disabled by default. If you wanted it working from launch you could change the code to assume users will want it on by default, but then you have to worry about making sure you correctly store the preference and can't rely on it defaulting to false like we do here. An easy way to determine if this is the first launch is to store a new Bool into UserDefaults that you set once inside the application delegate. This isn't perfect but will work in most circumstances.

Now if you run the app and take a new selfie you'll see that your location is no longer being determined or stored. If you open up the settings, turn on location support, and then take a selfie, it will have location data stored with it. If you then quit the app, launch it again, and go into the settings, you'll also see the switch is still correctly toggled to the on state. With that done, we now have the basics of our settings configured and working.

CHAPTER 11

Reminders and Notifications

In the last chapter we set up our settings view and wrote the code to let the user decide if they want to support location features in the app. Now we can add a new feature—a reminder to take a selfie each day that will display as a notification—and configure this to only be enabled based on the user choosing this setting. To do this we will need to write code to add a new row into the settings table view, write new code to generate a daily reminder notification, and enable and disable that reminder being fired based on the user's selection in the settings.

Adding a Reminder to the Settings

The first thing we want to do is set up a new row in the settings table view that we can use for toggling the reminder on and off as needed:

1. Open *Main.storyboard*.

2. Select the table view section (not the row or table view itself) from the settings view controller.

   The easiest way to select the table view section is by using the outline, as shown in Figure 11-1.

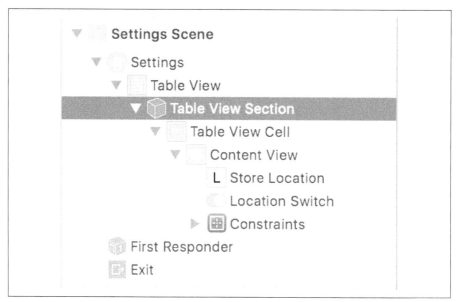

Figure 11-1. Select the table view section from the outline

3. Using the Attributes inspector, increase the number of rows from one to two. Doing this will create an exact duplicate of the location setting row, which will save us having to recreate the constraints. This does, however, have the drawback of *also* duplicating the actions, so we will have to change this if we don't want to find ourselves very confused why turning off the reminder setting also turns off the location setting.

4. Select the bottom cell's label.

5. Change the text to "Remind me at 10am".

6. Select the switch in the bottom cell.

7. Inside the Connections inspector, break the connection from the Value Changed event in the Sent Events section by clicking the small x button. This will have the effect of unlinking this switch from the action we wrote in Chapter 10.

8. Open the assistant editor.

9. Inside the `SettingsTableViewController` class create a new outlet for the switch called `reminderSwitch`.

10. Create a new action for the switch called `reminderSwitchToggled`.

We are now finished with our UI and can close the storyboard and assistant editor. The rest of what we are doing is going to be in code.

Creating a Notification

In Chapter 10 we used `UserDefaults` to maintain the state of the location setting. This time we are going to be doing something a little bit different. We will be creating a new user notification to actually *show* our reminder, and then we will be scheduling this reminder with the Notification Center, which will handle it from there. Because the Notification Center persists across multiple launches we can query it, asking if there is a reminder scheduled, and use that as the way of determining the appearance of the switch. This requires a bit more work than using `UserDefaults`, but we need to do the work anyway to configure the notification, so we might as well not add more work by also supporting `UserDefaults` for the reminder.

We will be creating a *local* notification—that is, one that only exists in the device itself. The other kind is a push notification, which is sent to your device by a remote server. The basic configuration of both is the same, but push notifications require a lot more work to get up and running. For a start, you need to have them sent remotely to your device, adding another layer to worry about, and even once you've done that it doesn't significantly change how you handle them in your app. For this reason, we aren't going to cover push notifications. Apple has very good documentation on how you can use notifications in your app (*https://developer.apple.com/notifications/*), and if you are curious as to how to get push notifications working it is worth checking out.

Let's get started creating our notification:

1. Open *SettingsTableViewController.swift* and include the `UserNotifications` module:

   ```
   import UserNotifications
   ```

   This will give us access to the `UserNotifications` library, which is what we will be using to create and present the notification.

iOS supports a few different types of notifications. We are going to be using *user notifications*, which are what most people think of when you say the word "notification." They appear on the lock screen or SpringBoard and allow your app to share information with your users when the app isn't at the forefront. There are also *system notifications*, which let users know when system-related events occur (such as the keyboard being dismissed, or an application moving to the background).

2. Add a new property to the `SettingsTableViewController` class:

    ```
    private let notificationId = "SelfiegramReminder"
    ```

    This will be used later by the notification system to uniquely identify our notification amongst all the others out there.

3. Add the following to the `reminderSwitchToggled` method:

    ```
    @IBAction func reminderSwitchToggled(_ sender: Any)
    {
        // Get the Notification Center.
        let current = UNUserNotificationCenter.current()

        switch reminderSwitch.isOn
        {
        case true:
            // Defines what kinds of notifications we send --
            // in our case, a simple alert
            let notificationOptions : UNAuthorizationOptions = [.alert]

            // The switch was turned on.
            // Ask permission to send notifications.
            current.requestAuthorization(options: notificationOptions,
                            completionHandler: { (granted, error) in
                if granted
                {
                    // We've been granted permission. Queue the notification.
                    self.addNotificationRequest()
                }

                // Call updateReminderSwitch,
                // because we may have just learned that
                // we don't have permission to.
                self.updateReminderSwitch()
            })
        case false:
            // The switch was turned off.
            // Remove any pending notification request.
            current.removeAllPendingNotificationRequests()
        }
    }
    ```

Here, we first get a reference to the current `UserNotificationCenter`. This is the singleton object that is responsible for managing user notifications. We then switch over the state of the reminder switch. If it is off, all we do is tell the Notification Center to cancel all unfired notifications, effectively purging our notification from the system. If the switch is on, however, we have to do a bit more. Like with location gathering, the user must grant the app permission to present notifications before we are allowed to do so, so we first have to check if we have permission to send notifications. Unlike with location, we use a closure to determine our authorization status. If permission is granted we then proceed to call a method to actually create the notification. If permission is denied we instead call a message to update the switch's UI. Don't worry about Xcode complaining about missing methods; we are going to be writing them now.

 In the preceding code there's a line that creates a new constant UNAuthorizationOptions array. When requesting permission for notifications you need to let the authorization method know what kind of notifications you intend on sending. This is so the users can decide whether or not they want to receive notifications of the various types. In our case we only care about sending alerts, the standard pop-up-style notifications, but the call expects a list of them so we bundle it up and pass that over.

4. Implement the addNotificationRequest method:

```
func addNotificationRequest()
{
    // Get the Notification Center
    let current = UNUserNotificationCenter.current()

    // Remove all existing notifications
    current.removeAllPendingNotificationRequests()

    // Prepare the notification content
    let content = UNMutableNotificationContent()
    content.title = "Take a selfie!"

    // Create date components to represent "10AM" (without
    // specifying a day)
    var components = DateComponents()
    components.setValue(10, for: Calendar.Component.hour)

    // A trigger that goes off at this time, every day
    let trigger = UNCalendarNotificationTrigger(dateMatching: components,
                                                repeats: true)

    // Create the request
    let request = UNNotificationRequest(identifier: self.notificationId,
                                        content: content,
                                        trigger: trigger)

    // Add it to the Notification Center
    current.add(request, withCompletionHandler: { (error) in
        self.updateReminderSwitch()
```

```
        })
    }
```

This method is the meat of the notification generation. First, we tell the Notification Center to purge all unfired notifications. This is to prevent the user toggling the reminder switch multiple times and at the next 10 a.m. being sent a whole heap of alerts to take a selfie.

There are few things more annoying to your users than spamming them with notifications—make sure you only send notifications for useful and important information! Pelting your users with hundreds of notifications because you forgot to keep track of what you are sending will not give your app a very professional appearance.

Then we create a notification content object, which we can configure however we like. In iOS you don't directly create the notification you want to send; instead, you set up how you want it to work and let the Notification Center take care of it. In our case all we are doing is giving it a title telling our user to take a selfie, although you can do quite a bit more, including using custom sounds and images. Next, we set up a trigger, which will be used to determine when the notification is delivered. We have set it to go off at 10 a.m. each day by using a Date Component.

With our content and trigger ready, we make a notification request. This is what the Notification Center will use to create the notification and fire it at the appropriate time. The request is basically just a bundled-up form of our trigger (10 a.m. each day), our content (the title "Take a Selfie!"), and the identifier we set up earlier. Then we pass the request to the Notification Center, and it will take it from there. Once all this is done we call a method to update the switch UI, which we are about to write.

When the appropriate moment is reached for the trigger to fire, the Notification Center will create a notification object with the content we set up and send it off.

The completion closure where we call our updateReminderSwitch method is run not when the notification trigger is fired but when the add method has finished adding our notification to the Notification Center.

5. Implement the updateReminderSwitch method:

```
func updateReminderSwitch()
{
    UNUserNotificationCenter.current().getNotificationSettings
```

```
    { (settings) in
        switch settings.authorizationStatus
        {
        case .authorized:
            UNUserNotificationCenter.current()
                .getPendingNotificationRequests(
                    completionHandler: { (requests) in

                    // We are active if the list of requests contains one
                    // that's got the correct identifier
                    let active = requests
                        .filter({ $0.identifier == self.notificationId })
                        .count > 0

                    // Our switch is enabled; it's on if we found our pending
                    // notification
                    self.updateReminderUI(enabled: true, active: active)
                })

        case .denied:
            // If the user has denied permission, the switch is off and
            // disabled
            self.updateReminderUI(enabled: false, active: false)

        case .notDetermined:
            // If the user hasn't been asked yet, the switch is enabled,
            // but defaults to off
            self.updateReminderUI(enabled: true, active: false)
        }
    }
}
```

This method is where we work out what state the reminder switch needs to be in —whether it's on, based on if there is a reminder scheduled, and whether it should be enabled, based on the user's permission setting for notifications. By determining if the switch should be enabled, we prevent it from being interactive even if the user has denied permission for notifications.

First we determine the permissions from the Notification Center. If permission has been given, we enable the switch and then check if the Notification Center currently has a scheduled notification that matches the notification ID we created earlier. Depending on this, the switch will then be toggled to true or false. If permission has been denied we set the switch to false and disable it, preventing user interaction. Finally, if permission hasn't yet been determined, we enable the switch but set it to false, allowing the first interaction with it to be possible.

6. Implement the updateReminderUI(enabled: active:) method:

```
private func updateReminderUI(enabled: Bool, active: Bool)
{
```

```
OperationQueue.main.addOperation {
    self.reminderSwitch.isEnabled = enabled
    self.reminderSwitch.isOn = active
}
}
```

This is a convenience method that sets the toggle and enabled states of the switch to those determined in the updateReminderSwitch method. The only interesting part here is that we are wrapping the calls inside a call to the main queue. The reason for this is that we don't know what queue the Notification Center will run the completion closure on when it completes adding a notification, but updates to the UI are only allowed on the main queue. Because of this we are making sure that changes to the state of our switch are explicitly run on the main queue.

7. Add the following to the end of viewDidLoad to set the switch state on first launch of the view controller:

```
updateReminderSwitch()
```

 Testing your notifications can be time-consuming and annoying. An easy way to quickly test your recent code changes is to set up a trigger that will fire quickly. For example, this is a nonrepeating trigger that will fire 10 seconds after it is sent to the Notification Center:

```
let trigger = UNTimeIntervalNotificationTrigger(
    timeInterval: 10,
    repeats: false
)
```

It is very important, however, that you make sure you test your notifications in situ. Fake triggers are good for quick testing but are insufficient for proper testing.

With that done, Selfiegram is now ready to start showing notifications. If you run the app, jump into the settings view, and turn that switch to "on" (Figure 11-2) a notification will be scheduled to fire at 10 a.m.!

Figure 11-2. Showing off our snazzy new notification

With all of this done, we have now completed the basic version of Selfiegram. We started with nothing and have implemented an entire app that is ready for people to start using and testing. In the next chapters we are going to look at adding some polish and advanced functionality to our working app.

PART III

Polishing Selfiegram

CHAPTER 12

Theming and Sharing Selfiegram

As it currently stands our app is in pretty good shape from a functionality perspective. Everything works properly and the interface of the app is solid—it is, however, a bit dull looking. While the default UIKit elements work very well and provide a consistent appearance with the Apple-provided apps, they aren't what we are after. We want our app to stand out.

There are loads of different ways we can go about this, but we are going to use *themes* to customize the appearance of our app. Themes allow us to design a universal appearance we want shared by each and every view in Selfiegram and have this automatically applied across the app. Our theme will be defined using the UIAppearance class. This class has a variety of different methods that let us dive into the guts of a view and set its appearance according to how we want it to look. Once this is done this theme will be applied to the entire view hierarchy, giving us a consistent interface for the whole app. As an added bonus, if we ever want to update the theming of our app all we need to do is modify the theme code and it will propagate out to the entire app at once, saving oodles of time.

 The UIAppearance class is a proxy object that exists on most view subclasses. It's designed to work on a class and not an instance, but we interface with it in the same fashion as if it were an instance. This means we won't be telling specific items in our interface, such as a particular button, to change how they look, but instead will be telling the whole UIButton class how to look.

We could do it the other way, but that would lead to scattering our theme's code across the entire app and make it a pain to change or tweak.

In the rest of this chapter we will be defining our theme and applying it to our interface. By the end we will have modified our app so that it will look like Figure 12-1, and once we've themed it we will add in support for sharing selfies with the wider world.

We are not going overboard with the theming of Selfiegram—we could spend days tweaking each and every detail, and in a real app you would do just that, but our goal here is teaching you *how* to theme, not making the best possible app we can. For this reason, we are only going to be doing basic theming, but you can run with it and polish it up later yourself.

Custom Fonts

The first step in making our app look a bit different is to give it a customized font. The default font for iOS 11, San Francisco, is a decent enough font and is very good for clean lines and readability on computer screens, but it isn't what we want.

San Francisco is only the default font on iOS devices where the language is one that uses the Latin alphabet character set; other languages have a different default font.

We are after something a bit more fluid and jovial feeling. Luckily enough iOS has a very good font handling system built into the operating system; it can handle common font formats and has a very good drawing engine in the form of Core Text to present them in a nice-looking way. This means we don't have to be concerned about using a third-party font—assuming the font itself is made correctly, it will present correctly.

We are demonstrating using a third-party font to show the steps involved, but you don't have to. Out of the box iOS comes with many fonts built in and ready to go, offering professionally made fonts to cover most scenarios.

If you want to see what you can play with there is a site called iOS Fonts (*http://iosfonts.com*) that shows every font on iOS, as well as what version of iOS it is supported on. You can see there just how many high-quality (and expensive) fonts Apple has purchased or created for use.

For Selfiegram we are going to be using three different fonts. The fonts we will be using are available from Font Squirrel under the SIL font license (*http://bit.ly/2GHPOWL*), which means (among other things) that it's fine to use them in our app.

 Fonts are released under their own licenses that determine how you are allowed to use them. If you can't meet the requirements of the font's license, you can't use it!

All of the Apple-provided fonts are available for use in your apps without any extra work required.

Let's get started:

1. Go to *https://www.fontsquirrel.com* and locate and download the following fonts:

   - Lobster
   - Quicksand

   This actually gives us eight different fonts (one regular-weight Lobster and seven variants of Quicksand). We only want three of these.

2. Add a Fonts group into the Xcode project.

   To do this, right-click the Selfiegram group inside the project navigation bar and select New Group. This will be where we store our fonts in the project structure.

3. Drag the following font files into the new Fonts group:

   - *Lobster_1.3.otf*
   - *Quicksand-Regular.otf*
   - *Quicksand-Bold.otf*

   Now that our fonts are included, it is time to hook them up to our app. To do that we will need a way to load them in our code. So far if you've wanted to change a font you'll have done so in the storyboard, but this isn't the only way.

4. Create a theme file.

   Create a new Swift file called *Theme.swift*. This is where we will be putting all our theming code, but for now all we'll be doing is creating the part that lets us load our fonts.

5. Import UIKit:

   ```
   import UIKit
   ```

6. Create an extension to UIFont to load our custom fonts:

   ```
   extension UIFont {
       convenience init? (familyName: String,
                          size: CGFloat = UIFont.systemFontSize,
                          variantName: String? = nil) {
   ```

```
// Note! This is how you'd figure out the internal font name
// using code. However, it introduces a bug if there's more
// than one font family that contains <familyName> in its name,
// or if the first font found isn't what you'd expect.

// We're doing it this way because otherwise we'd just be
// showing you the internal font names of the fonts we're
// using, and you wouldn't learn as much. In your real apps,
// you should manually specify the font name.

guard let name = UIFont.familyNames
    .filter ({ $0.contains(familyName) })
    .flatMap ({ UIFont.fontNames(forFamilyName: $0) })
    .filter({ variantName != nil ?
        $0.contains(variantName!) : true })
    .first else { return nil }

self.init(name: name, size: size)
    }
}
```

UIFont is the class that represents a font and all its associated font information. You don't create a font directly, like you would any other class; instead, you use the initializers to get a font back from the operating system. Here, we've made a new failable convenience initializer. We are making it failable because it is possible that for some reason we won't be able to load in our custom font.

 Because of how we are loading fonts, if two fonts have the same partial name match, such as "Lobster1" and "Lobster2", then loading them as "Lobster" will cause an issue as we don't know which we will get back. The general way to load a font is by its precise name—so, in the case of Lobster, "Lobster_1.3" —but showing you that wouldn't really teach you much about Swift or iOS's font system. So, just be wary in the future about using this exact code; if you know the precise name, you should use that!

We're doing a lot with closures here, but all our initializer is doing is getting a list of all the available fonts and filtering that by those that contain our desired font's name. Then we run flatMap over this to remove any nils and get it to a single-level collection. Once that is done we again filter for the specific font variant we want, and then return that.

We haven't really spoken much about flatMap. It's a special version of map that reduces the depth of the collection it is mapping over by one level. You can think of running flatmap as being the same as running map over a collection and then running flatten over it after that.

As an added bonus, you can use it to squish out any nils that might occur as a result of the transformation you are mapping.

Finally, we need some way of telling iOS about the new fonts—while they are in the project and we have our code ready to provide them, we haven't actually hooked them up in any way. For this we need to add a new entry into the *info.plist* file telling iOS that our font files are to be made available to our app.

7. Open *info.plist*.

8. Add a new entry into the file.

9. Set the key to "Fonts provided by application".

10. Set the type to Array.

11. Add a string into this array with the value "Quicksand-Regular.otf".

12. Add another string into this array with the value "Lobster_1.3.otf".

13. Open the project file.

14. Select the Build Phases tab.

15. Expand the Copy Bundle Resources section.

16. Click the plus button.

17. Select our font files. This will include them as part of the build process.

With that done, our fonts can now be used by our application. If we run it, however, nothing will change. This is because we haven't actually made use of our fonts yet. We'll be doing that next.

Making the Theme

The time has come to make our theme for Selfiegram. We'll be doing all of this inside a singe function call, using the UIAppearance class as our interface into the theme:

1. Inside of *Theme.swift*, create the theme struct:

   ```
   struct Theme {
   }
   ```

2. Create a static function called apply. This will be where we put all of our theme code:

```
    static func apply() {

    }
```

3. Add the following code inside the `apply` method:

```
guard let headerFont = UIFont(familyName: "Lobster",
                              size: UIFont.systemFontSize * 2) else {
    NSLog("Failed to load header font")
    return
}

guard let primaryFont = UIFont(familyName: "Quicksand") else {
    NSLog("Failed to load application font")
    return
}
```

This code is where we actually load in our fonts, using the convenience code we set up earlier. We are wrapping these checks inside `guard` statements because if we can't load our fonts we don't want the app to be half-themed. That would just look weird, so we bail out if we can't find them.

Next we want to change the *tint color* of our application. Most views in iOS have a tint color property, which is essentially their default coloring. This is that standard light blue coloring you've seen on the buttons we've been using so far.

4. Inside the `apply` method, add the following below the section on fonts:

```
let tintColor
    = #colorLiteral(red: 0.56, green: 0.35, blue: 0.97, alpha: 1)

UIApplication.shared.delegate?.window??.tintColor = tintColor
```

The first thing we are doing here is creating a *color literal*—notice that once you finished typing it it changed and was replaced with a small square of color. You can now click the square and use a color picker to select the color you are after. For Selfiegram we've gone with a nice-looking purple, which will be used as our new global tint color.

 Color literals are an easy way of creating colors that you can literally see and change, which is a much nicer way of adjusting color than using RGB or HSV values. The color literal returns an appropriate color object for your platform—so in the case of iOS, a `UIColor`. If we typed the same code on macOS it would still work but would instead return an `NSColor`. You can also create `UIColor` objects directly if you prefer, but then you don't get the nice little preview inside Xcode.

Then we set the tint color on the main window of our application. The main window is the one that all our views will be drawn into. As tint color is an inherited property, once we set it on our main window all of our views will inherit this, so we don't need to set it anywhere else.

Next we need to set the various appearance proxies for the different UIView subclasses we want to customize:

1. Add the following to the apply method:

```
let navBarLabel = UILabel.appearance(
    whenContainedInInstancesOf: [UINavigationBar.self]
)

let barButton = UIBarButtonItem.appearance()

let buttonLabel = UILabel.appearance(
    whenContainedInInstancesOf: [UIButton.self]
)

let navBar = UINavigationBar.appearance()

let label = UILabel.appearance()

// theming the navigation bar
navBar.titleTextAttributes = [.font: headerFont]

navBarLabel.font = primaryFont

// theming labels
label.font = primaryFont

// theming the buttons' text
barButton.setTitleTextAttributes([.font: primaryFont], for: .normal)
barButton.setTitleTextAttributes([.font: primaryFont], for: .highlighted)

buttonLabel.font = primaryFont
```

The first chunk of code here is getting references to the UIAppearances of each of the various different types we are planning on changing: navigation bar labels, bar buttons, button labels, navigation bars, and labels.

Then we give each of these different types the appearance we want them to have. In our case all we are doing is changing the font they are using to be one of our custom fonts.

We're using the `appearance(whenContainedInInstancesOf:)` variant of an appearance in several cases. This is because almost everything we are customizing is a `UILabel`, but we want it to have a different appearance when it is a label in a button versus when it is a label inside a navigation bar. This lets us modify the different label types independently of each other.

The last thing we need to do before all of this can take effect is to actually call the `apply` method somewhere. We'll be doing this inside our application delegate, as it is the logical entry point for our application and it makes sense to turn the theme on right from Selfiegram's launch.

2. Inside the application delegate's `didFinishLaunching` method, call the `apply` function right before the `return` statement:

```
Theme.apply()s
```

It's worth pointing out that if you don't like the design we've gone for here, you should feel free to change it. Now that your theme is set up it is easy to make changes to it.

There is one last part of the app we have yet to theme: the launch screen. You have probably noticed that when you launch the app there is a brief flash of white before the app launches. This white is launch screen, and we can customize it, too.

The launch screen is another separate storyboard called *LaunchScreen.storyboard* that iOS loads while it is getting the rest of the app loaded and ready. It only shows for a few brief moments, so there is no point in overly customizing the storyboard that gets displayed. Generally the app's logo is shown here, but as we don't have a logo we'll just change the color of the launch screen to be the same nice purple we've chosen as our tint color:

1. Open *Launchscreen.storyboard*.

2. Select the main view inside the view controller.

3. Using the Attributes inspector, change the background color of the view to the following custom color:

   - Red: 142
   - Green: 90
   - Blue: 247

- Opacity: Full

This is the same color as our tint color.

 As the launch screen is a storyboard you can control and interface with it through a view controller if you want. This is generally not worth doing, though, as it doesn't last long enough to bother showing anything beyond images and colors.

If you run the app again now, you'll see the result in Figure 12-1.

Figure 12-1. Our themed app

Sharing Selfies

Now that our app is looking snazzy, it's time to add in the ability to share our selfies—after all, what good is a selfie if we can't let others see how awesome we look in it?

There are two main ways to share to various social media channels. The first way requires you to either create a library from their API or use a premade library framework that supports them, and then handle the message crafting and all communication between your app and their service yourself. This is a whole bunch of work, pushes all the testing of unreliable services off onto you, and only supports the services you can find or create libraries for. There is another way, though: you can use the built-in iOS sharing functionality.

The `UIActivityViewController` provides a premade view controller that presents a standardized interface to any service on the device that provides an *activity*. An activity is anything that takes user data of some kind, performs a service on that data, and optionally returns the results of that service. An example is Twitter: the Twitter app provides an activity that takes in a short message and optional image and uploads them to Twitter, making the tweet on behalf of the user. Loads of different services provide these activities (in the form of `UIActivity` objects), and your own apps can provide activites too if you want.

> We won't be talking about making our own activities in this book, but the Apple documentation on the `UIActivity` class (*https://devel oper.apple.com/documentation/uikit/uiactivity*) has got you covered.

This means that any apps and services that your users have installed on their devices, such as Facebook, Twitter, Sina Weibo, Instagram, or email, can provide these services for you to use. All you need to do is configure the data you want to share, bring up an activity view controller, and let the user do the rest.

> The downside to doing our sharing this way is we lose control over the platforms that we can share to—but that isn't necessarily a drawback, as we put that power into our users' hands instead. Rarely is giving your users more agency in your applications a bad thing.

In Selfiegram we are going to set it up so users can share a selfie from two places, the selfie list view controller and the selfie detail view controller. These are the two most likely places someone will want to share a selfie from. Inside the selfie detail view controller we will add a new button to enable sharing, and inside the list view controller we will add in support for a custom swipe behavior on a selfie inside the table view.

Sharing from the Detail View Controller

The first step is to update the UI of the selfie detail view controller so that it has a button we can use for sharing:

1. Open *Main.storyboard*.
2. Select the selfie detail scene.
3. Drag a button into the righthand side of the navigation bar.
4. Select the button and change its System Item setting from Custom to Action.

    We will now have a button that looks exactly like the standard activity button used throughout iOS. The next step is to hook it up to an action.

5. Open the assistant editor and ensure the *SelfieDetailViewController.swift* file is open.
6. Control-drag from the button into the `SelfieDetailViewController` class.
7. Create a new action called `sharedSelfie`.
8. Close the assistant editor and open *SelfieDetailViewController.swift*.
9. Add the following code to the `shareSelfie` function we just created:

```
@IBAction func shareSelfie(_ sender: Any) {
    guard let image = self.selfie?.image else {

        // pop up an alert dialog letting us know it has failed
        let alert = UIAlertController(title: "Error",
                    message: "Unable to share selfie without an image",
                    preferredStyle: .alert)

        let action = UIAlertAction(title: "OK",
                                   style: .default,
                                   handler: nil)
        alert.addAction(action)

        self.present(alert, animated: true, completion: nil)

        return
    }

    let activity = UIActivityViewController(activityItems: [image],
                                    applicationActivities: nil)

    self.present(activity, animated: true, completion: nil)
}
```

In this method we first do a check to make sure that we actually have an image as part of our selfie. At this point in our app that should definitely be the case, but it is possible that it failed to load correctly. If there isn't an image, we pop up an error message and exit the sharing.

If there is an image, we create a new activity view controller. In this initializer are two important components. The first is an array of items we want shared. For a selfie all we are sharing is the image, but if we had support for multiple images or wanted to share text and an image we could add them to the array.

 The items inside this array will also determine what services the activity view controller will show. An activity defines what types of items and services it can support. For example, Twitter supports images and text, but not PDFs, so if you included a PDF inside that array Twitter would not appear as an option, but email (which supports *everything*) would.

The second component is the application activities array, which in our case is nil. This is where you can define what custom activities your application will be providing. Finally, we present the activity view controller, and now it is up to the user. And that's all there is to supporting sharing in iOS!

Sharing from the List View Controller

Now that we have a grasp on sharing itself, let's do it again from the selfie list view controller. This time we'll make it trigger from a different action. Instead of a button, we are going to add in support for a custom swipe action on a selfie in the table view. The sharing component will work exactly the same as in the preceding section, but now we'll get to do some more work inside our table view to make it all work:

1. Open *SelfieListViewController.swift*.

2. Delete the `tableView(UITableViewcommit editingStyle: forRowAt index Path:)` call. We will no longer need it.

3. Add in the following table view delegate method:

```
override func tableView(_ tableView: UITableView,
                    editActionsForRowAt indexPath: IndexPath)
                -> [UITableViewRowAction]? {

    let share = UITableViewRowAction(style: .normal, title: "Share")
    { (action, indexPath) in

        guard let image = self.selfies[indexPath.row].image else
        {
            self.showError(message:
```

```
                "Unable to share selfie without an image")
            return
        }
        let activity = UIActivityViewController(activityItems: [image],
                                            applicationActivities: nil)

        self.present(activity, animated: true, completion: nil)
    }
    share.backgroundColor = self.view.tintColor

    let delete = UITableViewRowAction(style: .destructive,
        title: "Delete")
    { (action, indexPath) in
        // Get the object from the content array
        let selfieToRemove = self.selfies[indexPath.row]

        // Attempt to delete the selfie
        do
        {
            try SelfieStore.shared.delete(selfie: selfieToRemove)

            // Remove it from that array
            self.selfies.remove(at: indexPath.row)

            // Remove the entry from the table view
            tableView.deleteRows(at: [indexPath], with: .fade)
        }
        catch
        {
            self.showError(message:
                "Failed to delete \(selfieToRemove.title).")
        }
    }

    return [delete,share]
}
```

This delegate call is responsible for telling the table view what actions it has to play with when a swipe occurs on a cell. The call needs to return an array of all the actions that are possible for a particular index path.

In here we create two new UITableViewRowActions; these are actions that will appear on a swipe event on a table view row and are very similar to what the table view itself ran when we added in support for swipe deletion in "Deleting Selfies" on page 155. All actions work the same: you create one with a style and a title, and give it a closure to run when the action occurs.

Our first action is for sharing. We've given it the normal style, which by default is a dull gray color for the background, and the code inside the closure is identical to our earlier code. We then change the color of the action to be the view's tint color, which if you remember from "Making the Theme" on page 217 will be purple.

Our second action is a delete action. We need this because by adding a custom action in we have overridden the normal delete we had working before. The code inside the closure is the same as the original deletion code we had, and by using the destructive style for the action we get an appearance that is identical to our original deletion.

Finally, we bundle up both of these actions into an array and return this.

Now if we run the app again, we can swipe across on a table view cell and both delete and share a selfie from here (see Figure 12-2).

Figure 12-2. Sharing from the table view

CHAPTER 13

Custom Views and View Controllers

Selfiegram is now themed and looking much nicer than before, but we still haven't really done much customization beyond some color tweaks and font changes. Let's take a look at building a custom `UIView` and `UIViewController` subclass to further improve our app.

The reason to make a custom view or view controller is to do something that isn't available in the ones Apple or third-party libraries provide. In our case we are going to be making a replacement for the image picker we are currently using to take photos.

 There are reams of third-party camera view controllers out there, each with its own strengths and weaknesses, but we are going to be creating our own. This is both because it is a good example of what it involves and because it lets us talk a bit about working with the camera in iOS, beyond what we could do with the image picker.

We will be using the `AVKit` framework to handle the communication with, and presentation of, the camera. `AVKit` is a framework that includes a great deal of classes and functions for interacting with, displaying, and creating audio and video content —hence the name `AVKit`. Using `AVKit` you could build yourself an entire video and audio editing suite, but we're going to start small and just capture images from the camera.

There is a lot to do to this chapter. We will need a custom view to show what the camera is seeing, we are going to need a custom view controller to perform the role of talking to the camera and returning an image, and we need to hook it into our existing application structure. Let's get started!

A Camera View

The first step in building our own camera controller is showing what the camera is seeing, as it is going to be terrifically hard to take a selfie if we can't see what the camera will end up saving. But we are going to need somewhere for our custom view code to exist. To get started, we are going to make a new view controller to hold our custom camera view:

1. Create a new Cocoa Touch Class file.

2. Name it *CaptureViewController.swift*.

3. Make it a subclass of `UIViewController`.

4. Save it into the project and ensure the Selfiegram target is selected.

5. Import the `AVKit` framework:

   ```
   import AVKit
   ```

6. Create a new `UIView` subclass called `PreviewView`:

   ```
   class PreviewView : UIView {

   }
   ```

7. Create the `previewLayer` property:

   ```
   var previewLayer : AVCaptureVideoPreviewLayer?
   ```

   This property holds an optional `AVCaptureVideoPreviewLayer` object, which is itself a subclass of `CALayer`. A `CALayer` comes from the Core Animation framework and is an important component of drawing views in iOS. Each `UIView` has a *layer* inside of it, which is responsible for the actual drawing of the view. They are called layers because they can be laid on top of one another to create a draw hierarchy. In our code here, the `AVCaptureVideoPreviewLayer` is a layer designed to show video content. Later we will be configuring our code so that this layer shows what the camera is seeing and adding it as a sublayer to this view's main layer.

 We are going to be showing a video layer because we want the view that is appearing to the user to be dynamic and reflect what the camera is seeing in real time. We could cobble together something ourselves using `UIImageViews` to create an approximation of what the camera sees, but it would be a bad hack and look terrible. It's much easier to stream in the camera output as a video and display it live, capturing only the relevant moments when the users want them.

---

8. Now we need to give our preview layer something to actually preview. Implement the setSession function:

```
func setSession(_ session: AVCaptureSession) {
    // Ensure that we only ever do this once for this view
    guard self.previewLayer == nil else {
        NSLog("Warning: \(self.description) attempted to set its"
        + " preview layer more than once. This is not allowed.")
        return
    }

    // Create a preview layer that gets its content from the
    // provided capture session
    let previewLayer = AVCaptureVideoPreviewLayer(session: session)

    // Fill the contents of the layer, preserving the original
    // aspect ratio
    previewLayer.videoGravity = AVLayerVideoGravity.resizeAspectFill

    // Add the preview layer to our layer
    self.layer.addSublayer(previewLayer)

    // Store a reference to the layer
    self.previewLayer = previewLayer

    // Ensure that the sublayer is laid out
    self.setNeedsLayout()
}
```

This method does a fair amount of work, and is intended to be called once we have set up the camera ready to display its content. The meat of the method is inside the session parameter that's passed into it. This is an AVCaptureSession object and represents a current capture session—essentially, it has all the information from the camera bundled up inside of it. This will be configured elsewhere; in our code here all we need to worry about is grabbing the camera data from it.

First we do a check to make sure that we haven't already set up the layer, and if we have, we abort. If we didn't have this check we could end up with multiple video layers being drawn into our view at once. Then we set the gravity of the layer so that it always keeps the input aspect ratio and resizes itself to fit the entire layer. Without this we would get distorted and squished video.

Finally, we add our video layer to the layer hierarchy of the view and then tell the view to redraw.

Technically we are telling the view to lay out itself and all of its child views, which isn't the same as a redraw but works well enough for our purposes. Additionally, the call to `setNeedsLay out` won't force an immediate drawing of the view and all its children. What it does is schedule a redraw, and in the next update of the drawing system iOS will cause the view to be redrawn. Most of the time this all happens so fast you won't even see it, but it is worth knowing it isn't actually instantaneous, although the method does return instantly.

The real advantage of this is that you can bundle up all your requests at once and get iOS to do all the redrawing in the next update, without having to wait for each call to finish drawing before moving on to the next.

With a call ready to redraw our view, we have to write the code to handle that redraw. We'll be overriding a `UIView` method call for this, `layoutSubviews`, which will be called by iOS when it comes time to lay out the view and its subviews. In our case this will be triggered by our call to `setNeedsLayout`.

You shouldn't ever call this method yourself. Trying to interrupt when and how iOS draws views is risky and will very likely result in unexpected behavior and crashes.

9. Implement the `layoutSubviews` method:

```
override func layoutSubviews() {
    previewLayer?.frame = self.bounds
}
override func viewWillLayoutSubviews() {
    self.cameraPreview?.setCameraOrientation(currentVideoOrientation)
}
```

All we do here is make the size of the preview layer the same as that of the view itself, essentially filling it completely.

Finally, we need to handle what happens when the device rotates. As it currently stands we aren't dealing with that, which could result in some very strange-looking results being shown on the preview layer. Correctly handling resizing and laying out a video layer based on orientation isn't an easy task, but luckily for us Apple has already handled all that for us.

10. Implement the `setCameraOrientation` method:

```
func setCameraOrientation(_ orientation : AVCaptureVideoOrientation) {
    previewLayer?.connection?.videoOrientation = orientation
}
```

All we do here is set the orientation of the video layer to the orientation of the parameter call—the video layer knows how to handle it from here—and we don't have to think about it. This method will be called by the view controller whenever the orientation changes on the device.

With that done, our custom view is ready to be used.

The Camera View Controller

The time has come to start creating our camera capture view controller. There is a fair amount of work we have to do in this section to build our view controller. We'll get started with the UI.

Building the UI

1. Open *Main.storyboard* and drag a navigation controller into the scene.
2. Delete the table view controller that came with the navigation controller.
3. Drag a view controller into the scene.
4. Control-drag from the navigation controller onto the view controller, and select Root View Controller from the Relation Segue section.

 We are using a navigation controller here because later we will be adding another view controller after the capture view controller, and we might as well set up the basics now rather than have to change the controller hierarchy later on.

5. Drag an empty UIView into the main view of the new navigation controller.
6. Resize the view so that it takes up the entirety of the screen.
7. Using the Add New Constraints menu, add the following constraints to the view:

   - Top edge: 0
   - Bottom edge: 0
   - Left edge: 0
   - Right edge: 0

When moving around and resizing regular views it can help to change their background color to something very obvious, such as full green or red, so that you can easily see how they differ from the views around them. Just make sure to set the background color back to the appropriate default when you finish.

Now our view is fully pinned to its parent view and will always be the same size as it. This view will be our camera preview view, and as such it needs to take up all the space available.

8. Select the new view and open the Identity inspector.

9. Change the type of the view from UIView to PreviewView.

We could have just changed the default view all view controllers have to be our custom preview class, but as we plan on having other UI elements laid out on top it makes more sense to have a separate view perform the role of the preview.

With that done, our preview view is ready to be configured. It's time for the rest of the UI:

1. Drag a button into the navigation bar.

2. Select the button and, using the Attributes inspector, configure it in the following way:

   • Set Style to Bordered.

   • Set the System Item to Cancel.

3. Select the navigation bar and, using the Attributes inspector, set its title to "Selfie!".

4. In the object library, search for a "Visual Effect with Blur" view.

5. Drag this into the main view (not the preview view!).

When you have a view that takes up most (or all) of the space of the main view, it can be hard to add new UI elements into their correct places in the hierarchy. It is often easier to drag the new UI element into the wrong view, and then manually move it out using the document outline.

6. In the Attributes inspector, change the Blur Style to Dark.

7. Using the Add New Constraints menu, add the following constraints:

- Height: 40 points
- Leading space: 0 points
- Trailing space: 0 points
- Bottom space: 0 points

    This will pin our effect view to the bottom of the view, making it 40 points high and as wide as the main view.

 UIVisualEffectView is a custom view class designed for presenting special visual effects as a mask over the top of a view and its contents. In our case we are using the blur form of the view to create a dark blurred area, so that we don't have a harsh line between our camera preview and the instructions on its use (which we are about to create). Visual effect views currently support both blur and vibrancy masks, but it is possible that more effects will be created over time.

8. Drag a label into the effect view.
9. Set the text of the label to "Tap to take a selfie".
10. Using the Attributes inspector, change the color of the label to white.
11. Control-drag from the label into the effect view, and in the menu that appears add the following constraints:

- Center vertically
- Center horizontally

12. Drag a tap gesture recognizer into the view controller.

 UITapGestureRecognizer is a specialized subclass of gesture recognizer designed to trigger when a tap is encountered. You can configure them to respond to single or multiple taps, as well as single or multiple fingers. The UIGestureRecognizer class in general can be used to recognize almost any form of gesture, from taps, to presses, to swipes.

With this done, our UI is complete.

Connecting the UI

The next step is to hook up our freshly made UI to our code:

1. Select the view controller and, in the Identity inspector, set the class to `Capture ViewController`.

2. Open the assistant editor and make sure that the *CaptureViewController.swift* file is open.

3. Control-drag from the preview view into the `CaptureViewController` class and create a new outlet called `cameraPreview`.

4. Control-drag from the cancel button into the `CaptureViewController` class and create a new action called `close`.

5. Control-drag from the cancel button into the `CaptureViewController` class and create a new action called `takeSelfie`.

Now we can start writing some code to set all this into action.

Talking to the Camera

Our UI is complete and hooked up; now it's time to give it some functionality. There are quite a few steps involved in this, however, and a lot of new libraries we haven't touched on so far. Our first step will be configuring a few properties for later use:

1. Create a completion handler property:

   ```
   typealias CompletionHandler = (UIImage?) -> Void
   var completion : CompletionHandler?
   ```

   This will be used later on as a way to signal to the rest of the application that we have successfully grabbed an image for use in the selfie. As this view controller is a replacement for the image picker, we will use this handler as the way of passing back information to the list view controller. When we have a photo, or the cancel button is pressed, we will call this completion handler and pass in the image (or `nil` in the case of a cancellation) to let the list view controller continue in its job of creating the rest of the selfie.

2. Create a session and an output property:

   ```
   let captureSession = AVCaptureSession()
   let photoOutput = AVCapturePhotoOutput()
   ```

   These two properties are our main interface into the camera (or will be). The capture session represents a live stream of what the camera sees, and the output provides an interface for taking a still photo from the camera. We will use the session for displaying into our custom preview view what the camera sees, and the output will give us our selfie image.

3. Create an orientation computed property:

```
var currentVideoOrientation : AVCaptureVideoOrientation {
    let orientationMap : [UIDeviceOrientation:AVCaptureVideoOrientation]

orientationMap = [
        .portrait: .portrait,
        .landscapeLeft: .landscapeRight,
        .landscapeRight: .landscapeLeft,
        .portraitUpsideDown: .portraitUpsideDown
    ]

    let currentOrientation = UIDevice.current.orientation

    let videoOrientation =
        orientationMap[currentOrientation, default: .portrait]

    return videoOrientation
}
```

This property uses the device's orientation to work out what the correct orientation for both the video and the photo will be. This is to prevent taking a photo and having it present sideways or upside down. The code first maps device orientations (of type `UIDeviceOrientation`) to AVKit orientations (of type `AVCaptureVideoOrientation`). Then we get the device's current orientation and use our mapping to return the same AVKit orientation, using portrait as the default.

 You might be wondering why iOS has both a device and an AV orientation. This is so that if you want you can change the orientation of the device but have the video not change.

Setting up the session

Our properties are done; our next moves are to set up our capture session and our preview to show what the camera is seeing:

1. Replace `viewDidLoad` with the following:

```
override func viewDidLoad() {
    let discovery = AVCaptureDevice.DiscoverySession(
        deviceTypes: [AVCaptureDevice.DeviceType.builtInWideAngleCamera],
        mediaType: AVMediaType.video,
        position: AVCaptureDevice.Position.front)

    // Get the first available device; bail if we can't find one
    guard let captureDevice = discovery.devices.first else {
        NSLog("No capture devices available.")
```

```
                self.completion?(nil)
                return
            }

            // Attempt to add this device to the capture session
            do {
                try captureSession.addInput(AVCaptureDeviceInput(device:
                    captureDevice))
            } catch let error {
                NSLog("Failed to add camera to capture session: \(error)")
                self.completion?(nil)
            }

            // Configure the camera to use high-resolution
            // capture settings
            captureSession.sessionPreset = AVCaptureSession.Preset.photo

            // Begin the capture session
            captureSession.startRunning()

            // Add the photo output to the session, so that
            // it can receive photos when it wants them
            if captureSession.canAddOutput(photoOutput) {
                captureSession.addOutput(photoOutput)
            }

            self.cameraPreview.setSession(captureSession)

            super.viewDidLoad()
    }
```

The first thing we do here is ask `AVKit` for all capture devices that are wide-angle cameras, are capable of capturing video, and are on the front. Essentially, we are asking for the front-facing camera. This returns a list of all devices that match these requirements.

 On every device Apple makes there is only a single camera that matches these requirements, but it is possible that it may add more front cameras in the future. This is why the API is set up in this way.

2. Then we try and get the first camera out of this list. If this fails (for example, if the front camera is unavailable or perhaps damaged) we bail out: we call the completion handler with `nil` and end here.

3. Once we have a device, we try and add it as the device for our capture session, essentially telling the session to be ready to stream video from the front camera. If we fail to do that, we again run the completion handler.

4. Next, we set the session preset (the quality) of the session to a level appropriate for taking photos (that is to say, a high level of quality) and then start the session running. This will begin the streaming of the camera data into the session property.

 The call to `startRunning` can take some time to return and will block the rest of the code that follows it until it finishes. We generally want our UIs to be snappy and responsive at all times, so having something block the rest of the method from completing is a bad thing. In our case, as we can't continue the loading of the view without the camera, we don't have to worry about it slowing down the view's setup—we need it to finish before continuing. Normally, however, it is worth running a call like this on a different queue to prevent it slowing down your UI.

5. With our session running, we then configure it to use our output property as a valid output for the session. We need to do this so we can grab photos out of the session while it is running.

6. Finally, we configure our custom preview view to show the session.

Handling interaction

Our session is now configured, and our UI is ready to show the camera. So how do we interact with it all?

1. Create the `viewWillLayoutSubviews` method:

   ```
   override func layoutSubviews() {
       previewLayer?.frame = self.bounds
   }
   override func viewWillLayoutSubviews() {
       self.cameraPreview?.setCameraOrientation(currentVideoOrientation)
   }
   ```

   This will be called whenever the device orientation changes; all we do is update the orientation of the video preview.

2. Now we need to handle when the cancel button is tapped. Add the following to the `close` method:

   ```
   self.completion?(nil)
   ```

If the user taps the cancel button all we need to do is call the completion handler with nil passed in. When we replace the image picker in the list view controller (see "Calling the Capture View Controller" on page 240) we will be using the value from the completion handler to work out what to do. This means that we don't have to worry about dismissing ourselves from the view hierarchy, as the selfie list view controller will be handling that task.

3. Next we need to handle when the user wants to take a selfie. In our app we are making it so that when the user taps on the screen it will take the picture. This is different from the image picker, where there was a dedicated button for taking the photo. Add the following to the takeSelfie method:

```
// Get a connection to the output
guard let videoConnection
    = photoOutput.connection(with: AVMediaType.video) else
{
    NSLog("Failed to get camera connection")
    return
}

// Set its orientation, so that the image is oriented correctly
videoConnection.videoOrientation = currentVideoOrientation

// Indicate that we want the data it captures to be in JPEG format
let settings =
 AVCapturePhotoSettings(format: [AVVideoCodecKey: AVVideoCodecType.jpeg])

// Begin capturing a photo; it will call
// photoOutput(_, didFinishProcessingPhoto:, error:) when done
photoOutput.capturePhoto(with: settings, delegate: self)
```

You are probably getting an error warning you that the Capture ViewController class doesn't conform to the AVCapturePhotoCaptureDelegate protocol. Don't worry about it for now; we are just about to fix that.

The first thing we are doing in this code is getting a connection to the video stream inside our output property. We are getting this so we can then set its orientation correctly.

Then we set up the settings we want for our output—in this case, a single JPEG photo.

There's a rather impressive amount of flexibility in the settings format. While we are just creating a JPEG, it is worth checking out the documentation (*https://apple.co/2HMSljz*) on the available format options if you ever need more precise output control. Amongst the different formats Apple supports both JPEG and HEIF, both of which are great for photos. As it gains more adoption in the future it will be well worth considering supporting the newer HEIF (High Efficiency Image File Format) in your apps, in places where you would otherwise use JPEG. Until that future, though, we'll stick with JPEG.

Finally, we tell the output that we want it to capture a photo. Its delegate (soon to be the `CaptureViewController` class) will take it from here.

Conforming to the AVCapturePhotoCaptureDelegate protocol

Earlier, we made a call on our output property to `capturePhoto(with: delegate:)`, which requires a delegate to handle the results of trying to save out an image. Now we need to actually conform to this protocol:

1. Create a new extension on the `CaptureViewController` class:

    ```
    extension CaptureViewController : AVCapturePhotoCaptureDelegate {
    }
    ```

2. Implement the `photoOutput(didFinishProcessingPhoto photo:, error:)` delegate method:

    ```
    func photoOutput(_ output: AVCapturePhotoOutput,
                     didFinishProcessingPhoto photo: AVCapturePhoto,
                     error: Error?) {
        if let error = error {
            NSLog("Failed to get the photo: \(error)")
            return
        }

        guard let jpegData = photo.fileDataRepresentation(),
              let image = UIImage(data: jpegData) else {
            NSLog("Failed to get image from encoded data")
                return
        }

        self.completion?(image)
    }
    ```

This method will be called once the output has either managed to create an image or failed to do so. If it fails, the error variable will have a value; in our case all we are doing is logging this, but you could present a dialog box to the users to let them know. If it doesn't fail, we instead get the image out of the data that was sent over, in the form of an AVCapturePhoto object, and convert it into a UIImage for use in creating a selfie.

Then we call the completion handler, passing in the image we just collected. From this point onward it is the responsibility of the selfie list view controller.

Calling the Capture View Controller

Our capture view controller is now complete—it is time to hook it into our existing app. Currently, we are using the prebuilt image picker to collect images. We need to strip that part of our code out and add code to call our view controller in its place.

Now, we could create a normal segue in the storyboard to present the capture view controller, but we've already seen how to do that. Instead, we'll take a look at how to create and display a view controller from a storyboard through code:

1. Open *Main.storyboard* and select the navigation controller of the capture view controller.

2. In the Identity inspector, set the storyboard ID to CaptureScene.

 Setting a Storyboard ID will also get rid of the warning Xcode is showing about an unreachable scene.

   We will be using the storyboard ID as a means of finding the view controller inside the storyboard to instantiate a copy of it.

3. Open *SelfieListViewController.swift*.

4. Inside the createNewSelfie method, delete all references to the image picker controller, its instantiation, its configuration, and its presentation.

5. Add the following to the createNewSelfie method:

```
guard let navigation = self.storyboard?
        .instantiateViewController(withIdentifier: "CaptureScene")
        as? UINavigationController,
      let capture = navigation.viewControllers.first
        as? CaptureViewController
else {
    fatalError("Failed to create the capture view controller!")
}
```

We are using the instantiateViewController(withIdentifier:) method call to instantiate a copy of the navigation controller that encapsulates our capture view. This works by diving into the storyboard, finding a scene with that identifier, and returning an instance of that view controller. Once we have that we then get a reference to the capture view controller inside of it. If either of these two actions fails we exit using the `fatalError` call, as failure to load either of these means the flow of the app is compromised. However, as we've named our storyboard scene correctly and the first view controller of our navigation controller is the capture view, the `else` should never run. As you start writing your own apps, bear in mind that while using `fatalError` and similar dangerous and crashing calls is fine at the start of development, as you get closer to releasing your app out into the world you want to limit this, even in cases where you are sure it can't happen—a crash rarely looks good. What to do when something unexpected happens will change on an app-by-app basis, so we haven't implemented anything here.

 Most of the time using the built-in means of linking scenes together through storyboard segues is the correct way of moving between view controllers. We're doing it differently to show off the technique, but normally you wouldn't do this and would instead use a segue. As a rule of thumb, you should only be creating view controllers through code when it isn't easily done or logically sensible via segues.

6. Below the `guard` statement we just wrote, add the following:

```
capture.completion = {(image : UIImage?) in

    if let image = image {
        self.newSelfieTaken(image: image)
    }

    self.dismiss(animated: true, completion: nil)
}
```

Here we are setting the completion handler closure of the capture view controller. We check if we have an image, and if we do we run the method to create a new selfie. Then we dismiss the capture view controller. As we are using the image property to determine if the image creation worked, our completion handler is thankfully very small. Now we need to present our newly configured view controller.

7. Add the following after the closure we just wrote:

```
self.present(navigation, animated: true, completion: nil)
```

With that done our capture view controller will now be presented, allow you to take photos, and then be dismissed. The last thing we need to do is a bit of cleanup.

As the image picker required delegate callbacks and our capture view instead uses a completion handler, we no longer need that part of our codebase.

 We know deleting code can seem a little scary, but as you are of course using version control in your apps (right?), you should never be afraid of deleting code. If it turns out you need it back, just use your version control system to bring it back.

8. Delete the `SelfieListViewController` extension that made it conform to the `UIImagePickerControllerDelegate` and `UINavigationControllerDelegate` protocols.

Now our replacement of the image picker is complete! Check out the new functionality in Figure 13-1.

Figure 13-1. Our custom capture view controller

At this point we are at the stage where we can't test the functionality of Selfiegram without a device. The simulator has no cameras, only a photo library. The image picker we originally used had the fallback of the photo library, but our capture view controller does not.

Image Overlays

Now that we have a replacement for our image picker working it is time to start adding a new feature into Selfiegram. We are going to add in support for overlaying cartoon eyebrows onto the selfie images—after all, what good is a selfie app if it lacks comedic eyebrows? If we were to save the eyebrows into the app itself, any time we wanted to add new eyebrows we'd have to make a new build of the app, so instead we will make it so that the eyebrows are downloaded from a server.

There are quite a few steps involved in this. In this chapter we will be building the model component, which will entail downloading eyebrow images, saving them locally, and presenting an interface that our UI can later talk to. Then in the next chapter we will create the UI to show the list of eyebrows, preview them on a selfie, and save the results.

 We are storing our eyebrows in the GitHub repository (*https://github.com/thesecretlab/learning-swift-3rd-ed*) where we are making our code available. We can get away with this because our server needs are very minimal and we are trying to show off downloading and URL handling in Swift, not proper file server configuration.

Creating the Overlay Model

The basic structure for our overlay model will follow a pattern very similar to how we structured our selfies. There will be an `Overlay` object that will have the relevant overlay information inside it, which in our case will be three images: a left and a right eyebrow, and a preview image. Unlike the selfies, however, which are saved to the disk, we won't be saving overlays directly; instead, they will be created dynamically as needed. There will also be a manager singleton that will handle the saving, loading, and downloading of the overlays and their information, creating them dynamically based on that information. Finally, there will be an overlay information type that will hold relevant information about each overlay, such as its image location, and will be used by the manager to create overlays as necessary.

The manager will download an overlay information file containing information about the various overlays, save this information locally, and when needed create overlays that it can then return based on this information. A great deal of the design of our manager is based around caching the overlays—we want Selfiegram to be nice and snappy, and downloads take time. For this reason, wherever possible we are going to be caching our overlays. Let's get started:

1. Create a new Swift file called *OverlayStore.swift*. This will be where we store our Overlay class and information and is synonymous with *SelfieStore.swift*.

2. Create the OverlayInformation struct:

   ```
   struct OverlayInformation: Codable {
       let icon : String
       let leftImage : String
       let rightImage : String
   }
   ```

   This will be used later on in the manager as a quick lookup for the names of the different parts of an overlay. The reason for creating this struct is to prevent us having to pass around the much larger image objects that an overlay would otherwise need. From this information overlays will be created with their images.

3. Create the overlay errors:

   ```
   enum OverlayManagerError: Error {
       case noDataLoaded
       case cannotParseData(underlyingError: Error)
   }
   ```

   Much like with the selfies, there are numerous occasions for errors to occur in our downloading and saving of overlays and their images. If we set up some errors now, we can throw them later on when we encounter issues. Our two errors relate to when we haven't managed to successfully download an overlay, and when we fail to parse an overlay we've downloaded.

4. Create the overlay manager class:

   ```
   final class OverlayManager {



   }
   ```

This will be our manager and will also be following the singleton pattern we discussed in "The SelfieStore" on page 127. This class is responsible for the meat of the work around overlays.

5. Create the shared instance of our singleton:

```
static let shared = OverlayManager()
```

This will be our main interface into the overlay manager class and functions identically to how our selfie store singleton does.

6. Create a property to hold the list of overlays we currently know about:

```
typealias OverlayList = [OverlayInformation]
private var overlayInfo : OverlayList
```

Whenever we download a list of overlays we are going to want to keep around a reference to them. This property will then be used later to build the actual overlays themselves.

We are using a type alias here to save a tiny bit of typing time later on, and more importantly to make the code look a bit nicer. Type aliases are used all over the place in Swift and Cocoa for these very reasons, as they share a philosophy that emphasizes readability. It's worth aliasing common types when they have a specific role to play, such as the Double struct being type-aliased to CLLocationDegrees when used inside of Core Location to represent a latitude or longitude. Readability may be the most important aspect of any code you write, and type aliases are just one tool to help improve your code's readability.

7. Create the two data URLs:

```
static let downloadURLBase = URL(
    string: "https://raw.githubusercontent.com/"
    + "thesecretlab/learning-swift-3rd-ed/master/Data/")!
static let overlayListURL = URL(string: "overlays.json",
                        relativeTo: OverlayManager.downloadURLBase)!
```

We've broken the base URL into multiple strings concatenated together because we need it to be visible in the book. You can break it up like this if you want, but there is no difference in the workings of the code if you write it all on one line.

The first is the base URL where we store all our overlay data, and the second is the location of the file that describes the overlays. These will be used numerous times when we need to download the overlay data.

Just like we did with `SelfieStore`, we are using `static` variables inside our class. Swift supports both `static` and `class` properties that are made available to the entire class, not just instances of the class. The main difference between them is that `class` properties can be overridden by subclasses and `static` properties cannot. This means that if we wanted to support subclassing we could rewrite our `overlayListURL` property to be a `class` property. To do this, however, we would need to make it a computed property, as stored `class` properties are not supported in Swift:

```
class var overlayListURL : URL {
    return URL(string: "overlays.json",
            relativeTo: OverlayManager
                .downloadURLBase)!
}
```

If you intend on having class variables that are configurable and overrideable in subclasses, they have to be computed properties. In our case, as our overlay manager class is `final` it can't be subclassed anyway, so there is no point in doing this, but we thought it was worth pointing out.

8. Create the two cache URLs:

```
static var cacheDirectoryURL : URL {
    guard let cacheDirectory =
        FileManager.default.urls(for: .cachesDirectory,
                                in: .userDomainMask).first else {
        fatalError("Cache directory not found! This should not happen!")
    }
    return cacheDirectory
}
static var cachedOverlayListURL : URL {
    return cacheDirectoryURL.appendingPathComponent("overlays.json",
            isDirectory: false)
}
```

These are the URLs for our local cached versions of the content at the server URLs. The first is the URL for the cache directory for Selfiegram. We are force-unwrapping the optional here because the cache directory is created by the operating system, not our app. If we are unable to find it, something horrible and out of our control has happened. The second URL is the location of the data file that describes the overlays inside the cache.

The *Caches* directory is very similar to the *Documents* directory we've already been using. It's a place where we can store
downloaded and created assets we will need in our app. The
difference between the two is that *Caches* is, as its name
implies, for caching items, not for storage of user-created data.
This means this directory isn't saved into backups and its contents will be deleted by the device whenever it needs more
space. You should only save things into the cache that are able
to be recreated as needed should they go away!

9. Create the two asset URL functions:

```
// Returns the URL for downloading a named image file
func urlForAsset(named assetName: String) -> URL? {
    return URL(string: assetName,
            relativeTo: OverlayManager.downloadURLBase)
}

// Returns the URL for the cached version of an image file
func cachedUrlForAsset(named assetName: String) -> URL? {
    return URL(string: assetName,
            relativeTo: OverlayManager.cacheDirectoryURL)
}
```

These functions will be used later to load specific overlay images based on their
names. The names of the assets come from the overlay information files. We have
two versions of the function, one for cached assets and the other for those we'll
have to download. In both cases we are returning optional URLs as the assets that
are being requested may not exist.

10. Create the initializer:

```
init() {
    do {
        let overlayListData =
            try Data(contentsOf: OverlayManager.cachedOverlayListURL)
        self.overlayInfo =
            try JSONDecoder().decode(OverlayList.self,
                from: overlayListData)

    } catch {
        self.overlayInfo = []
    }
}
```

All our initializer has to do is attempt to create a list of overlays based on what is
stored inside the cache. On the first run there will be no cached overlays as none
will have been downloaded; in this case, we initialize our list of overlays as an
empty array.

11. Create the method stubs:

```
func availableOverlays() -> [Overlay] { return [] }
func refreshOverlays(
    completion: @escaping (OverlayList?, Error?) -> Void){}
func loadOverlayAssets(refresh: Bool = false,
                        completion: @escaping () -> Void) {}
```

You might be wondering what adding the @escaping attribute to the closures in those method stubs does. This is a part of Swift and closures we haven't spoken about before. Swift has two types of closures. An *escaping closure* is one that runs after the function it is a part of has returned (as is the case with our methods). It is called "escaping" because it *escapes* the function; it exists after the function has completed. By default in Swift all closures are *nonescaping*, which means they have to be run before the function completes. There are a lot of advantages to having closures be nonescaping by default, especially when it comes to functional programming, so this is what the Swift community opted for. In a nutshell, this means if you are using closures as completion handlers in functions, they have to be marked as escaping closures using the @escaping attribute.

12. Our final step in the manager is to create method stubs. Much like with our selfie store, we are going to be building the class up as a series of method stubs we can write tests for, filling in the stubs, and then using the tests to check our work.

Don't worry about that Overlay type that Xcode will be complaining doesn't exist; we are just about to create it.

13. Import the UIImage class:

```
import UIKit.UIImage
```

As the overlay itself will be a wrapper around images, we need to import the ability to use images. We are just importing the parts of UIKit that relate to images here, as we don't need the entire module.

14. Create the Overlay struct:

```
// An Overlay is a container for the images used to present
// an eyebrow choice to the user
struct Overlay {
```

```swift
    // The image to show in the list of eyebrow choices
    let previewIcon: UIImage

    // The images to draw on top of the left and right eyebrows
    let leftImage : UIImage
    let rightImage : UIImage

    // Creates an Overlay given the names of images to use
    // The images must be downloaded and stored in the cache,
    // or this initializer will return nil
    init?(info: OverlayInformation) {
        // Construct the URLs that would point to the cached images
        guard
            let previewURL = OverlayManager
                .shared.cachedUrlForAsset(named: info.icon),
            let leftURL = OverlayManager
                .shared.cachedUrlForAsset(named: info.leftImage),
            let rightURL = OverlayManager
                .shared.cachedUrlForAsset(named: info.rightImage) else {
                return nil
        }

        // Attempt to get the images.
        // If any of these fail, we return nil.
        guard
            let previewImage = UIImage(contentsOfFile: previewURL.path),
            let leftImage = UIImage(contentsOfFile: leftURL.path),
            let rightImage =
            UIImage(contentsOfFile: rightURL.path) else {
                return nil
        }

        // We've got the images, so store them
        self.previewIcon = previewImage
        self.leftImage = leftImage
        self.rightImage = rightImage
    }
}
```

This struct represents a single overlay and contains the three images necessary to present it. Overlays are created based on overlay information and are just wrappers around the images. They are designed to be short-lived and as such are made only when needed.

With this done, we can now start writing our tests for the overlay manager.

You might be wondering why we have done so much work in the manager class without writing any tests. In a proper test-driven development world we wouldn't have done this, but nearly all the work we have done so far was just configuring unchanging URLs, and there isn't really any point in testing those.

Testing the Overlay Manager

With our manager all stubbed out, it is time to make some tests:

1. Create a new unit test:

   a. Go to File → New File.

   b. Select Unit Test Case.

   c. Name the test `DataLoadingTests`.

   d. Make it a subclass of `XCTestCase`.

   e. Make it target the SelfiegramTests build target and save it into the Tests group.

2. Delete the two example tests.

3. Import the testable form of the `Selfiegram` module:

   ```
   @testable import Selfiegram
   ```

Writing the Tests

Now that we are set up, we can start writing our tests. The first step is to perform some setup on our overlays:

1. Add the following to the bottom of the `setUp` method:

   ```
   // Remove all cached data
   let cacheURL = OverlayManager.cacheDirectoryURL

   guard let contents = try?
       FileManager.default.contentsOfDirectory(
           at: cacheURL,
           includingPropertiesForKeys: nil,
           options: []) else {
       XCTFail("Failed to list contents of directory \(cacheURL)")
       return
   }

   var complete = true
   for file in contents {
       do {
           try FileManager.default.removeItem(at: file)
   ```

```
            } catch let error {
                NSLog("Test setup: failed to remove item \(file); \(error)")
                complete = false
            }
        }
        if !complete {
            XCTFail("Failed to delete contents of cache")
        }
```

This method will be called before every test is run, deleting any existing overlays we may have created as part of the other tests. This gives us a clean sheet for every test case to use.

2. Add the `testNoOverlaysAvailable` test case:

```
func testNoOverlaysAvailable() {

    // Arrange
    // Nothing to arrange here: our start condition is that
    // there's no cached data

    // Act
    let availableOverlays = OverlayManager.shared.availableOverlays()

    // Assert
    XCTAssertEqual(availableOverlays.count, 0)

}
```

This test case is to see if we correctly handle having no overlays (effectively what happens when there is no cache).

3. Add the `testGettingOverlayInfo` test:

```
func testGettingOverlayInfo() {

    // Arrange
    let expectation = self.expectation(description: "Done downloading")

    // Act
    var loadedInfo : OverlayManager.OverlayList?
    var loadedError : Error?
    OverlayManager.shared.refreshOverlays { (info, error) in

        loadedInfo = info
        loadedError = error

        expectation.fulfill()
    }

    waitForExpectations(timeout: 5.0, handler: nil)
```

```
// Assert
XCTAssertNotNil(loadedInfo)
XCTAssertNil(loadedError)
}
```

This test case is to ensure we can correctly download the overlay information data from the server. We are using a new technique in this test, because as a download will take a nontrivial amount of time we can't just write our test like we would normally. If we tried this it would always fail, because the test assertions would be run before the download had time to finish. Instead we use an *expectation*, which is a way of setting up something to occur later on in the test. In our case we create an expectation that the download will be finished, and we fulfill that expectation when it is.

Then we add a call to waitForExpectations(timeout: handler:) to make the test case wait for the estimated time to complete the expectation. Failure of an expectation to be completed in the time allotted causes the test to fail.

4. Add the testDownloadingOverlays test:

```
// The overlay manager can download overlay assets, making them
// available for use
func testDownloadingOverlays() {

    // Arrange
    let loadingComplete = self.expectation(description: "Download done")
    var availableOverlays : [Overlay] = []

    // Act
    OverlayManager.shared.loadOverlayAssets(refresh: true) {

        availableOverlays = OverlayManager.shared.availableOverlays()

        loadingComplete.fulfill()
    }

    waitForExpectations(timeout: 10.0, handler: nil)

    // Assert
    XCTAssertNotEqual(availableOverlays.count, 0)
}
```

This test case works in a very similar fashion to the previous one, but instead of downloading the overlay information it downloads the overlay data itself. Because this test case has more work to do we've also given it a fairly large window of opportunity to complete the download before the expectation fails.

5. Add the testDownloadedOverlaysAreCached test:

```
// When the overlay manager is created, it has access to all previously
// cached overlays
```

```
func testDownloadedOverlaysAreCached() {

    // Arrange

    let downloadingOverlayManager = OverlayManager()
    let downloadExpectation =
        self.expectation(description: "Data downloaded")

    // Start downloading
    downloadingOverlayManager.loadOverlayAssets(refresh: true) {
        downloadExpectation.fulfill()
    }

    // Wait for downloads to finish
    waitForExpectations(timeout: 10.0, handler: nil)

    // Act

    // Simulate the overlay manager starting up by initializing a new
    // one; it will access the same files that were downloaded earlier
    let cacheTestOverlayManager = OverlayManager()

    // Assert

    // This overlay manager should see the cached data
    XCTAssertNotEqual(
    cacheTestOverlayManager.availableOverlays().count, 0)
    XCTAssertEqual(cacheTestOverlayManager.availableOverlays().count,
                    downloadingOverlayManager.availableOverlays().count)
}
```

Our final test is a test of the caching ability of the overlay manager. In this test we initially download all the overlay data and then do it again. In the second run, we check to see if the cached data is there.

Of interest here is that we are creating a new copy of the overlay manager for this test. Even though we have it set up to be accessed as a singleton, we can still create instances like this for testing.

Now we have to fill in the method stubs so that our tests pass.

Returning Available Overlays

The first method we want to fill out is availableOverlays. This returns an array of overlays that are ready to use—that is, that are already in the cache and require no further downloads to present.

Replace the availableOverlays method stub with the following:

```
func availableOverlays() -> [Overlay] {
    return overlayInfo.flatMap { Overlay(info: $0) }
}
```

As we have already set up a property that will hold all the overlay info, here we use that information to generate new overlays. Then we return that list of overlays.

Downloading Overlay Information

The next method we need to fill out is `refreshOverlays`. This method is responsible for downloading the list of overlays from the server. Once it has completed that, or failed to do so, it runs the completion handler parameter as its means of sending back the data it collects.

Replace the method stub with the following:

```
func refreshOverlays(completion: @escaping (OverlayList?, Error?) -> Void) {
    // Create a data task to download it.
    URLSession.shared.dataTask(with: OverlayManager.overlayListURL) {
        (data, response, error) in

        // Report if we got an error, or for some other reason data is nil
        if let error = error {
            NSLog("Failed to download \(OverlayManager.overlayListURL): " +
                "\(error)")
            completion(nil, error)
            return
        }

        guard let data = data else {
            completion(nil, OverlayManagerError.noDataLoaded)
            return
        }

        // Cache the data we got
        do {
            try data.write(to: OverlayManager.cachedOverlayListURL)
        } catch let error {
            NSLog("Failed to write data to " +
                "\(OverlayManager.cachedOverlayListURL); " +"reason: \(error)")
            completion(nil, error)
        }

        // Parse the data and store it locally
        do {
            let overlayList = try JSONDecoder()
                .decode(OverlayList.self, from: data)

            self.overlayInfo = overlayList

            completion(self.overlayInfo, nil)
            return
```

```
        } catch let decodeError {
            completion(nil, OverlayManagerError
                .cannotParseData(underlyingError: decodeError))
        }

    }.resume()
}
```

This method relies heavily on the URLSession class, which is designed for handling network tasks you are likely to want to do such as downloading and uploading of files. The intent with this class is that you configure it for the types of tasks you need, give it some tasks to perform, and let it go. It will inform you once it has succeeded or failed to complete the tasks. In our case we are going to be using the preconfigured singleton form of the URL session, which is designed around simple HTTP and HTTPS download tasks.

The URLSession class is extraordinarily flexible, and if it is possible to do something over the network, it can probably do it. It supports numerous different protocols (including FTP), has delegate callbacks for all manner of events, and is one of those APIs you could build almost any networking tool with. Most of the time all you really want is to download some files, though, and it is for this reason that a singleton instance is set up for this very purpose.

In this method we first create a new data task for the URL session to handle. The URL of this task is the location of the overlay data file on the server. The completion closure for this task will be run when the task completes or fails to complete. The closure has three components: the data that was collected in the download, the response from the server, and an error. All of these are optional.

The response is the server's response to the task and represents those HTTP status messages and codes you've likely seen before, such as 404 File Not Found or 500 Server Error. A great number of these responses look like errors (and are, from the perspective of downloading the correct file) but aren't technically in the sense of failing to complete the task. It completed, just not how you expected. This means in the case of a status of 404, the error parameter will be nil as nothing went wrong from an HTTP perspective, but the data variable will contain the server's 404 error message page instead of the data we were after.

Inside the closure we first do a check to see if there is an error. If there is, we run our completion closure, passing back the error. If there isn't an error, we try and grab the data we were after, and once we have it we save it, parse it, and return it. If any of these steps fails, we send the error back up through the completion closure. At the end of this we have either given the completion handler valid overlay info or sent an error.

 You might notice how all the URLs we've been using use the HTTPS protocol instead of HTTP. This is because HTTP has all manner of security issues and vulnerabilities associated with it. HTTPS fixes some (not all) of these issues, so Apple has made it the default. This is part of what Apple calls App Transport Security (ATS). If you want to talk to a server over HTTP you need to set a specific flag (*https://developer.apple.com/library/content/documentation/General/Reference/InfoPlistKeyReference/Articles/CocoaKeys.html#//apple_ref/doc/uid/TP40009251-SW33*) in your *info.plist* file to tell iOS that it is okay to support HTTP in your app.

The final part of the method is a call on the data task to resume. This tells the URL session to begin the download. Data tasks wait until they are told to start before beginning as they consume resources (in this case, network resources).

 Forgetting to tell a task to start is a fairly easy and common mistake to make. If you ever find yourself wondering why a task you've written doesn't seem to be running, it might well be because you never told it to start.

Downloading Overlay Images

The final method we need to create is the one that is responsible for downloading the images that make up the overlays themselves. Each overlay has three images: a preview, and a left and right eyebrow image. This means for each overlay we need to perform three download tasks, and we are going to need some way of coordinating these downloads. For this, we are going to be using a *dispatch group*.

A dispatch group is a way of combining several different tasks together into a group that can be synchronized and controlled with regard to how they work. Our dispatch group will contain numerous different download tasks that will each run and, when it completes, tell the dispatch group about it. Once every task inside the dispatch group is complete, the dispatch group will let us know. The great thing about using a dispatch group for this is that we don't have to worry about what queues the work will be run on; it handles all that for us.

Replace the `loadOverlayAssets` method with the following:

```
// A group for coordinating multiple simultaneous downloads
private let loadingDispatchGroup = DispatchGroup()
```

```swift
// Downloads all assets used by overlays. If 'refresh' is true, the list of
// overlays is updated first.
func loadOverlayAssets(refresh: Bool = false,
                       completion: @escaping () -> Void) {

    // If we're told to refresh, then do that, and rerun this function with
    // 'refresh' set to false
    if (refresh) {
        self.refreshOverlays(completion: { (overlays, error) in
            self.loadOverlayAssets(refresh:  false, completion: completion)
        })
        return
    }

    // For each overlay we know about, download its assets
    for info in overlayInfo {

        // Each overlay has three assets; we need to download each one
        let names = [info.icon, info.leftImage, info.rightImage]

        // For each asset, we need to figure out:
        // 1. where to get it from
        // 2. where to put it
        typealias TaskURL = (source: URL, destination: URL)

        // Create an array of these tuples
        let taskURLs : [TaskURL] = names.flatMap {
            guard let sourceURL
                = URL(string: $0,
                      relativeTo: OverlayManager.downloadURLBase)
            else {
                return nil
            }

            guard let destinationURL
                = URL(string: $0,
                      relativeTo: OverlayManager.cacheDirectoryURL)
            else {
                return nil
            }

            return (source: sourceURL, destination: destinationURL)
        }

        // Now we know what we need to do, start doing it
        for taskURL in taskURLs {
            // 'enter' causes the dispatch group to register that a job is not
            // yet done
            loadingDispatchGroup.enter()

            // Begin the download
            URLSession.shared.dataTask(with: taskURL.source,
```

```
            completionHandler: { (data, response, error) in

                defer {
                    // This job is now done, so indicate that to the
                    // dispatch group
                    self.loadingDispatchGroup.leave()
                }

                guard let data = data else {
                    NSLog("Failed to download \(taskURL.source): \(error!)")
                    return
                }

                // Grab the data and cache it
                do {
                    try data.write(to: taskURL.destination)
                } catch let error {
                    NSLog("Failed to write to \(taskURL.destination): \(error)")
                }
            }).resume()
        }
    }

    // Wait for all downloads to finish and then run the completion block
    loadingDispatchGroup.notify(queue: .main) {
        completion()
    }
}
```

The first line of code here creates a new property, our dispatch group.

Next we jump into the method itself. It works in a similar fashion to the overlay information download, with data passed back through a completion handler. There is also a refresh parameter; when this is true, we also perform an update of the overlay information.

The first part of the method refreshes the overlay information if necessary based on the refresh parameter. Then we start looping over all the overlays we have information about. For each one we work out where it is stored online, and where we will be caching it. We bundle up all of this information into a tuple and return an array of them.

Now that we know where each image is currently and where it needs to be, we can start downloading and saving them. Looping through all of the tasks we have to perform works more or less the same as it did in refreshOverlays. The interesting parts are the calls to loadingDispatchGroup.enter() and, inside the defer block, loading DispatchGroup.leave(). These are how we add a job to the dispatch group and how we then signal that it is complete.

The final part of the method is the call to `loadingDispatchGroup.notify()`. This is where we can write code that will be executed when the work inside the group has finished. One of the interesting parts about this call is the `queue` parameter, which indicates what dispatch queue we want to the closure to be run on. In our case we are choosing the main queue, but you can pick another depending on the needs of your app.

With that done we can run the tests once more, and this time they'll all succeed (Figure 14-1)!

Figure 14-1. Successful tests!

In the next chapter we will start hooking our new overlay model into a UI and see how we can place the eyebrow overlays onto our selfie images.

CHAPTER 15

Overlay UI

At this point we have a fully tested and working overlay manager and model. It's time to make use of them! We are going to be adding an editing view controller that will allow us to select which overlay we want (if any) on our selfie. This view controller will sit after our capture view controller and will be automatically presented after taking a photo.

 Our editing view is intentionally simple. We could add in all sorts of additional features, such as different overlays, touchups, cropping, color changes, and so on, but as these all take a rather long time to make, and wouldn't teach you anything new beyond how to manipulate and draw image data, we are going to just stick with our eyebrow overlays.

Building the UI

Without further ado, let's get started on building the UI:

1. Open *Main.storyboard* and drag in a new view controller.

2. Create a *manual segue* from the capture view controller to the new view controller:

   a. Select the capture view controller from the scene.

   b. Control-drag from the capture view controller to the new view controller.

   c. From the segue menu that appears, select the Show option.

All of our segues to date have been automatic segues that are triggered by actions. A manual segue works identically to an automatic
segue, but instead of being fired due to an action in the UI, you
trigger it yourself in the code. This means you don't have to hide a
button somewhere in your UI just to get a segue. We'll be calling
our manual segue when the user takes a photo a little later on in
this chapter.

3. Select the segue and, using the Attributes inspector, set its identifier to
   `showEditing`.

4. Drag an image view into the scene, and stretch it to make it fill the entire view.

5. Inside the Attributes inspector, set the content mode of the image view to Aspect
   Fill to prevent the photo being distorted.

6. Using the Add New Constraints menu, pin all four sides of the image view to the
   superview, ensuring it will always fill the main view.

7. Drag a scroll view into the scene and place it near the bottom of the view.

8. Using the Add New Constraints menu, pin the scroll view in the following way:

   • Set the left edge to 0 points away from the superview.

   • Set the right edge to 0 points away from the superview.

   • Set the bottom edge to 0 points away from the superview.

   • Set the height of the scroll view to 128 points.

`UIScrollView` is another very common view class in iOS
programming. It provides, as the name implies, views that
can scroll—or rather, the views inside a scroll view can
scroll (it's intended to be a container view, with other views
placed inside it).

Scroll views can be a bit tricky as you have to worry about
the size and position of not only the scroll view itself, but
the views inside of it. Most of the time this isn't as bad as
you might think, and there are already plenty of subclasses
premade and ready to use. In fact, we've already been using
scroll views quite a lot without mentioning it—`UITableView`
is a subclass of `IUScrollView`.

9. In the object library, search for a horizontal stack view and drag one into the
   scroll view.

A stack view is a custom view subclass designed for showing subviews that are laid out in a stacked pattern, either vertically or horizontally. The idea behind a stack view is that you place any UI elements you need aligned inside it and let it handle the layout, size, and positioning. You can specify the axis (either vertical or horizontal), the alignment, and the distribution, which lets you control the positioning and size of the subviews across the perpendicular and main axes, and the spacing between the subviews.

We'll be using this stack view to place a preview image of our overlays.

 As most UIs are composed of vertically or horizontally aligned elements, the stack view is a perfect class to use to position components of your UI that need to be near each other but for which would be tedious to set up the constraints manually. You can instead pop them all inside a stack view and just place the stack in the proper location.

10. Stretch the stack view so that it fills the entire size of the scroll view.

11. Using the Add New Constraints menu, set all four edges to be 0 points away from the superview.

12. Control-drag from the stack view onto the scroll view and, from the constraints menu that appears, select Equal Height.

13. Using the Attributes inspector, set the following attributes on the stack view:

- **Alignment**: Center
- **Spacing**: 8

14. Using the Size inspector, set the intrinsic size of the stack view to Placeholder.

So far we have been setting constraints that hard-lock the position and size of elements, but we can't easily do that with our stack and scroll view combo. We need the stack view to fill the size of the scroll view, but also to be able to stretch as far to the trailing edge as possible, as we may have a very large number of overlays to present. As the size of the stack view will be determined by the elements inside, its size will change. A normal view wouldn't work with the scroll view even if we'd set up the constraints correctly, as it won't be prepared for the width of the stack view to change. As such, we have to tell the constraints that they are placeholders and will be changed at runtime based on what is inside the stack view. This resolves the warning from Xcode.

With that done, we now have a stack view that arranges its subviews horizontally (centered vertically), with a gap of 8 points between them, and will fill out the available space of the stack view. As we've also put this inside a scroll view, we will have a list of overlays that scrolls and handles new images, no matter how many of them we have.

Hooking Up the UI

Our UI is done, and it is time to hook it up to our code. First, we need a place for that code to go:

1. Create a new Cocoa Touch class.

2. Make it a subclass of `UIViewController`.

3. Name it `EditingViewController`.

4. In the storyboard, select the new view controller we've been working with, and in the Identity inspector set the class to be `EditingViewController`.

5. Using the Attributes inspector, set the title of the editing view controller to "Edit".

6. Open the assistant editor and ensure the *EditingViewController.swift* file is open.

7. Control-drag from the image view and create a new outlet called `imageView`.

8. Control-drag from the stack view and create a new outlet called `optionsStack View`.

We are now ready to start writing some code to put our model and UI into action.

Creating the Overlay View

Before we can start showing different overlays we need a view to show them in, so now we're going to create a new custom view class that will be responsible for showing the content of an overlay and handling what happens when it is tapped:

1. Inside the *EditingViewController.swift* file create a new `UIImageView` subclass:

   ```
   class OverlaySelectionView : UIImageView {

   }
   ```

2. Create an overlay property for the class, which will be used later to extract the requisite images for the overlay:

   ```
   let overlay : Overlay
   ```

3. Create a new closure handler property. This will run when the user taps the overlay:

   ```
   typealias TapHandler = () -> Void
   let tapHandler : TapHandler
   ```

4. Create an initializer for the class:

```
init(overlay: Overlay, tapHandler: @escaping TapHandler) {

    self.overlay = overlay
    self.tapHandler = tapHandler

    super.init(image: overlay.previewIcon)

    self.isUserInteractionEnabled = true

    // The method we'll be calling when tapped
    let tappedMethod = #selector(OverlaySelectionView.tapped(tap:))

    // Create and add a tap recognizer that runs the desired method
    // when tapped
    let tapRecognizer = UITapGestureRecognizer(target: self,
                                               action: tappedMethod)
    self.addGestureRecognizer(tapRecognizer)
}
```

This initializer has two parameters, the overlay for this overlay view and the handler to be run when it is tapped upon. Inside the initializer we store the two parameters into our properties, call our superclass's initializer with the value of the overlay preview image, and then set up a new tap gesture recognizer. We are using a tap gesture recognizer here as it is the easiest way to handle user input in a class that doesn't normally support user interaction.

The call to self.isUserInteractionEnabled = true in the preceding code is very important. By default image views aren't set to handle user interaction, so they have no reason to receive events. Without this set to true we wouldn't be able to receive user-generated events, such as a tap.

5. Write the code to handle when a tap occurs:

```
@objc func tapped(tap: UITapGestureRecognizer) {
    self.tapHandler()
}
```

Whenever a tap comes in, we want to run the tap handler that was passed in as a part of our initializer. This will be used a bit later to actually draw the eyebrows onto the image.

6. Finally, implement the required initializer:

```
required init?(coder aDecoder: NSCoder) {
    fatalError("init(coder:) has not been implemented")
}
```

This initializer is necessary to conform correctly to the image view subclass and all its protocols, but it will only be used when this class is being initialized from a storyboard, which will never happen for us. As we need both an overlay and a handler and we are going to be dynamically creating this view in code we don't have to worry about this; we're just doing the minimum necessary to make our class compile.

 It is good practice to make sure that your custom subclasses correctly conform to the requirements of their parents and don't just crash when they don't, especially if your code is to be reused outside of a single project. This is because you can never really predict what will happen with your code once it is out there. The easiest way to do this in our case would be to make the overlay and tap handler properties optional, but as we know this call can never happen it isn't worth dealing with optionals everywhere in a class where they really shouldn't be optional.

Presenting the Overlays

We are now at the point where we can start looking at drawing the eyebrows onto the image, but there are a few steps involved, so we'll be building this up in small pieces.

Initial Setup

First, we need to set up our types and properties:

1. Import the Vision framework:

   ```
   import Vision
   ```

   Vision is the framework that gives us access to facial detection code, which we'll be using to identify where on the image the eyebrows are located. We'll talk more about Vision and how it works when we start using it; for now, we just want to make sure we include it.

2. Inside the EditingViewController class, add the following:

   ```
   // There are two kinds of eyebrows: the left, and the right
   enum EyebrowType { case left, right }

   // An eyebrow is a combination of its type and its position
   typealias EyebrowPosition = (type: EyebrowType, position: CGPoint)

   // DetectionResult represents either a successful detection or a failure;
   // it uses associated values to carry additional context
   enum DetectionResult {
       case error(Error)
       case success([EyebrowPosition])
   }
   ```

```
// We have one type of error: we didn't find any eyebrows
enum DetectionError : Error { case noResults }

// A detection completion is a closure that's used to receive
// a detection result
typealias DetectionCompletion = (DetectionResult) -> Void
```

These are a bunch of convenience types and aliases we'll be using later on, so it makes sense to set them up now.

Of most interest are the eyebrow type and position. The type is a normal enum for indicating if an eyebrow is a left or right eyebrow, and the position is a tuple that wraps up the type of the eyebrow as well as the center point of the eyebrow. These will be used later, when it comes time to position the eyebrow images on the selfie. We've set it up like this so that we can independently position the left and right eyebrows.

3. Create the two image properties:

```
// The image we received from the CaptureViewController
var image : UIImage?

// The image that we'll create by drawing eyebrows on top
var renderedImage : UIImage?
```

The first of these properties will be given to this class by the capture view controller when it segues into this view controller. This will hold the image from the camera itself. The second property will hold the edited image with the eyebrows placed on top. When it comes time to return the edited image, this property will be the one returned, or if the user aborts the editing the original image will be returned instead.

4. Create the eyebrow property:

```
// The list of eyebrow positions we detected.
var eyebrows : [EyebrowPosition] = []
```

This is a list of all eyebrows that we know about, and will be created on the fly from the overlays extracted from the overlay manager.

5. Create the overlay properties:

```
var overlays : [Overlay] = []

var currentOverlay : Overlay? = nil {
    didSet {
        guard currentOverlay != nil else { return }
        redrawImage()
    }
}
```

The first property here is a list of all overlays that we know about and will come from the overlay manager. The second holds the currently selected overlay. Initially it will be nil but whenever an overlay is selected it will be set, and after that it will call a method to redraw the image based on the newly chosen set of eyebrows. We will get to the redrawImage method in a moment, once we finish our setup.

 There are going to be plenty of times where you know you will need a method to do something but you haven't written it yet, and don't want to be bogged down writing it while you are still in a different headspace. In these cases it is really useful to write a quick method stub so that Xcode stops complaining about it, and lets you get back to work.

6. Create the completion handler property:

```
var completion : CaptureViewController.CompletionHandler?
```

This will be the same completion handler that the capture view controller uses, and we will pass this as part of the segue.

With our properties and types ready, we still have a few small pieces of setup left to do. We need to configure these properties and give our image view and overlay stack view something to show:

1. Add the following to the end of the viewDidLoad method:

```
guard let image = image else {
    self.completion?(nil)
    return
}
self.imageView.image = image

// setting up the overlay information
overlays = OverlayManager.shared.availableOverlays()

for overlay in overlays {

    let overlayView = OverlaySelectionView(overlay: overlay) {
        self.currentOverlay = overlay
    }

    overlays.append(overlay)

    optionsStackView.addArrangedSubview(overlayView)
}

// adding in a done button
```

```
let addSelfieButton = UIBarButtonItem(barButtonSystemItem: .done,
                                      target: self,
                                      action: #selector(done))
navigationItem.rightBarButtonItem = addSelfieButton
```

First, we are performing a check that we have an image. If an image wasn't passed in there is no point in continuing, so we run the completion handler with nil and exit the function.

This will dismiss us and the capture view and return control to the selfie list view controller. As the image will always be passed in from the capture view controller, however, this will never happen. Once we have an image, we set it to appear in the image view. Next, we run through all the overlays we know about, create an overlay view for them, and then add them to the options stack view ready to be selected. Finally, we add a done button to the navigation bar; this will be how the user will let the program know she is happy with the image as it appears.

2. Create the done function:

```
@objc func done(){
    let imageToReturn = self.renderedImage ?? self.image

    self.completion?(imageToReturn)
}
```

This function will be run when the user taps on the done button. Inside here we work out whether we will be sending back the edited image or the original image. Once we've determined this we call the completion handler with the value of the image. This will result in the editing and capture view controllers being dismissed, control being returned to the selfie list view controller, and the creation of a new selfie with our newly edited image.

That's the setup of our editing view controller done—now it is time to start editing the images.

Drawing Eyebrows

All of our drawing code is neatly encapsulated within the redrawImage method, which we'll be writing now. This method is responsible for taking the existing image and placing the eyebrows over the top of it, in their correct positions.

 UIImage data is immutable, so technically we won't be changing the existing image at all. Instead, we will be creating a new image that is a composite of the original image with the overlay images on top. This will be saved and stored locally.

Create the `redrawImage` method:

```
func redrawImage(){
    // Ensure that we have an overlay to draw, and an image to draw it on
    guard let overlay = self.currentOverlay,
        let image = self.image else {
        return
    }

    // Start drawing and when we're done, make sure we cleanly stop drawing
    UIGraphicsBeginImageContext(image.size)

    defer {
        UIGraphicsEndImageContext()
    }

    // Start by drawing the base image
    image.draw(at: CGPoint.zero)

    // For each eyebrow that we know about, draw it
    for eyebrow in self.eyebrows {

        // Pick the appropriate image to use, based on which eyebrow it is
        let eyebrowImage : UIImage

        switch eyebrow.type {
        case .left:
            eyebrowImage = overlay.leftImage
        case .right:
            eyebrowImage = overlay.rightImage
        }

        // The coordinates we receive are flipped (i.e., (0,0) is at the bottom,
        // right, not the top left), so we flip them to account for that
        var position = CGPoint(x: image.size.width - eyebrow.position.x,
                               y: image.size.height - eyebrow.position.y)

        // Drawing an image at a position places that image's top-left
        // corner at that position. We want the image to be centered on
        // that position, so we adjust by 50% of the width and height.
        position.x -= eyebrowImage.size.width / 2.0
        position.y -= eyebrowImage.size.height / 2.0

        // We're finally ready to draw this eyebrow!
        eyebrowImage.draw(at: position)
    }

    // We're now done drawing the eyebrows, so grab the image and store it
    self.renderedImage = UIGraphicsGetImageFromCurrentImageContext()

    // Also display the image in the image view
```

```
        self.imageView.image = self.renderedImage
    }
```

There is a lot going on in this method. First, we make sure we have a currently selected overlay and an image to draw on. Without both of these, we can't continue.

Then we create a new *image context*. This needs a size (which we want to be the same size as the original image). An image context is essentially a buffer that draw calls get written into.

 UIGraphicsBeginImageContext is a convenience function that we call instead of the more flexible UIGraphicsBeginImageContextWi thOptions. In the full version of the function you can set not only the size, but also the scale factor and whether the image is opaque. The call we have made assumes a scale factor of 1.0, which is fine in our case as we are using an existing image as our basis, but if you were doing custom image creation from scratch a scale of 1.0 would look distorted when shown on a device with a higher scale factor—such as every iOS device.

iOS manages a stack of graphics contexts, and the topmost context is the one that gets sent draw commands. At the end, we can then ask for an image out of the context. This will take all the draw commands and bake them into an image. We are using defer here to close off the image context, as until the image context is closed any draw calls will go here. This also means we get to have our setup and teardown for the context in the one spot.

 Failure to close an image context can result in all manner of weird things happening. As iOS does a great amount of bitmap drawing, leaving a dangling context is a very risky thing to do. Make sure you always close off your image contexts.

The first thing we do is draw the existing image into the context. We set it to draw from position (0, 0), and as both the image and the graphics context have the same size it will fill the entirety of our edited image.

Next we go through each eyebrow image (for the left and right eyebrows) in the selected eyebrow and work out its position in the image. We have to flip the image coordinates, as when drawing the origin is at the bottom right as opposed to the top left, and find the center position of the eyebrow. Once we have that we can then draw the eyebrow image at the appropriate spot.

For simplicity's sake we are just centering the eyebrows where the image detection system says eyebrows are located. This means they won't be appropriately scaled and positioned for all images. This is not a limitation of the image detection (which we will talk about shortly) but a deliberate choice to avoid having to spend a great deal of the book talking about how you correctly conform and distort an image to map it to a series of points.

Finally, we get the new image from the context with the call to `UIGraphicsGetImage FromCurrentImageContext`, store it into our edited image property, and also set the image view to display this rendered image. With that done, our drawing code is complete, and it is time to do some eyebrow detection.

Vision and Image Detection

Our eyebrow detection will be broken up into three main parts. The actual image detection will be done using the Vision framework provided by Apple, which we imported back in "Initial Setup" on page 268.

We will have a method called `detectEyebrows`, which will be the main interface into the image detection system. This will be a simple method that calls the more complex code and presents a clean interface to the detected eyebrow positions. There'll also be a method to detect facial landmarks. As the Vision framework is designed for more than just finding eyebrows, this method will be responsible for setting Vision up for looking for facial landmarks. Finally, there will be a dedicated function for finding just the eyebrows from the facial landmarks Vision detects, determining their position, and returning this information.

This may seem a bit convoluted, but it makes more sense once you see how Vision is designed to operate. Vision isn't just a point-of-interest facial detection system—it can do that and has built-in helpers for it, but that isn't its main purpose. Vision is an image detection system. It uses machine learning to take in one or more images and try to find relevant information inside of them based on various requests. This means you could pass Vision an image and ask it to find both eyebrows and chairs in the same image, assuming you had models capable of doing this detection.

Vision is designed to work with Core ML machine learning models. This is well beyond the scope of this book, but if you are interested in doing more with Vision, check out the Apple documentation on using Vision with Core ML. (*https://apple.co/2HPUHOW*)

So, in our case, this means we will make a single request asking to find facial landmarks inside the image. The request will have a handler that is run once it finds facial landmarks, which will then in turn find the eyebrows among all the landmarks it found.

The reason Vision is set up like this is because it has to be flexible to support arbitrary detection models over many different images, all of which can take some time to process. As such, this approach is very much by design, although at first glance it does look a bit weird.

We'll be writing our code from the bottom up to match this design. First, create the locateEyebrowsHandler request handler method:

```
private func locateEyebrowsHandler(_ request: VNRequest,
                                   imageSize: CGSize,
                                   completion: DetectionCompletion) {

    // If we don't have one, then we have no eyebrows to detect, and must
    // error out
    guard let firstFace = request.results?.first as? VNFaceObservation else {
        completion(.error(DetectionError.noResults))
        return
    }

    // Landmark regions contain multiple points, which describe their
    // contour. In this app, we just want to know where to stick the
    // eyebrow image, so we don't need the whole contour, just an
    // idea of where the eyebrow is. We can get that by taking the
    // average of all points. This internal function does that.
    func averagePosition(for landmark: VNFaceLandmarkRegion2D) -> CGPoint {

        // Get all of the points in the image
        let points = landmark.pointsInImage(imageSize: imageSize)

        // Add up all the points
        var averagePoint = points.reduce(CGPoint.zero, {
            return CGPoint(x: $0.x + $1.x, y: $0.y + $1.y)
        })

        // And divide by the number of points, producing the average point
        averagePoint.x /= CGFloat(points.count)
        averagePoint.y /= CGFloat(points.count)

        return averagePoint
    }

    // Start building a list of eyebrows
    var results : [EyebrowPosition] = []

    // Try and get each eyebrow, calculate its position, and store it in
    // the list of results
    if let leftEyebrow = firstFace.landmarks?.leftEyebrow {
        let position = averagePosition(for: leftEyebrow)
        results.append( (type: .left, position: position) )
```

```
        }

        if let rightEyebrow = firstFace.landmarks?.rightEyebrow {
            let position = averagePosition(for: rightEyebrow)
            results.append( (type: .right, position: position) )
        }

        // We're done! Pass a value indicating success, with its associated
        // results.
        completion(.success(results))
    }
```

locateEyebrowsHandler will be responsible for grabbing the eyebrow positions once the request to find them has been run. This method has three parameters. The first and most important is the request that we want to handle the result of—in our case, this will be a facial landmark detection request. It is from this request that we will extract the facial landmark information. The other two parameters are the size of the image, which we will need to work out where the eyebrows map to the image itself, and a completion handler to run when the eyebrow positions have been determined.

The first thing we do in this method is attempt to get the landmarks for the first face detected in the image. Vision can identify landmarks for multiple faces in a single image; we are assuming here that as this is a selfie app there will only be a single face.

If we did want to deal with multiple faces, we would have to change our app's overlay structure or allow the user to select which face in the image he wants to have the fancy eyebrows.

We then have an internal function that will take in a VNFaceLandmarkRegion2D object (in our case an eyebrow) and, using the image size, determine the center point of that eyebrow. It does this by averaging all the points of the eyebrow landmark. The landmark itself comprises a collection of points that describe the contour of the eyebrow, and if we were doing more advanced overlaying we certainly would be keeping that information instead squishing it down to a single point.

If you want to extend Selfiegram to have better eyebrow positioning, this function would be a decent starting point.

With this all set up we then collect the left and right eyebrows out of the landmarks, determine their center positions, and bundle this information into an array of Eye browPosition tuples. We include this array of eyebrow positions inside the completion handler when we call it to run.

With that done, we can move on to the next level up, detecting facial landmarks inside the image. Create the detectFaceLandmarks method:

```
// Given an image, detect eyebrows and pass them back to a completion handler
func detectFaceLandmarks(image: UIImage,
                         completion: @escaping DetectionCompletion) {

    // Prepare a request to detect face landmarks (e.g., facial features like
    // nose, eyes, eyebrows, etc.)
    let request =
        VNDetectFaceLandmarksRequest { [unowned self] request, error in

            if let error = error {
                completion(.error(error))
                return
            }

            // The request now contains the face landmark data. Pass it off to our
            // handler function, which will extract the specific info this app
            // cares about.
            self.locateEyebrowsHandler(request,
                                       imageSize: image.size,
                                       completion: completion)
        }

    // Create a handler that uses the image we care about
    let handler = VNImageRequestHandler(cgImage: image.cgImage!,
                                        orientation: .leftMirrored,
                                        options: [:])

    // Attempt to perform the request on the handler, and catch any errors
    do {
        try handler.perform([request])
    }
    catch {
        completion(.error(error))
    }

}
```

Inside this method we first create a new facial landmark request. This is a specialized Vision request for finding facial landmarks, such as eyes, mouth, eyebrows, and so on. This takes a closure to run once the request has been performed; this is where we call our method to extract the eyebrows from the landmarks.

Next we create an image request handler. This is the class that will actually perform the facial landmark analysis request.

The specific handler we've created is designed for processing requests on a single image. If you need multiple images at once there is another class for that, VNSequenceRequestHandler.

To create this handler, we have to give it an image, orientation, and options. We don't have any necessary options so we're passing in an empty dictionary here, but we also include our image (as a CGImage) and the left mirroring set for the orientation.

Vision operates on CGImages as opposed to UIImages. CGImage is the underlying image structure of a UIImage. The UIImage class is designed for the presentation of images, not analysis. A UIImage is effectively a high-level object representing an image. CGImage is a bit closer to the metal and contains the bitmap data that makes up the image. As such, it is more appropriate than UIImage for something that needs to look at an image as a grid of pixels, such as Vision.

Finally, we attempt to have our handler perform the facial landmark request.

This method takes in an array of requests to perform—we only have a single request, but we could have bundled up lots of them. As we've seen a few times across different classes, Cocoa often takes the approach that it's better to do everything at once instead of performing multiple calls.

We are now at the last stage: writing the detectEyebrows method, which calls these methods and presents a nice interface to the results. Create the detectEyebrows method:

```
func detectEyebrows(image: UIImage,
                completion: @escaping ([EyebrowPosition])->Void) {
    detectFaceLandmarks(image: image) { (result) in
        switch result {
        case .error(let error):
            // Just pass back the original image
            NSLog("Error detecting eyebrows: \(error)")
            completion([])
        case .success(let results):
            completion(results)
        }
    }
}
```

This method takes in the image we want analyzed and the completion handler we want run once it finishes the analysis. We make our call to detectFaceLandmarks inside the method and either run the completion handler with an empty array or the array of eyebrow positions, depending on the results of that method and Vision.

With that done our code to do the image detection is complete—but we still need to call it. Add the following to the end of `viewDidLoad`:

```
self.detectEyebrows(image: image, completion: { (eyebrows) in
    self.eyebrows = eyebrows
})
```

Here, we call the eyebrow detection code and then save the positions into our property.

Connecting It into the App

Our editing view controller is now complete, but we still need to add it into our existing app layout. The first move is to make it so that the capture view controller segues into this view when a photo is taken instead of dismissing itself:

1. Open *CaptureViewController.swift*.

2. Replace the `photoOutput(didFinishProcessingPhoto: error:)` method with the following:

```
func photoOutput(_ output: AVCapturePhotoOutput,
                 didFinishProcessingPhoto photo: AVCapturePhoto,
                 error: Error?) {
    if let error = error {
        NSLog("Failed to get the photo: \(error)")
        return
    }

    guard let jpegData = photo.fileDataRepresentation(),
          let image = UIImage(data: jpegData) else {
        NSLog("Failed to get image from encoded data")
        return
    }

    self.captureSession.stopRunning()
    self.performSegue(withIdentifier: "showEditing", sender: image)
}
```

This is the same as before, except instead of running the completion handler we are telling the capture session to stop running and calling the manual segue we set up earlier. Now we need to handle this segue occurring.

3. Add the `prepare(for segue:, sender:)` method to the `CaptureViewController` class:

```
override func prepare(for segue: UIStoryboardSegue, sender: Any?) {
    guard let destination =
```

```
        segue.destination as? EditingViewController else {
        fatalError("The destination view controller"
+ "is not configured correctly.")
    }

    guard let image = sender as? UIImage else {
        fatalError("Expected to receive an image.")
    }

    // Give the view controller the image we just captured, and
    // the completion handler it should call when the user has
    // finished editing the image
    destination.image = image
    destination.completion = self.completion
}
```

In here, we ensure we have the correct view controller class and image data. Once we have both of these we can configure our editing view controller. We set the image to be the photo we just took and the completion handler to be the capture view controller's handler. This way when the user has finished editing the image he can run the same completion handler that is already set up correctly from "Handling interaction" on page 237.

4. Add the `viewWillAppear` method to the `CaptureViewController` class:

```
override func viewWillAppear(_ animated: Bool) {
    super.viewWillAppear(animated)

    if !self.captureSession.isRunning {
        DispatchQueue.global(qos: .userInitiated).async {
            self.captureSession.startRunning()
        }
    }
}
```

The `viewWillAppear` method will be called whenever this view controller's view is about to appear on the device. As we now can move away from and back to the capture view controller, we need to make sure that we are turning the capture session back on. If we didn't do this, if we took a photo, went to the edit view, and then changed our mind and went back, the camera preview wouldn't update.

As we mentioned earlier on, the call to start the session can actually take a little while to complete. For this reason we are running it on a different queue than the main queue, to prevent the call slowing down our UI. We are still running it with a high level of importance (`.userInitiated`), as we don't want a great deal of lag between going back and the session starting back up.

Our next step is to make sure that we have some overlays. While we have tested our overlay manager and are using the overlays it will provide in the editing view controller, we haven't ever told it to start downloading the overlays:

1. Open *AppDelegate.swift*.

2. Inside the `application(didFinishLaunchingWithOptions:)` method, add the following after the call to apply the theme:

   ```
   OverlayManager.shared.loadOverlayAssets(refresh: true, completion: {})
   ```

   This will start our overlay manager off on downloading the overlay assets from scratch and caching them for later use.

Now we can run the app and add snazzy eyebrows onto our selfies! Figure 15-1 shows the result.

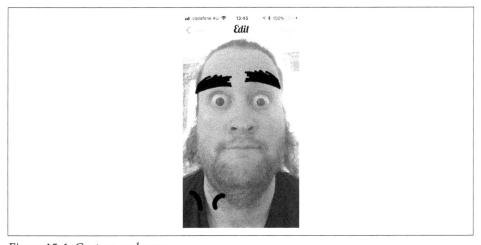

Figure 15-1. Custom eyebrows

CHAPTER 16

Localization and Internationalization

Selfiegram is shaping up into a pretty nice little app—we've got reams of features, a solid tested codebase if we want to add more, and some custom appearances set to make it stand out. What we don't have is support for anything outside of the English language.

Because all of this book's authors speak English, it made sense for our app to be developed primarily in English. What doesn't make sense is for this to be the *only* language we support. While English is one of the most popular languages out there, it isn't the only one—literally billions of people don't speak it. And even if English were spoken as a secondary language by everyone on the planet, that wouldn't mean they wouldn't prefer their apps to be in their native languages.

Apple cares a great deal about localization and internationalization and offers excellent support. *Internationalization* is the process of preparing an app for localization. You do this by separating the text used in your app from the app itself, making it load any user-facing language resources at runtime based on the user's language preferences, and adjusting your user interface to support different lengths of text. In addition, your app should take into account whether the user's language displays text in a left-to-right direction (such as English and French) or in a right-to-left direction (such as Hebrew and Arabic). Once you've internationalized your application, you can *localize* it into a specific language. The majority of this work involves providing new text for your internationalized strings.

In this chapter we are going to be fully internationalizing our app and then localizing it into French. This will involve touching almost every part of the app but the process itself is (mostly) smooth. Apple has invested a lot of time and effort into this and done a great deal of the work for us—for example, common terms provided by the operating system, such as button names, are already translated. Even though French is a left-to-right language like English, if we decided to translate the app into Arabic or Hebrew Apple would provide support for this too by automatically flipping the left and right edge constraints.

This is also the reason why the left and right constraints are technically called "leading" and "trailing."

The majority of the work we have to do is provide some text for our own strings.

While we've done our best to ensure our translations are accurate, they were still done using a variety of methods by people who don't speak the language. As such, they might seem a bit wonky at times to those of you who speak French.

We realize there may be some lines that are wrong, and we apologize for this—if you spot any errors please let us know so we can fix them! The process of localizing Selfiegram is correct, even if us language troglodytes have made a mistake with the specific translations used in this book.

Internationalization

The first step in our internationalization process is to configure Selfiegram to support multiple languages. This means we need to go through and modify any user-facing strings.

There are a lot of user-facing strings in Selfiegram, or any project really. It's for this reason that when you're building an app it's best to include internationalization support from the start, even if you don't currently have any plans for additional languages.

We make strings available for localization through the NSLocalizedString function. This function takes in a key and a comment: the key is the string we want the localized version of and the comment is a place for us, as the developers, to write any additional information that might help the translator understand the context of the text. This method will return the localized form of the string based on a lookup in a string table and the device's current locale.

As there are so many different strings to be internationalized in our app we won't list them all, but will instead show an example of how it's done. The same process should be repeated throughout the entire app:

1. Open *SelfieListViewController.swift* and go to the section where we create new selfies.

2. Find the line where we create a new `Selfie` object. It should look like:

```
let newSelfie = Selfie(title: "New Selfie")
```

3. Replace that line with the following:

```
let selfieTitle = NSLocalizedString("New Selfie",
    comment: "default name for a newly-created selfie")
let newSelfie = Selfie(title: selfieTitle)
```

Now when we get around to adding in support for French, whenever we hit this line of code iOS will dig into the strings file looking for that line of text, and return the French version of it. If we were to repeat this process across the entire app, we would get a French version of the app…with one exception.

We did go to the effort of localizing all the strings in Selfiegram. If you are curious, take a look at our example repository (*https:// github.com/thesecretlab/learning-swift-3rd-ed*) to see what this looks like.

Back in Chapter 11, when we created the settings view controller, we added in support for sending a reminder. This reminder has a user-facing string as part of it. Now, we could just use the `NSLocalizedString` function again to translate this string, but this approach has a flaw. If we did this and then changed the locale of the device, when the notification popped up it would be in the wrong language.

Instead, we'll use a different way of localizing this string:

1. Open *SettingsTableViewController.swift*.

2. Find the line where we set the notification title.

3. Replace it with the following:

```
content.title = NSString.localizedUserNotificationString(
    forKey: "Take a selfie!",
    arguments: nil
)
```

This is using a method call from the `NSString` class, which comes with Objective-C. This call works almost identically to the `NSLocalizedString` function, but it waits until the notification is being delivered before it performs the lookup in the string table.

It is these sorts of tiny details that, when overlooked, make your app seem inferior to the other ones out there. When you do things like this right, no one will ever know or even think about it, but when you do them wrong your users will notice.

In our app, we don't have to bother localizing log messages or segue identifiers. As these aren't user-facing, there is no point in going through the effort of having them translated.

Generating the String Table

We've explained that iOS will use a string table to work out what line of text to show, but we haven't actually created one yet. Let's fix that now. If we wanted to, we could manually write out a strings file as it is just text, but that is slow, clunky, and error prone. Instead what we are going to do is automatically generate one using a command-line utility Apple provides called `genstrings`, which can read our project and create a string table with all the relevant entries:

1. Open up *Terminal.app*.

2. Navigate to the Selfiegram project folder with the following command (swapping in the correct path):

   ```
   cd /path/to/selfiegram/project/folder
   ```

3. Navigate to the source code folder inside the project with the following command:

   ```
   cd Selfiegram
   ```

4. Run the `genstrings` utility over the project:

   ```
   find . -name \*.swift | xargs genstrings -o .
   ```

   We are doing a little bit of command-line magic here, but basically in the first half of that line we are searching for every *.swift* file, and in the second half we are asking `gen strings` to identify all the localized strings inside these files and generate a string table from them.

   This will create a new file called *Localizable.strings*. This is our string table.

5. Drag the strings file into the Xcode project navigator to add it to the Xcode project.

6. Click Finish in the dialog box that appears.

   We now have our strings file loaded into the project and we can see that inside it are the localized lines, including our new selfie title line:

```
/* default name for a newly-created selfie */
"New Selfie" = "New Selfie";
```

There is an issue, however—you might notice that our notification string isn't in the table. This is because `genstrings` only creates strings for calls to `NSLocalized String`, so we'll have to manually add in the extra call.

7. Open *Localizable.strings*.

8. Add the following to the end of the file:

```
/* Notification title */
"Take a selfie!" = "Take a selfie!";
```

The idea of the string table is that you can send out a copy of this table to your translators, and it has all the information and context required for them to be able to perform the translation—all without preventing you from continuing development. Now we are ready to start localizing Selfiegram into French!

Localization

With our app internationalized, it is time to add support for another language—in this case French—to our project.

 By default the only language that your app supports when you create the project is the same as the system language, which in our case is English.

We can do this in just a few steps:

1. Open the project file and select the project itself, as shown in Figure 16-1 (not the Selfiegram target).

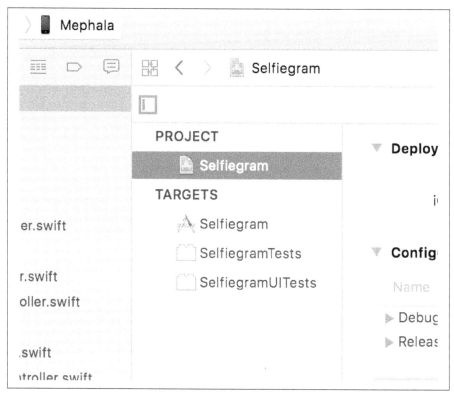

Figure 16-1. Selecting the project file

2. On the Info tab, under Localizations, click the + button to add in support for another language.

3. From the menu that pops up, select "French (fr)".

You might notice that there are multiple variants of some languages. This is because some languages that share a common root have diverged a great deal. For example, the Spanish spoken in Costa Rica is different to the Spanish spoken in Spain, and the English spoken in the United States is different to the English spoken in Australia (ours is better, though). This means you can customize not only what languages your app supports but even what variants of languages.

iOS is also clever enough to fall back to the related language if the user's dialect is not supported—so when we add in French, even if we don't add the version for a particular locale, such as Senegal, iOS will still use the French version included instead of the development language (English) for users in that locale.

4. A window will appear asking if you want to localize the two storyboard files. Ensure both are ticked and click Finish.

At first glance it might not seem like much has changed, but under the hood Xcode has made quite a few changes, especially to our storyboard files. If you look at *Main.storyboard* in the project navigator you'll see a small expansion arrow. If you click this arrow you'll see a new file underneath, called *Main.string*. If you open this file you'll find another string table like the one we made earlier, but unlike our *Localizable.strings* keys, the keys inside here look like gibberish. These are the unique identifiers for each UI element inside our storyboard. For example, the key `"lex-nC-JFD.text"` maps to the label with the text "Tap to take a selfie" in our capture view controller. Quite often, though, you won't be able to work out which labels and titles relate to what elements in your storyboard. This is where the description comes in handy—Xcode has generated a comment to give you a bit of context. Even this won't always be enough, though, and in those cases we can use the `ObjectID` shown in the comments and at the start of the key to dig in deeper. For instance, using our example of `"Iex-nC-JFD"`, if we open the storyboard and select the "Tap to take a selfie" label and then open the Identity inspector, we can see the object ID there matches our object ID.

Your object IDs are going to be different from ours, so don't worry if you can't find `"Iex-nC-JFD"` in your storyboard.

With this knowledge we can now translate all the lines in this file, and when the app loads the storyboard it will swap out the hardcoded text in the storyboard for the correct version at runtime. But before we do that, there are a few extra things to take care of. Selfiegram now supports the base development language (English) and French. However, it's good practice to localize into the development language, too, so that you have a separation between the development language and your spoken language:

1. Select the *Localizable.strings* file.

2. In the Localization section of the File inspector, tick both French and English.

3. Select the *Main.storyboard* file.

4. In the Localization section of the File inspector, tick English.

Xcode will create additional string tables automatically, and now Selfiegram is localized into English and French. It is time to start the translation.

Translating the Strings

If you want to see the completed string tables, check out our code repository (*https://github.com/thesecretlab/learning-swift-3rd-ed*). Rather than showing each and every translation, we'll just go through a few examples:

1. Open *Main.strings (french)*.

2. Replace the string "Tap to take a selfie" with "Appuyez pour prendre une photo."

   This will replace the label text for our custom camera capture view controller class.

3. Open *Localizable.strings (french)*.

4. Replace the line `"New Selfie" = "New Selfie";` with the following:

   ```
   "New Selfie" = "Nouvelle photo";
   ```

   Now whenever a new selfie is taken, the default name for it will be in French.

5. Replace the line `"Take a selfie!" = "Take a selfie!";` with the following:

   ```
   "Take a selfie!" = "Prendre un selfie!";
   ```

Now whenever a reminder notification comes in it will also be in French. Repeat this process for every user-facing string, and at the end Selfiegram will fully support the French language!

 The string tables are *not* Swift, even though they look pretty similar. Failing to include the semicolon at the end of each line will result in the file not being parsed correctly.

Testing Locales

So, Selfiegram is now in French—but how can you test this? Currently you are just trusting us when we say what we've done will result in the app being localized.

One option would be to change your system language to French. But unless you speak French, this would complicate everything else. What you can do instead is change the language you run Selfiegram in:

1. Next to the simulator selector, select the current build target and choose Edit Scheme from the drop-down menu (Figure 16-2).

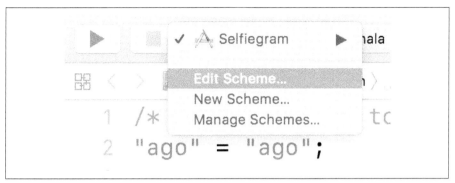

Figure 16-2. Editing the scheme

2. Select the Run section.

3. Under the Options tab, change the application language from System to French (Figure 16-3).

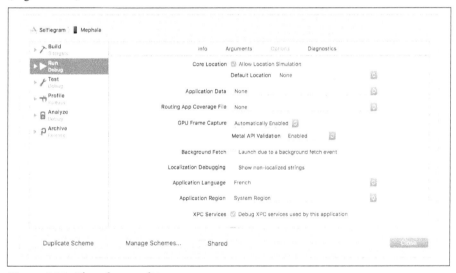

Figure 16-3. The scheme editor

Now if you run the project again, Selfiegram will be in French! Check out Figure 16-4.

Figure 16-4. French Selfiegram

 You can also create a new scheme with French set as the language only for that scheme. That way you can switch between schemes when testing different languages. Having custom schemes is a good way to set up different configurations of your apps when testing different features.

Pseudolanguages

While French and English are different languages, they share quite a few commonalities—both are left-to-right languages, and both use similar-length words. Indeed, this is part of the reason why we chose French as our localization language; we knew we didn't have to worry about sentences being too long or misaligned. But there are plenty of languages that don't share these similarities with our development language. Arabic, for example, is displayed right to left, and German sentences are often significantly longer than their English counterparts. How can we test that our app will work with these languages?

While we could create localizations for each different language and test them, this approach has a very large overhead, requiring a huge amount of translation work to be done before we can see how the results will look. There is another option: using *pseudolanguages*. A pseudolanguage is a fabricated language that has specific properties you wish to test. Apple provides two: double length and right to left (see Figure 16-5). Both of these simply modify the development language for testing purposes (so, the double length language doubles each string). You can enable the pseudolanguages in your app the same way that you changed it to French, through the scheme editor.

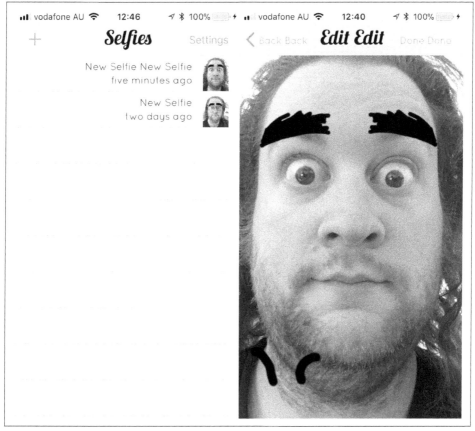

Figure 16-5. Selfiegram running in the right to left (left) and double length (right) pseudolanguages

Pseudolanguages are designed to help you test your layout, to aid in later testing when you do localize your app to other languages. You shouldn't just test your app in the double length pseudolanguage, make it look fine, and then assume German will also look fine. You still have to do your normal testing for each localization variant.

Previewing Localizations

It can be a bit of a pain to have to build and run your application every time you want to see if your constraints work correctly, especially if all you want to check is something like how the layout looks in the double length pseudolanguage. To help with this Apple has created a *preview mode* in the assistant editor. This mode allows you to see how a particular view controller inside a storyboard will look on different devices with different language settings (see Figure 16-6).

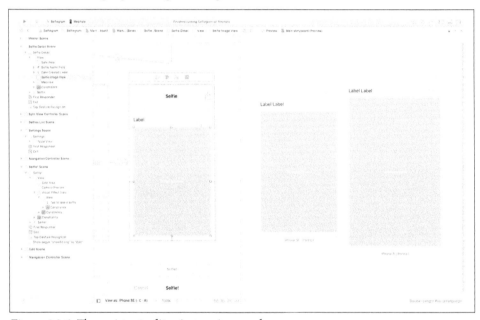

Figure 16-6. The assistant editor in preview mode

Let's take a look at how to use it now:

1. Open *Main.storyboard* and select any view controller you want to preview.

2. Open the assistant editor.

3. Using the assistant editor's jump bar, select Preview → Main.storyboard (Figure 16-7).

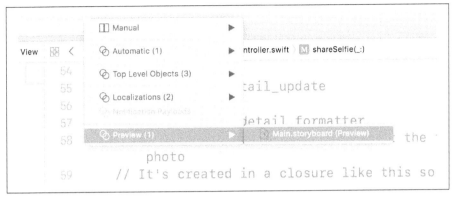

Figure 16-7. Selecting preview mode

Now the assistant editor will be showing a rendered preview of what the view controller will look like when it is run. You can configure what device you are previewing on by using the devices menu in the bottom-left corner of the assistant editor (see Figure 16-8).

iPhone 4s
iPhone SE
iPhone 8
iPhone X
iPhone 8 Plus
iPad Pro 9.7" | Full Screen
iPad Pro 9.7" | Split View 1/3
iPad Pro 9.7" | Split View 2/3
iPad Pro 10.5" | Full Screen
iPad Pro 10.5" | Split View 1/3
iPad Pro 10.5" | Split View 2/3
iPad Pro 12.9" | Full Screen
iPad Pro 12.9" | Split View 1/3
iPad Pro 12.9" | Split View 2/3

+

Figure 16-8. Configuring preview devices

You can also set what language you want to preview from the menu at the bottom right (Figure 16-9).

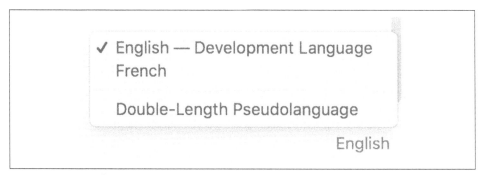

Figure 16-9. Configuring preview languages

While preview mode is a great feature, it can't replace fully testing on real devices.

Conclusion

Now that Selfiegram is internationalized and localized into French, we are finished with our development. We started with an iOS template and have gone on to make an entire app. In the next part of the book we will look at what we have to do now that we've finished working on the app and are ready to get it out into the world.

PART IV

Beyond Developing Selfiegram

CHAPTER 17

Debugging

Selfiegram is complete, and we're at the point where we want to start shipping it off for people to start testing—right? But what if there are bugs in the code? How would we go about finding and squashing them? What about the performance of Selfiegram? Is the app snappy and responsive? Are we leaking memory or taking too long to load resources? In this chapter we are going to be looking at how we can use the debugger in Xcode to find bugs, and the Instruments app to monitor and performance-test our app.

The Debugger

No one is perfect, especially not when it comes to writing code. There are so many tiny pieces all in play that small mistakes can easily get lost in the codebase. Eventually these little bugs will cause issues, and you'll have to fix them—but they can be buried many layers deep in your code, so how do you find them?

This is where the debugger comes in. The debugger lets you move through your code line by line, action by action, inspecting and querying the running program as you go.

 Depending on your previous experience with debuggers, this section might be a bit dull. The Xcode debugger (LLDB) is very similar in design and function to all other debuggers.

The basic operation of the debugger is the same regardless of what you are debugging. You run your app through the debugger, and it will run the program like normal but will halt execution at certain points to let you inspect the code and give you control over how to continue execution.

Breakpoints

The primary means of using the debugger is through *breakpoints*. A breakpoint is a mark in your code that tells the debugger to pause execution at this point and await further instructions.

To add a breakpoint, click inside the line gutter where you want to pause the execution. On the line where you clicked in the gutter Xcode will add a small blue pentagon indicating where the execution will halt (see Figure 17-1).

```
163      /// - Throws: `SelfieStoreObject` if it fails to save to disk
164      func setImage(id:String, image : UIImage?) throws
165      {
166          // Figure out where the file would end up
167          let fileName = "\(id)-image.jpg"
168          let destinationURL =
169              self.documentsFolder.appendingPathComponent(fileName)
170
171          if let image = image
172          {
```

Figure 17-1. Adding a breakpoint

 Xcode will halt the program on this line *before* it executes, not after it has run.

You can disable a breakpoint by clicking the blue pentagon in the line gutter. This will leave it in place, but Xcode will no longer halt execution upon reaching this breakpoint (see Figure 17-2). You can also disable and enable breakpoints live inside Xcode while debugging your running program.

```
163      /// - Throws: `SelfieStoreObject` if it fails to save to disk
164      func setImage(id:String, image : UIImage?) throws
165      {
166          // Figure out where the file would end up
         let fileName = "\(id)-image.jpg"
168          let destinationURL =
169              self.documentsFolder.appendingPathComponent(fileName)
170
171          if let image = image
172          {
```

Figure 17-2. A disabled breakpoint

A common reason to disable a breakpoint is when you know it will trigger, but you aren't focusing currently on that particular area of the code. So, rather than having to keep telling the debugger to continue execution when it reaches that breakpoint, you can disable it for now, and the debugger will act as if it isn't there. This lets you set up breakpoints for various issues, or potential causes for a bug, and only be affected by those that you are currently interested in.

You can see all your project's breakpoints inside the breakpoint navigator (the second icon from the right in the navigation selector bar). This displays a list of every breakpoint, showing where it is located and if it is currently enabled or disabled (see Figure 17-3).

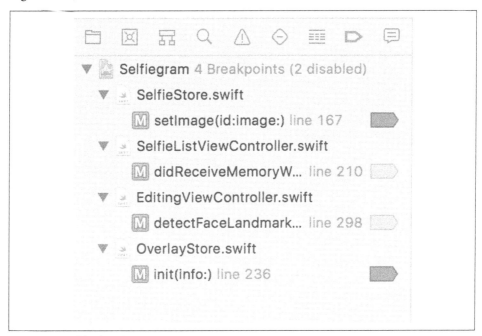

Figure 17-3. The breakpoint navigator

From the navigator you can select a breakpoint to jump directly to that line of code in the editor. You can also click the pentagon to toggle its enabled or disabled status, giving you an easy way to disable or enable breakpoints during testing.

You can edit a breakpoint from the navigator, too. If you right-click a breakpoint in either the navigator or the editor and select Edit Breakpoint, you can apply conditions to the breakpoint that restrict whether or not it will fire. The conditions can take the form of a Swift expression, which must evaluate to true or false. When the breakpoint is reached, Xcode checks the condition; if it's true, it will halt execution on that breakpoint. You can also add actions to be performed when the breakpoint is encountered, such as playing a sound, printing out a message, or running a custom command (see Figure 17-4). Finally, you can set the breakpoint to not halt execution of the program—it will still be hit by the debugger and its actions will run, but program execution will continue as if it were not there.

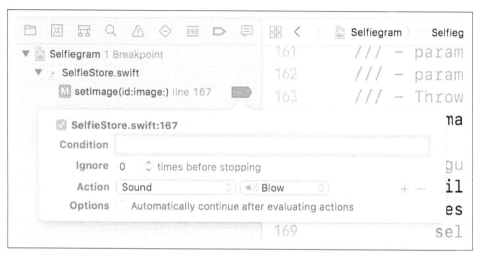

Figure 17-4. Editing a breakpoint

Breakpoint conditions can also be written in Objective-C if you like.

After you've edited a breakpoint, the blue pentagon will have a slightly altered appearance to make it clear that it has been modified and is no longer a normal breakpoint (see Figure 17-5).

```
163   /// - Throws: `SelfieStoreObject` if it fails to save to disk
164   func setImage(id:String, image : UIImage?) throws
165   {
166       // Figure out where the file would end up
167       let fileName = "\(id)-image.jpg"
168       let destinationURL =
169           self.documentsFolder.appendingPathComponent(fileName)
170
171       if let image = image
172       {
```

Figure 17-5. An edited breakpoint

Combining the play sound action with automatically continuing execution after a breakpoint is a good way to see if parts of your code are being reached. If you don't hear a sound when you expect one, something is wrong with your logic. You can use the various sounds to let you differentiate between breakpoints.

You can also create breakpoints for specific types of events occurring. At the bottom of the navigator is a + button; clicking this lets you create breakpoints that trigger when the selected type of event is reached (see Figure 17-6).

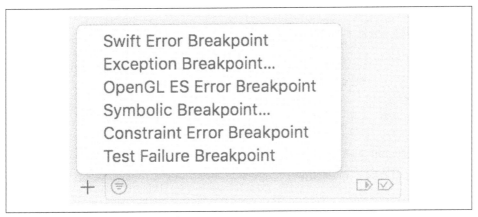

Figure 17-6. The event type breakpoint menu

These breakpoints will be triggered by any event of the correct type, even by code outside of your influence. Make sure you don't spend too much time tracking phantom breakpoint issues beyond your control.

To delete a breakpoint, you can drag it out of the line gutter into the editor; upon releasing the drag, Xcode will delete it. You can also delete a breakpoint by right-clicking it in the breakpoint navigator or the editor and selecting Delete Breakpoint.

If you have previously used the debugger in older versions of Xcode, you might remember the lovely little puff of smoke animation that played when deleting a breakpoint and be wondering where that has gone. Unfortunately in Xcode 9 Apple removed this animation; the breakpoints are still gone, even if you no longer get the feedback.

Inspecting Code

Now that we know about breakpoints, let's take a look at what we can do once a breakpoint is triggered. As the program's execution is halted by the debugger, breakpoints give us plenty of time to inspect the workings of our code without having to worry about losing our place.

To show this off we are going to be adding a breakpoint into the `SelfieStore` class, inside the `setImage(id:, image:)` method:

1. Add the breakpoint to the `if-let` line that checks that we have an image to save:

    ```
    if let image = image
    ```

    As execution halts before the line is run we won't be looking at the `if-let` clause itself, but the lines above it.

2. Run Selfiegram as normal.
3. Attempt to take a new selfie.

When the code hits the breakpoint it is triggered and the debugger halts all execution. Even tapping on buttons won't work; it will look as though the program has frozen (and it has).

Don't be too concerned about removing all the breakpoints from your code before shipping it off to the App Store. Breakpoints are only triggered when running your programs through the debugger, which only happens when you are running the project through the Debug scheme. Any program that gets shipped to App Store (or TestFlight) will be in Release mode. Release mode automatically strips out all debugging information and states like breakpoints. Your users will never run into a breakpoint-induced freeze because you left a breakpoint in the project.

Now that the execution has been halted, we can start taking a look at the program as it currently stands. The Debug area should have automatically appeared once the breakpoint was hit; if it didn't you can bring it up using the buttons at the top-right corner of the Xcode window (see Figure 17-7).

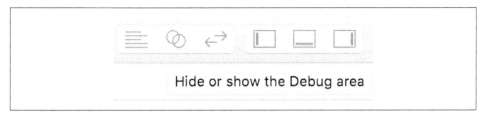

Figure 17-7. Hiding and showing the Debug area

The Debug area is split into two main parts, the Variables view and the Console view. With our program frozen we can see a breakdown of all the variables it is using at this point in the code in the Variables view (Figure 17-8).

Figure 17-8. The Variables view

These can be expanded out to see the details of everything inside a variable as well (Figure 17-9).

Figure 17-9. Expanding a variable

A nice feature of the Variables view is that we can use the macOS Quick Look feature to see a preview of the value inside a variable. This works for simple variables such as Strings (Figure 17-10), as well as more complex ones like UIImage (Figure 17-11).

Figure 17-10. Quick Look on a string

Figure 17-11. Quick Look on an image

The Console view on the other side is for inputting commands directly into the debugger and receiving the output of these commands. A great deal of the functionality of the Variables view and the way you control program flow (discussed in the next section) is performed by Xcode injecting commands into the debugger for you, but if you like you can type commands straight into this view yourself and they will be run by the debugger. For example, the po command prints the value of the object name that follows the command (see Figure 17-12), or to show the global variables of the current file you could type target variable.

```
(lldb) po fileName
"0AC619D0-7691-465E-BF20-AF7D3D66DFEF-image.jpg"

(lldb) |
```

Debugger Output ◇

Figure 17-12. Running a command in the debugger

 The LLDB debugger is a very complex piece of software—we are only scratching the surface of what it can do, and could write a whole book on it alone. For more details on its functionality and commands, check out Apple's documentation on the debugger (*https://apple.co/2HOX0BM*) or the official LLDB project site (*https://lldb.llvm.org*).

Controlling Program Flow

Finally, we have to look at controlling program flow once a breakpoint has been hit. After all, if we were stuck on a single line it would be very hard to track down certain problems.

To demonstrate controlling application flow using the debugger, let's step through the setImage(id:, image:) method from before:

1. Move the breakpoint up to the line where we declare the fileName variable:

        let fileName = "\(id.uuidString)-image.jpg"

2. Start the program as normal.

3. Attempt to take a new selfie.

    As before, the program will halt at the breakpoint, and we can look at controlling the program flow from here. Inside the debug bar there are four relevant buttons that we care about (see Figure 17-13):

    • Continue or pause program execution
    • Step over
    • Step into
    • Step out

Figure 17-13. The debug bar

Continue or pause works as its name implies: it either continues the execution or pauses it where it is. Continuing execution after a breakpoint won't prevent another breakpoint halting execution. Step over will run the current line and then continue on to the next; it's called "step over" because if that line is a function (or a line that can be jumped into) the debugger won't jump into the function. Step into runs the current line and *does* jump into the code (assuming it can do so). Step out leaves a jumped-into routine, such as a function. Through these buttons we can move about in our program line by line, function by function, querying it as we go to learn what it is doing.

> To the left of the control buttons is a global breakpoint enable/ disable toggle. This can be very handy when used in conjunction with the continue execution action.

4. Press the step over button to move on to the next line.

   The debugger has just run the line we were on and has paused execution on the next line, where we determine the URL for saving our selfie. The current line has a bit more going on in it than the earlier line, giving us a jump point.

> As we move about through the program the Variables view will be updating. For example, the fileName variable now has a value.

5. Press the step into button to move into the call in the line.

   The debugger has moved us into the first part of the line, the call to the docu mentsFolder variable, and moved Xcode to that point as well. We could jump into the FileManager class, but seeing as Apple made that we don't really want to go digging around in there.

6. Press the step out button to return to where we jumped from.

   Now we are back at the line where we jumped and can continue execution.

7. Press the step over button to continue execution.

   This takes us to the if-let statement. At this point we could continue using the debugger to move from line to line, controlling the entire program one click at a time, if we were curious.

8. Press the continue execution button to let the program run as normal.

Performance

Debugging is a great way to dive into what your program is doing, but it doesn't tell you everything. Sometimes slowdowns and crashes aren't the result of a mistake in the program or the logic but are a side effect of the performance of the code.

 There is an old line by Donald Knuth about premature optimization being the root of all evil. Humans are inherently bad about correctly guessing where and when to optimize programs. We like to solve problems and often waste time writing cleverly optimized code for problems that never actually occur.

Only optimize code that needs it, and only when it needs it. Simple code is nearly always better than clever code.

Even in an app as straightforward to explain as Selfiegram, there are numerous areas where performance can be a bottleneck. We have networking, file I/O, camera access, and the ubiquitous CPU, battery, and memory to worry about. Luckily, Xcode has a variety of tools designed to help us look at the performance of our apps.

When running an application through the debugger, the debug navigator (accessed via the third button from the right, shown in Figure 17-14) shows the various *debugger gauges* for the application.

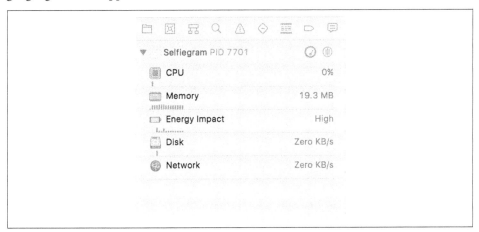

Figure 17-14. The debugger gauges

The gauges show a simple breakdown of the current resource use of the app (CPU, memory, energy, disk, and network). They also show a small timeline for each, allowing you to identify spikes in usage. Clicking any of these gauges displays a larger and more detailed version of the same resource information in the editor view (see Figure 17-15).

Figure 17-15. The memory gauge

The gauges are useful for an at-a-glance investigation into app performance, but they lack any sort of fine breakdown to precisely identify performance issues. This is where *Instruments* comes in.

Instruments

Instruments is a separate app included as part of the Xcode download and is designed for digging into precisely what is happening in your app.

The easiest way to start Instruments is to activate it through an Xcode debugger gauge. At the top-right corner of the editor view, you'll notice a small "Profile in Instruments" button. Clicking this button will launch Instruments. Let's try it out now:

1. Click the "Profile in Instruments" button.

This isn't the only way to connect Instruments into your app, but it is the simplest.

A dialog box will appear confirming you wish to transfer the session from Xcode to Instruments.

2. Click Transfer to launch *Instruments.app* and begin profiling.

Instruments works by adding *profiles* to the current session. A profile is a tool that measures certain aspects of your application, such as memory or CPU use. As we launched Instruments from the memory debugger gauge, it has the memory allocation and memory leaks profiles running (see Figure 17-16).

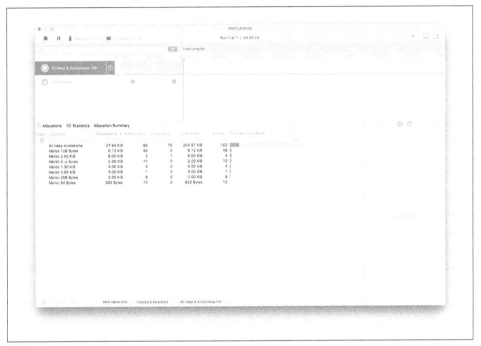

Figure 17-16. The Instruments app

Apple calls profiles "instruments," but we thought talking about instruments while discussing the app called Instruments would get a bit confusing. For this reason, we are going to be calling them profiles.

As we use the app as normal, we can see more detailed information from the selected profile. The top half of the Instruments window is a timeline; we can click anywhere inside the timeline and Instruments will show the information about that moment in the bottom half of the window. This gives a precise breakdown of what is happening, so in the case of the memory allocation profile it is showing the exact calls that are allocating memory in the program, as opposed to the aggregate we were given in Xcode.

To add a new profile into Instruments, we have to first stop the current session:

1. Press the Stop button in Instruments (the square at the top left).

This stops the current profiling session, not the app itself.

2. Press the Library button (the + at the top right of the Instruments window).

   This brings up the list of profiles Instruments supports. While the Xcode debugger gauges support only a few types (albeit the most common ones), Instruments has profiles for almost everything you could ever want to look at.

3. Select the Activity Monitor profile.

   This profile tracks CPU use, and it will be placed after the leaks test.

 You can drag the profiles around to change their order. This doesn't affect their functionality, just how they are shown.

4. Press the Record button (the red circle) to begin the profiling session.

   Instruments will start a new session, and as you use the app as normal now both the memory and CPU use will be profiled and stored. Once you've finished with Instruments you can save the sessions; these saved sessions can later be analyzed or shared.

Instruments and the debugger are powerful tools and can be used in a variety of ways far more complex and different than what we have done here. In the next chapter, we will take a look at a different tool available inside Xcode to help us with our testing: UI tests.

CHAPTER 18

UI Tests

We spoke about unit tests back in "Testing the SelfieStore" on page 130, but there is another type of testing Xcode can perform. *UI tests* are a way to run tests on the UI itself. Up to this point, any time we've wanted to test something in our UI, such as toggling the states of the settings switches or testing the UI flow for our custom capture view controller, we have had to do so manually. The problem with this is that it obviously doesn't scale very effectively and can get very boring very quickly for the developer. UI tests are an answer to this: essentially, they give you access to a virtual hand you can script, giving it orders and expectations for it to fulfill. It's like having your own army of testers you can make do all the tapping and swiping about for you.

 Throughout this chapter we will be making some assumptions about the permissions and setup of Selfiegram. Normally you would not do this and instead would provide setup code to ensure everything is ready for the tests, but as we are interested in showing off how to write UI tests and not general testing methodology we are skipping some of this. In your own apps, make sure you do perform your test setup correctly!

UI Testing Classes

There are three main types we interact with when doing UI testing:

XCUIApplication
A proxy object for the app being tested (in our case, Selfiegram).

XCUIElement
A single UI element we can interact with and query. This can be almost any type, including buttons.

```
XCUIElementQuery
```
A class for locating and identifying specific elements so we can interact with them.

Because of how UI testing works, we won't be testing Selfiegram directly. Everything goes through the application proxy. This means we won't be able to tell the UI test system to perform actions like "tap on the button that will cause the settings view to appear"; instead, we will be saying something like "tap the button with the label *Settings* that exists inside the navigation bar."

This may seem a bit odd at first glance, but you can't assume that your users will be able to dive into the guts of the app to use it, so neither should your testing. Additionally, this approach works well with one of the main uses of UI tests, *functional testing*. Whereas unit tests can check the correctness of a single piece of the code, functional testing ensures that the code and all the bits hooked together perform as the design says they will. This all boils down to a design philosophy based around writing queries to identify specific elements inside the app, and then interacting with them, or asking for information about them.

Writing UI Tests

Way back in "Creating the Project" on page 115, when we created our Selfiegram project, we told Xcode to include UI tests. Xcode dutifully generated a *SelfiegramUITests.swift* file for our UI tests. This is where we will put our test code. The UI tests work in a similar manner to the unit tests: there is some setup, followed by the test and then the tear down.

A Basic Test

To show off how UI tests work, let's make a basic test. Let's say, for example, we wanted to make sure the persistence of the app is working correctly, so we expect that the number of selfies in the selfie list stays the same between launches of the app:

1. Open the *SelfiegramUITests.swift* file.

2. Replace the testExample test with the following:

   ```
   func testExample() {
       let app = XCUIApplication()
       let currentSelfieCount = app.tables.element(boundBy: 0).cells.count

       app.terminate()
       app.launch()

       let tables = app.tables.element(boundBy: 0)
       XCTAssertEqual(currentSelfieCount, tables.cells.count)
   }
   ```

First our test gets a hold of the application proxy for the app we are testing. We then work out how many cells are in the table view. We do this in several parts. First we query for table views in the app (`app.tables`), and then we get an element from that query by asking for the first one (`element(boundBy: 0)`). Once we have our table view, we make another query for its cells and then get their count.

3. Then we terminate and relaunch the app.

 Using the application proxy gives you huge amounts of power you normally wouldn't have for your testing. Being able to invoke apps to launch and close them at will is not something iOS generally lets you do.

4. Once that is done, we get a reference to the table view and check the number of cells hasn't changed.

If we run this test, Selfiegram will launch, then terminate, then launch again, and then the test will pass.

Recording UI Actions

Now that we understand the basics of using queries to access elements, let's take a look at taking a photo using the UI tests. This requires some interaction with various elements, and while we could do this by making queries ourselves, this is a bit of a clunky action to write out. Instead, we will record our UI actions and save them. Recording our actions lets us directly inject what we do into a test as the appropriate queries and interactions, and then we can edit or play them back as needed.

For this test we are making an assumption about the setup of Selfiegram. On first launch we will need camera permission—we could handle that the same way, using UI recording, but after the first launch this would no longer work and would cause all sorts of headaches. So for now, make sure whatever device you are testing on has previously granted camera access.

 In "Handling UI Interruptions" on page 319 we will talk about how you can handle getting permission.

Then follow these steps to test taking a photo:

1. Create a new test, and call it `testPhotos`:

```
func testPhotos () {

}
```

2. Click inside the test function.

   At the bottom of the Xcode window you'll see a red circle. This is the Record button (see Figure 18-1).

Figure 18-1. The Record button

Xcode knows when you are inside a test function and makes the recording functionality available. When you're outside of a test, the button will be greyed out (see Figure 18-2).

Figure 18-2. The disabled Record button

3. Click the Record button to begin recording.

 Xcode can sometimes take a little while to notice that a test function has been written, and until it does it won't allow recording. Clicking outside of the test function and then back inside it generally fixes this.

Xcode will launch the app and start recording everything you are doing. As you interact with the app your actions will be recorded and appear as code inside the test function. We'll now perform the steps necessary to take a selfie.

4. Tap the + button.

5. Tap the photo preview.

6. Tap the done button.

7. Back in Xcode, click the active recording button (Figure 18-3) to stop it recording your actions.

Figure 18-3. The active recording button

 The recording system is a nifty little feature, but it can be a bit buggy. Occasionally it will fail to record any interaction—in these cases, the easiest thing to do is stop the app and the recording, and start recording again.

Xcode will have generated the following code:

```
let app = XCUIApplication()

let currentSelfieCount = app.tables.element(boundBy: 0).cells.count

app.navigationBars["Selfies"].buttons["Add"].tap()

app.children(matching: .window).element(boundBy: 0)
    .children(matching: .other).element.tap()

app.navigationBars["Edit"].buttons["Done"].tap()
```

In here, first we get access to the app. Then we tap the plus button inside of the navigation bar. The next big blob of code is what we need to say we are tapping on the camera preview. Unlike table views, buttons, or navigation bars, there is no nice, neat interface into normal views. As such, Xcode has to dive into the nesting of views to tap on the camera preview. Finally, we press the done button inside of the navigation bar.

This code does exactly what we just described we were doing, only now it is in a form that Xcode can perform over and over without us needing to do it manually.

 There are often multiple ways to perform a single action; as such, Xcode in your case may have generated slightly different code. If yours works functionally the same, feel free to use it. Otherwise, you might want to copy ours in its place.

With our actions ready, we can now write the test. In this case we are making sure that after performing the actions to take a selfie, a new selfie appears in the list.

8. Below the line where we get a reference to the application proxy, add the following:

```
let currentSelfieCount = app.tables.element(boundBy: 0).cells.count
```

This is collecting the current number of selfies inside the selfie list.

9. At the bottom of the test, add the following:

```
let tables = app.tables.element(boundBy: 0)
XCTAssertEqual(currentSelfieCount + 1, tables.cells.count)
```

Here we are getting a reference to the table view, and testing to see that it now has one more cell than before.

Checking if Elements Exist

Our next test will be to see if UI elements that we expect to exist do exist. In our case we expect that a selfie taken with location information should show a map preview when we look in the detail view. For this test to work we are making two assumptions:

- Location permission has previously been granted.
- The first selfie in the list has location information stored with it.

We could write code to ensure all of this, but that doesn't really show off how to check for the existence of UI elements, which is the point here:

1. Add a new test called `testExistence`:

```
func testExistence() {

}
```

2. Add the following to the test:

```
let app = XCUIApplication()
app.tables.element(boundBy: 0).cells.element(boundBy: 0).tap()

let mapView = app.maps.firstMatch
```

This will select the first element in the list of selfies, and grab a reference to the map view inside the selfie detail view controller. We are using the `firstMatch` variable in our maps query, which will return the first element that is a map to us. In our case this is fine as we know there is only one, but depending on your situation you may need to do more querying to ensure you've got the right one.

3. Now we need to write our assertions. Add the following to the end of the test:

```
XCTAssert(mapView.exists)
XCTAssert(mapView.isHittable)
```

In here we are asserting two things. The first is that the element exists. This is important as we may not have set up our code correctly and the map view may not be loaded, or we could be in the wrong view entirely, where there is no map view. Next we are checking that the map view is in a place where the user can interact with it. With these two things done, we can run the test.

Assuming the first element in the table view is a selfie with a location, the test will pass.

Handling UI Interruptions

Earlier on we glossed over dealing with getting camera and location permission, or for that matter dealing with pop-ups at all. There is a general rule of thumb that says alerts should be used sparingly, and the fact that they are hard to handle in UI tests contributes to this. We could write code to tap on the alert buttons when we expect them to appear, but this is clunky. After the first run of Selfiegram the camera permission dialog will never appear again. This means we'll have code in our test that we'll have to wrap in logic to make sure that we aren't running outside of the first time. Suddenly, instead of testing the functionality of the app we are testing the functionality of our test code. There is a better way, however: using *interruption handlers*. An interruption handler is a piece of code that gets run when Xcode detects that the UI has been interrupted, such as the camera permission dialog box appearing. By using an interruption handler we ensure that the interruption will only be handled should it occur. In our case this means that on first launch it will deal with the permission dialog, but it won't interfere otherwise:

1. Add the following to the start of the `testPhotos` test function:

   ```
   addUIInterruptionMonitor(withDescription: "Camera Permission Dialog")
   { (alert) -> Bool in
       alert.buttons["OK"].tap()
       return true
   }
   ```

2. Delete Selefiegram from your test device.

3. Run the test.

   You'll notice that the permission dialog appears and is handled automatically. If you run the test again, the dialog won't appear, the handler won't run, and the test is otherwise the same as before.

With that done, we are finished with our UI testing. We could write more tests to properly evaluate the entirety of the app's functionality, but it wouldn't show off any new functionality of the testing framework. In the next chapter, we are going to look at getting the app out of Xcode and into our users' hands for some testing, as well as automating a lot of the tricky parts of doing this.

CHAPTER 19

Automating Chores with Fastlane

A large number of the things we do during development aren't directly tied to creating the software. It's fun to build new features, and (slightly less) fun to squash bugs, but on top of that constructive work are all of the chores that surround it: managing the app's presence on the App Store, generating and code signing the builds, and deploying the builds to distribution channels. If you're doing active development, a significant fraction of your time might be taken up with this work.

Fastlane is a collection of tools that automate many of these tasks. Starting life as a set of helper scripts to speed up small tasks, it's grown into a huge project that can perform extremely sophisticated work in a single step.

 Fastlane is not made by Apple. Instead, it's an open source project that's currently owned by Google. The Fastlane developers do a great job of keeping the tools up to date with the latest releases, but if you're using a prerelease version of Xcode, Fastlane might not support your environment. Fastlane isn't the only way to do the sorts of tasks we'll talk about, but it is in our opinion the best way. Apple's Xcode Server, which has a large amount of feature overlap with Fastlane, is worth checking out if Fastlane isn't what you are after.

In this chapter, we'll introduce the Fastlane tools and walk through the process of installing and using them. Along the way, we'll talk about what they're useful for, and where you might want to use them.

The Fastlane Tools

A relatively little-known fact about Xcode is that, in addition to its regular macOS UI, it can be controlled via the command line. That is to say, you can invoke the `xcode build` command and pass in the path to a project's *.xcodeproj* file, and it will build the project just as if you'd opened it in Xcode and pressed Command-B.

The problem with Xcode's command-line interface is that it comes with a very large number of options and parameters, and it can be challenging to remember them all when you want to perform a build multiple times a day during a project's development. Frequently, what people do is write a small script that automates the invocation of Xcode's command-line tools. But eventually, a developer might notice that their automation needs to grow in complexity. If you were to spend lots of time on improving your automation tools, you'd probably end up with something like Fastlane.

Fastlane is a collection of Ruby scripts that interact with Xcode and the App Store. It includes tools for, among many other tasks:

- Building your app
- Managing your code signing signatures
- Taking screenshots of your app
- Delivering signed builds to the App Store
- Submitting metadata to the App Store
- Submitting builds for review
- Managing your beta testers

Fastlane is a collection of separate programs, called *actions*, that are all managed through a single central script. Each of the subprograms is its own project, but they're all designed to work together.

Importantly, Fastlane allows you to chain multiple actions together into a *lane*. You can have multiple lanes in your project: one for submitting a beta copy for testing, another for submitting a build for release to the App Store, and so on. Fastlane doesn't make many assumptions about how you want to use it, but it does provide you with building blocks that you can use in whatever way you want.

To speed things up, Fastlane stores information about the things you'd like to automate (and how to do it) in a file called *Fastfile*, which is stored within your project's file structure. This file can be stored in your version control repository, which means that if you're working on a project with others, they'll be able to use your automation setup as well.

Fastlane works through the command line. It helps if you're comfortable using command-line tools; if you aren't, Tania Rascia has written a very good tutorial (*http://bit.ly/2HPTIOq*).

Installing Fastlane

To get started with Fastlane, you need to install it on your computer.

There are three ways you can do this: via the Homebrew package manager, through RubyGems, or through direct download.

Of these three, the one that we recommend is Homebrew. Homebrew is a third-party project, unrelated to Fastlane, that acts as a package manager for macOS. It's extremely good, and is an awesome way to install command-line utilities and development libraries while still being able to keep them up to date. It's so good, in fact, that Homebrew's original author, Max Howell, was hired by Apple to work on the Swift Package Manager.

You can get Homebrew by following the instructions on the Homebrew website (*https://brew.sh*).

Before you install Fastlane, you should double-check to see if the Xcode command-line tools are ready to use. To do this, follow these steps:

1. Open the Terminal app, and type the following command: **xcode-select --install**.

2. One of two things will happen. If you've already installed the software, you'll be told that this is the case, and you can skip the rest of this list. If not, read on.

3. An alert will appear, asking you to confirm that you'd like to download and install the Xcode command-line tools. Click the Install button.

4. Next, you'll be asked to read and agree to the license for these tools. Read the terms thoroughly, and then click Accept if you do. (Accepting the terms or not is up to you; if you don't accept the terms, you won't be able to use the Xcode command-line tools or, as a consequence, Fastlane.)

5. macOS will download and install the tools.

Installing via Homebrew

To install Fastlane via Homebrew, follow these steps:

1. Open the Terminal app, and type the following command: `brew cask install fastlane`.
2. There's no step 2.

Installing via RubyGems

To install Fastlane via RubyGems, follow these steps:

1. Open the Terminal app, and type the following command: `sudo gem install fastlane -NV`.
2. If prompted, enter your password. Fastlane will then download and install itself.

Installing via Direct Download

If you prefer to install Fastlane manually, you can do so by following these steps:

1. Download the installer (*https://download.fastlane.tools*). This is a ZIP file that contains Fastlane, as well as scripts that install the project.
2. Unzip the file, and open the resulting folder.
3. Double-click on the *install* file. A terminal window will appear, and Fastlane will install itself.

 If you install manually like this, Fastlane will install itself into your home directory, rather than into a system-wide directory like */usr/ local*. If you share your computer with other users, they'll need to install it themselves if they want to use it.

Once Fastlane is installed, you're ready to start using it in your projects.

Setting Up a Project

Fastlane needs to be set up for each project that you're using, because each project usually has its own slightly unique requirements.

When you set up Fastlane for your project, it will detect the location of its *.xcodeproj* file and create a new directory called *fastlane* next to it. Inside this folder, Fastlane will store all related files.

 If you're using version control, the *fastlane* directory should be added to it so that other people working on your project can use Fastlane in the same way as you.

To set up Fastlane for your project, follow these steps:

1. Open a Terminal window, and `cd` to the folder containing your project's *.xcodeproj* file.

2. Run the following command: `fastlane init`.

3. Follow the prompts for information when they appear.

   As part of the setup process, Fastlane will ask you for the credentials for the Apple ID you'd like to use for development. It will then use those to sign in to the Apple Developer Portal and to iTunes Connect, and set up the entries for the app on both.

    Fastlane will also save the password in your Mac's keychain, which means that you won't have to provide the password for your Apple ID when you next use it.

4. Once this is all done, a directory will appear in your project's main directory. It'll contain a few files, all of which will be plain text and editable in any editor, including Xcode. Notably, it will contain an *Appfile*, which contains information about your app's details on the App Store, the Apple ID used to access Apple's developer services, and so on.

Doing a Build

As mentioned earlier, Fastlane is comprised of multiple separate tools called actions. Fastlane's actions are designed to be chained together, but they can also be invoked separately. This means that you can explore the various parts of Fastlane one at a time, without having to have a perfect setup in place before you can start getting stuff done.

The first tool we'll look at is gym, which automates the build process of your app. Specifically, it kicks off a build of your app, using the build settings contained inside your Xcode project. Using gym, you can also produce the signed *.ipa* file, which is the final built product that's delivered to a device and sent to the App Store for distribution.

gym is designed to be reusable across multiple people in a development team. To that end, it'll only work with build schemes that are marked as shared. By default, the build scheme that's used by Xcode when you create a new project isn't marked as shared, which means that gym won't see it.

To solve this, follow these steps:

1. Open your project, and open the scheme selector at the top left of the window.
2. Choose Manage Schemes. The scheme management sheet will appear.
3. By default, your app will have a single scheme. At the far right of the window, you'll see the Shared checkbox. Select it, and close the sheet.

When you've followed these steps, gym will be ready to build your app. To test it out, follow these steps:

1. In the Terminal, enter the directory that contains your *.xcodeproj* file.
2. Run the command `fastlane gym --skip_package_ipa`.
3. Your app will build. Assuming there aren't any errors in your code, the action will complete successfully.

The `--skip_package_ipa` argument tells gym to just do a build, and not export the built app for distribution. We're doing that here because exporting builds from gym doesn't work with automatic code signing, which is the default. In Chapter 20, we'll be setting up more advanced code signing with `match`.

Congratulations! You've just run your first command-line build. When you run gym without any other details, it'll try to pick sensible defaults for building. However, you can be more specific when invoking it. Some common options include:

Selecting a scheme
    If your project contains multiple schemes, you can specify which one to use with the `--scheme` option.

Performing a clean

You can instruct `gym` to perform a clean, which removes the temporary build files from the last build, by passing the -c option.

Specifying the output

You can specify the folder in which to store the built file that `gym` generates with the -o option.

Configuring a Fastfile

On its own, `gym` doesn't do much that you can't do just as easily by hitting the Build button in Xcode. Fastlane's real power is the fact that `gym` can be chained together with other actions in a lane.

Lanes are sequences of actions that are defined in your project's *Fastfile*, a file that's created in your project's *fastlane* directory when you first set up Fastlane. The *Fastfile* is a Ruby script that defines the lanes available for your project; by default, it contains examples of the kinds of lanes that Fastlane was designed for.

The contents of the *Fastfile* look something like this:

```
platform :ios do
  before_all do
    # Any actions you want to run before all lanes are put here
  end

  desc "Runs all the tests"
  lane :test do
    # Perform all of the tests in the project
    scan
  end

  desc "Submit a new Beta Build to Apple TestFlight"
  desc "This will also make sure the profile is up to date"
  lane :beta do
    # Build the app
    gym

    # Submit the app to TestFlight
    pilot
  end

  desc "Deploy a new version to the App Store"
  lane :release do
    # Build the app
    gym

    # Submit the app to the App Store
    deliver(force: true)
  end
```

```
end
```

To run a lane, you run the command `fastlane [name of lane]`. For example, the `beta` lane is run via the command `fastlane beta`. When you do this, each of the actions defined in the lane are run. If any action fails, the whole lane stops.

 You can define your own lanes, or rename the existing ones. You can also run the actions on their own; while important actions like `gym` can be run just by giving their name, you can also get a list of the dozens of extra actions available by running `fastlane actions`. To run any of these actions, you use the command `fastlane action [name of action]`.

With all of this in mind, you're now ready to start exploring the real power of Fastlane. In the next chapter, we'll look at some of the other tools included in the Fastlane suite, and explore how they can be used in real-world development and deployment.

Using Fastlane's Tools

Fastlane contains a number of useful tools for automating development. In this chapter, we'll be taking a close look at the most important components in the Fastlane collection, and how you can use them.

In particular, we'll be looking at the following tools:

- `match`, which manages your code signing setup, making it easier to deal with code signing across multiple computers and multiple team members
- `snapshot`, which automates the creation of preview screenshots for the App Store
- `deliver`, which submits your application to the App Store, as well as managing the contents of your app's page

In the examples in this chapter, we'll be looking at these tools in action using the Selfiegram app that we built in Part II and Part III; however, if you have your own project to use, the examples will work just as well with that. In all cases, we'll assume that you've already set up your project for use with Fastlane, by following the steps in "Setting Up a Project" on page 324.

Code Signing with match

`match` is a tool that manages the code signing setup for your application. In order to discuss what `match` does, we have to first briefly chat about what code signing is, and how you'd go about doing it without `match`.

The Problem That Match Solves

In order to run on a device, your code must be signed with a certificate endorsed by Apple. If the code's not signed, Xcode will refuse to install it—and even if it did manage to get installed on the device through some other means, the iOS kernel would refuse to execute it.

Code signing is done automatically by Xcode at build time, as long as your project is configured for it correctly.

Using Xcode alone, there are two ways you can set up code signing. The first way is to tell Xcode to do it for you, by turning on the "Automatically manage signing" setting in your project's settings (Figure 20-1). When this is enabled, Xcode will automatically set up the application on the Developer Portal, generate a certificate for you (if you don't already have one), and generate a provisioning profile for you that tells the code signing system to use your certificate to sign your code for running on your devices.

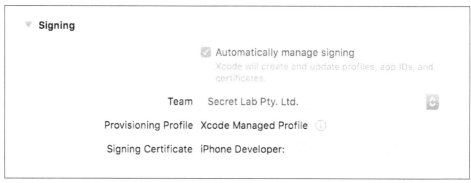

Figure 20-1. The Project page in Xcode with automatic code signing enabled

This is extremely convenient, and works most of the time. However, it takes control away from you, and doesn't give you the ability to choose the finer details of your provisioning profile—something that matters when your app needs access to certain Apple-provided features, which are configured in that profile.

In these cases, you could do the code signing setup manually. This is not a hugely onerous task; it basically involves manually generating a Certificate Signing Request file, uploading it to Apple, downloading the produced certificate, creating a provisioning profile, downloading it, and finally configuring the project in Xcode to use the profile (Figure 20-2).

Figure 20-2. The Project page in Xcode with automatic code signing disabled and a provisioning profile manually selected

In the cases of both automatic and manual code signing, the certificate and private key used to sign the application are kept in your machine's keychain, where they're secure. This is necessary because anyone with the certificate and the private key is able to generate code that has your name attached to it. If someone breached your computer and got a copy of the certificate and key, they could conceivably create malicious software and pin the blame on you.

However, it does mean that if you need to perform the code signing on another machine that you own, you need to transfer the certificate and key into the recipient's keychain, which is a slightly fiddly process involving exporting the certificate and key into an encrypted container file and importing it on the destination.

It gets more complex when you have more than one person working on your app. Each person on your team ends up needing to create their own signing certificate; additionally, you end up needing to ensure that the provisioning profiles used by your code signing setup are configured to be aware of all of the certificates in use by your team. On top of this, each person can end up needing more than one certificate —one for development and one for distribution—which further adds to the burden of management.

Additionally, the reference to the specific provisioning profile that's being used will change from person to person, and you can end up with code signing errors if the project is configured to use a provisioning profile that you don't have. Eventually, the process can become quite messy.

match's Solution

The match tool takes a different approach. Rather than having each team member work with their own individual certificate, match creates a *shared* certificate, which is encrypted and stored in a private Git repository. All team members have access to this certificate and the password with which it's encrypted. When match is invoked, it downloads the certificate from the repository, decrypts it, and installs it into the keychain. Additionally, match will create the necessary certificates and provisioning profiles for you, and ensure that Xcode uses them in your project.

To begin using match, you first need to have a Git repository. This repository should be one that's private to your team; while the certificates and keys are encrypted, there's no sense in inviting trouble by making the repository accessible to the world.

You can use the same repository across multiple projects. Importantly, this repository should *not* be the same one that you keep any source code in. It should be a separate repository.

There are a variety of third-party providers that you can use to host a private Git repository. Recently we've been using BitBucket (*https://bitbucket.org*), which provides free private Git repositories for up to five users.

Instructions on setting up a Git repo are beyond the scope of this book, but a great introduction to this is in *Pro Git* by Scott Chacon and Ben Straub (Apress). It's available to read for free on the official Git site (*https://git-scm.com/book*).

Using match doesn't involve very many steps. All you need to do is run the fastlane match command:

- If you want to set up code signing for submission to the App Store, run the command `fastlane match appstore`.

- If you want to set up code signing for distribution (ad hoc or submitting to the App Store), run the command `fastlane match distribution`.

Each time you run the command, match will check out a copy of the private Git repository and see if a certificate and provisioning profile are available for your app in it. If so, it will check with the Developer Portal to see if they're still valid, and if they are, the certificate and profile will be installed into your keychain. If either of those components doesn't exist, match will create it for you and add it to the Git repo.

You usually won't have to manually deal with the private Git repo yourself. match manages its contents for you.

Once match has done its work, you need to set up your project to use the provisioning profile that match has created. To do this, you open the Project page, turn off the "Automatically manage signing" option, and then select the provisioning profile that match created. The profile name will always begin with the word "match," to make it easier to spot; it will also contain the type of the profile (such as "Development" or "AppStore"), as well as the bundle identifier of the app.

With this done, your code signing setup is ready for use. From now on, you (and anyone else you work with) will use the same certificate; if it breaks, you can run fastlane match again to ensure that your local copy of the certificate and profile are correct.

Generating Screenshots Using snapshot

Screenshots are an important part of your app's presence on the App Store. They're you're primary way of telling your users what your app's all about, any many users make decisions about whether to buy or download apps based largely on what they see in the screenshots.

However, app screenshots need to be taken at multiple sizes (once for each iOS screen size), and, if your app has been localized into other languages, for each language you support. This means that you often need to repeat the same actions multiple times in order to get the app into the right state for the screenshots. As you might imagine, this can get tedious.

snapshot allows you to automate the creation of these screenshots, by using UI tests (which we discussed earlier, in Chapter 18) to perform the same actions over and over again to get your app into the right state. snapshot reruns these for every combination of your desired app sizes and supported languages.

To begin using snapshot, you first need to ensure that your project includes a UI test target. This is included in new applications by default, but if your app doesn't include it, you can add one. To do so, follow these steps:

1. Open the File menu, and select New → Target.
2. Scroll down to Test, and select the iOS UI Testing Bundle. Click Next.
3. Give the new target a name, and make sure that its "Target to be Tested" is your application (see Figure 20-3 for an example).

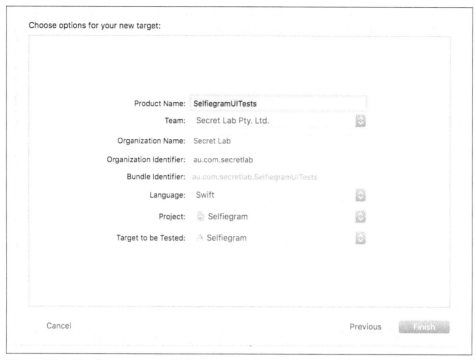

Choose options for your new target:

Product Name:	SelfiegramUITests
Team:	Secret Lab Pty. Ltd.
Organization Name:	Secret Lab
Organization Identifier:	au.com.secretlab
Bundle Identifier:	au.com.secretlab.SelfiegramUITests
Language:	Swift
Project:	Selfiegram
Target to be Tested:	Selfiegram

Cancel   Previous   Finish

Figure 20-3. Configuring a new UI test target

Once that's ready, you're all set to start setting up snapshot. To do so, follow these steps:

1. Run the fastlane snapshot init command.

   This will create a new file called *Snapfile*, which snapshot uses to control which screenshots it creates, as well as a Swift file called *SnapshotHelper.swift*, which contains the code that actually triggers the taking of screenshots. Both of these files will be stored inside the *fastlane* folder, along with Fastlane's other configuration.

2. Next, you'll need to add this Swift file to your UI test target. Reveal the file in the Finder by running the following command:

   ```
   open -R fastlane/SnapshotHelper.swift
   ```

3. Drag and drop the *SnapshotHelper.swift* file into the UI Tests group in Xcode.

4. In the sheet that appears, select the UI Tests target in the list of targets, and ensure that the other targets are deselected. Turn off "Copy items if needed" (Figure 20-4).

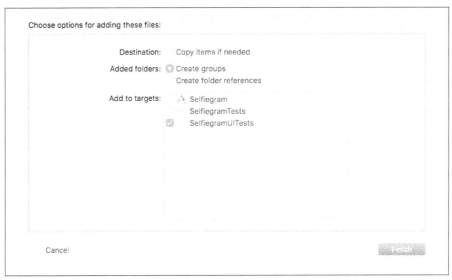

Choose options for adding these files:

Destination: Copy items if needed

Added folders: ○ Create groups
                 Create folder references

Add to targets: Selfiegram
                   SelfiegramTests
                 ☑ SelfiegramUITests

Cancel   Finish

Figure 20-4. Adding the SnapshotHelper file to the UI Tests target

5. Open your UI test Swift file, and replace the contents of the setUp method with the following code:

```
let app = XCUIApplication()
setupSnapshot(app)
app.launch()
```

6. You're finally ready to start recording the actions that you want to take screenshots of. Create a new method in your Swift file called testScreenshots:

```
func testScreenshots() {

}
```

7. Place the cursor inside this method, and click the Record button at the bottom-left corner of the editing window. Your app will launch; as you interact with the app, code will start to appear.

8. When you're done, click the Record button again to stop recording.

Depending on what you did in the app, the code inside your testScreenshots method will vary. However, you should be able to read the code and figure out what it does. Here's an example of some code that taps a button in the navigation bar, and then taps the back button (which is labeled "Photos"):

```
func testScreenshots() {

    let app = XCUIApplication()

    app.navigationBars["Photos"].buttons["Settings"].tap()
```

```
        app.navigationBars.buttons["Photos"].tap()
    }
```

9. Run the UI test, and verify that it repeats the steps you just took.

10. Add a call to the `snapshot` function at the points in the interaction where you'd like to take a screenshot. This function takes a single parameter, the name of the screenshot:

```
func testScreenshots() {

    let app = XCUIApplication()
    snapshot("MainApp")

    app.navigationBars["Photos"].buttons["Settings"].tap()
    snapshot("Settings")

    app.navigationBars.buttons["Photos"].tap()
}
```

The `snapshot` method signals the `snapshot` tool to take a screenshot of the app in its current state, and give it a name.

11. The last bit of configuration you need to do is to set up your *Snapfile* so that the devices and languages you want screenshots for are listed. Here's an example *Snapfile*:

```
# Put the list of devices you want screenshots for here.
# The names should be the same as they appear in the
# list of simulators in Xcode.
devices([
    "iPhone 7",
    "iPhone 7 Plus",
    "iPhone 8",
    "iPhone 8 Plus",
    "iPhone X",
    "iPad (5th generation)",
    "iPad Pro (9.7-inch)",
    "iPad Pro (12.9-inch)",
    "iPad Pro (10.5-inch)"
])

# Put the list of languages you want screenshots for here.
languages([
    "en-US",
    "fr-FR",
])
```

12. Finally, you're ready to fire off `snapshot`. Run the command `fastlane snapshot`. `snapshot` will compile your UI tests and run them on the simulators. The resulting screenshots will be saved to the *fastlane/screenshots* folder.

If you remove everything from the *Snapfile*, `snapshot` will take screenshots using all available simulators, and using the current locale.

Using Boarding to Add Testers to TestFlight

Apple's TestFlight service allows you to distribute beta copies of your app to testers. At the time of writing, you can add up to 1,000 testers; however, each tester must be manually invited, through iTunes Connect.

`boarding` is a web service that speeds up this process by allowing people to sign up as testers.

Because `boarding` needs access to your iTunes Connect account, it's not a shared web service. Instead, you host your own copy of the system. The easiest way to do this is by using a platform like Heroku.

Heroku is free if you don't expect a heavy amount of load on the service (which is probably true for this use case).

Follow these steps:

1. Ensure that your app has an entry in iTunes Connect. To do this, you can go to the iTunes Connect web app, navigate to My Apps, and click the + button at the top left.

Alternatively, you can use `fastlane produce`, which will set up the app for you via the command line.

2. Go to this Heroku page (*http://bit.ly/2p4XzzL*). This will start the process of deploying a copy of the `boarding` software to Heroku that's under your control.

3. Either sign up for a Heroku account or, if you already have one, sign into it.

Heroku refers to the services that run on it as "apps," but that's also the word we use to refer to iOS software. To remove ambiguity, for the rest of this discussion, the word *app* means "the copy of boarding that is running on Heroku."

4. Name the app something appropriate. For example, for Selfiegram, we used the name "selfiegram-boarding". This name will be included as part of the app's URL.

5. Choose a region to host it in. At the time of writing, Heroku supports two regions: the United States and Europe.

6. Finally, you'll need to configure the app by providing credentials for iTunes Connect, as well as the information that identifies which iOS app you want to add testers to:

   a. Set the ITC_USER option to your iTunes Connect username.

   b. Set the ITC_PASSWORD option to the password for this account.

   c. Set the ITC_APP_ID option to your app's bundle ID.

   d. If you want potential testers to enter a password in order to sign up, set the ITC_TOKEN option to the password you want them to enter.

 Your iTunes Connect password will never be shown to your end users, but it will be shown in the clear when you enter it on the configuration page, and it won't be stored in an encrypted form on Heroku's end. This is *generally* not a problem, but be aware of it.

7. Click the Deploy button. Heroku will create and deploy the application for you.

 If you get an error, double-check your username, your password, and the bundle ID, and ensure that you've created the entry for the app in iTunes Connect.

8. Click the View App button and you'll be taken to the live app, where you can enter credentials and be added as a tester (Figure 20-5).

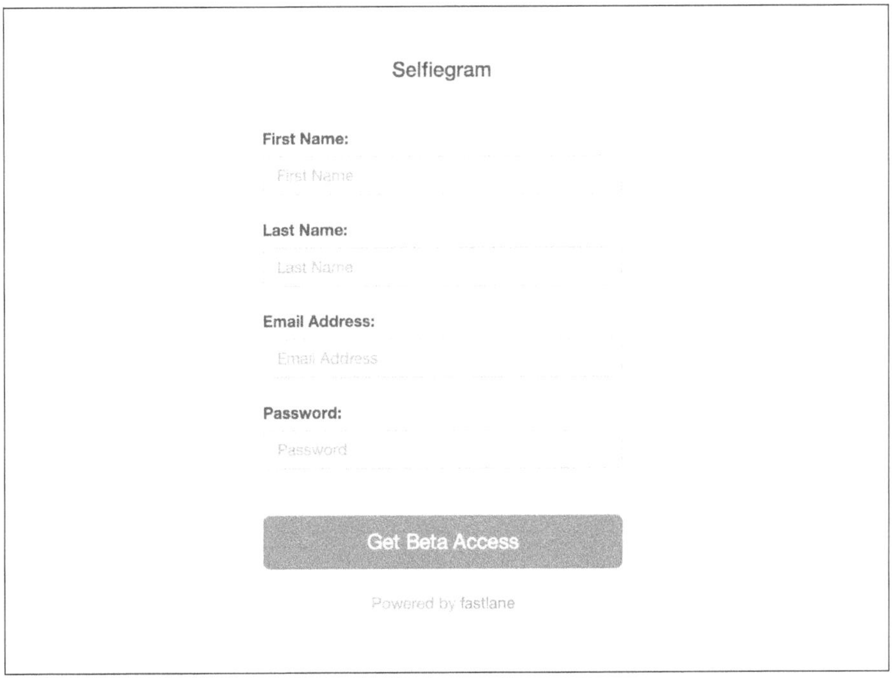

Figure 20-5. The boarding interface

You can now give the link to this page to anyone you want to invite; they can then enter their information, and `boarding` will communicate with iTunes Connect to send an invitation to them.

Managing Your App's Presence on the App Store Using deliver

The `deliver` tool manages the contents of your app's page on the App Store. Using `deliver`, you can upload built binaries for distribution, as well as metadata like the application name, description, and screenshots.

While `deliver` was originally designed for submitting builds for Apple's review, we've found that we tend not to use it for that.

Because builds that have been submitted to TestFlight can also be submitted to review for release, our process for releasing apps tends to follow the pattern of uploading one or more builds to Test-Flight, doing our external testing of them, and then submitting the build that we're happy with via iTunes Connect. (Another reason for doing this is that viewing the app's metadata all in one place in iTunes Connect is more convenient than reviewing the metadata that's kept locally, which `deliver` stores as multiple separate text files.)

However, something that `deliver` does extremely well is aiding in the *management* of that metadata. For this reason, we'll be demonstrating how to use `deliver` to work with, and submit, metadata.

Getting the Metadata

To start using `deliver` to manage your app's metadata, you'll first need to ask it to download the existing metadata. To do this, run the command `fastlane deliver download_metadata`. `deliver` will retrieve the metadata for the most recent version of your app from iTunes Connect and store it in a collection of text files, which it keeps inside the *fastlane/metadata* folder.

Each one of these files represents a different editable field in the app's entry in iTunes Connect. You can edit them as much as you like; when you're done, you can deliver the metadata to iTunes Connect.

Submitting New Metadata

To submit new metadata to iTunes Connect, run the command `fastlane deliver`. `deliver` will upload the local copy of the metadata to iTunes Connect. This includes both the text files, as well as any screenshots that `snapshot` has generated.

Fastlane will gather the metadata it's about to submit and present it to you as an HTML file in your browser. It will then ask you if you're happy to proceed; if you are, it will go ahead with the submission.

If you'd prefer to skip this check, add the `--force` option to the command. Additionally, you can add the `--skip_binary_upload` option to the command if you only want to submit metadata and don't want to upload a binary.

When you submit metadata using `deliver`, Fastlane will also run the `precheck` tool. This tool looks over your metadata and alerts you if it contains anything that might make your submission fail the review process. This can include things like including curse words in your description, making any references to future functionality, or suggesting that this build is a demo or test version.

Looking Further

There are many, many more tools in the Fastlane suite. If you want to get up to speed quickly, go read the Fastlane documentation (*https://docs.fastlane.tools*). Additionally, for inspiration on the kinds of things that Fastlane is being used for in real-world apps, take a look at the `fastlane-examples` project on GitHub (*https://github.com/fastlane/examples*), which showcases some of the *Fastfiles* that other developers have contributed.

Index

Symbols

! (exclamation mark)
  general meaning in Swift, 51
  unwrapping optional variable to get its
    value, 49
!= (inequality) operator, 30, 177
& (ampersand), prefacing variables passed as
    inout parameters, 56
() (parentheses) in function calls
  closure outside of, 59
  passing parameters to functions, 54
* (multiplication) operator, 30
+ (plus sign), addition operator, 30
  combining strings, 40
  overloading, example, 78
+= (addition and assignment) operator, com-
    bining strings, 40
- (minus sign), subtraction operator, 30
-> (arrow) operator, 53
. (dot) operator, accessing methods and proper-
    ties, 31
..< (range) operator, 36
/ (division) operator, 30
/* */, delimiting multi-line comments, 27
//, beginning single-line comments, 27
; (semicolon), ending lines of code and between
    statements, 30
< (less than) operator, 30
<= (less than or equal to) operator, 30
== (equality) operator, 30, 177
  comparing strings, 41
  in Swift vs. other languages, 42
==(lhs: rhs:) method, 177
=== (identity) operator, 42

> (greater than) operator, 30
>= (greater than or equal to) operator, 30
? (question mark)
  general meaning in Swift, 51
  in optional variables, 49-50
?? (nil coalescing) operator, 51
@escaping attribute to closures, 250
@objc in function definitions, 159
[] (square brackets)
  creating arrays with, 31
  creating dictionaries and accessing contents,
    33
  subscripting arrays and dictionaries, 80
  using to access an array element, 32
\() syntax, string interpolation, 42
_ (underscore) in Swift, 39
  before function parameters, 54
{} (curly braces)
  enclosing body of if statements and loops,
    35
  in computed property declarations, 67
… (closed-range) operator, 36
… in variadic parameters, 55

A

access control, 75-78
accuracy, configuring for locations, 188
actions
  creating expandMap action, 184
  creating for reminder switch, 202
  creating for selfie detail view controller text
    field, 172
  creating for switch in SettingsTableView
    Controller, 197

different ways to create, 168
Fastlane programs, 322
swipe event on table view row, 225
target-action mechanism, 158
activities, 222
addNotificationRequest method, 205
alerts, 205
(see also notifications)
for failure to load selfies list, 148
handling in UI tests, 319
aliases (type), 247
Any type, 52
APIs, guidelines for designing, creating, and
naming, 61
app ID, 117
App Store
and breakpoints in your code, 304
distributing apps to, 16
managing your app's presence on, using
deliver, 339-341
appearance proxies, setting for customized
UIView subclasses, 219
appearance styles for table view cells, 152
Appfile, 325
Apple Developer Program, 16
Apple developer website, 16
Apple library and API documentation, 97
application language, changing, 290
application(didFinishLaunchingWithOptions:),
281
applicationDidEnterBackground method, 93
apply function (for themes), 217-220
apps
App Transport Security (ATS), 258
configuring to support location, 186-187
resource use by, 309
structuring, 97-101
applications and delegates, 97
storyboards and nibs, 100
UIViewController, 99
views, 98
arithmetic operators, 30
array literals, 31
creating sets with, 43
arrays, 31
as generics, 81
as sorted function parameter, 58
iterating over, with for-in loops, 35
subscripting, 80

treating stings like arrays, 41
using sets instead of, 44
arrow symbol (->), 53
as! operator, 53
as? operator, 53
Aspect Fit content mode (UIImageView), 166
assertions, writing for test of UI element existence, 318
asset URL functions, 249
assistant editor (Xcode), 167, 172
preview mode, 294
associated values, storing in enumerations, 45
Attributes inspector
changing cell style for table view cells, 152
setting Return Key to Done, 172
authorization for location manager to use location hardware, 190
automating chores with Fastlane (see Fastlane)
autosynthesis of protocol conformance (in
Swift 4), 177
AVCapturePhoto object, 240
AVCapturePhotoCaptureDelegate protocol, 238
CaptureViewController class conforming to,
239
AVCaptureSession object, 229
AVCaptureVideoOrientation, 235
AVCaptureVideoPreviewLayer, 228
AVFoundation library, 97
AVKit framework, 227

B

bash, 103
BitBucket, 332
Blur Style, changing, 232
boarding (Fastlane), using to add testers to
TestFlight, 337-339
Bool type, 40
bounds (UIView), 98
breakpoint navigator (Xcode), 11, 301
breakpoints, 300-303
adding into SelfieStore class, setImage(id:,
image:) method, 304
hitting, and controlling program flow after,
307
removal from code before distribution, 304
bundle identifiers, 117

C

cache URLs, creating for Selfiegram and image overlays, 248
Caches directory, 249
caching, testing for overlay manager, 254
CALayer class, 228
camera
    checking for availability and permission to use, 159
    interactions with, handling by image picker, 158
camera preview view, 232
camera view, 228-231
camera view controllers
    creating, 231-240
        building the UI, 231
        connecting the UI, 234
        talking to the camera, 234-240
    third-party, 227
canEditRowAt indexPath:, 155
capture view controller (example), calling, 240-243
captured variables, using in functions, 58
captureSession, creating, 234
CaptureViewController class, 234
    conformance to AVCapturePhotoCapture-Delegate protocol, 239
    image property given to EditingViewController, 269
    prepare(for segue:, sender:) method, 279
    segueing into EditingViewController, 279
    viewWillAppear method, 280
case keyword, 44
cases (in switches), 37-39
cellForRowAt indexPath: method, 149
    updating to show time and image, 151
certificates (code signing), 15, 331
CGImage, 278
CGRect object, 98
character sets (different), combining, 40
class keyword, access level specified before, 76
class properties vs. static properties, 248
classes and objects, 63-82
    access control
        private or fileprivate levels, 76
        public and open access levels, 76
    classes as reference types vs. structures as value types, 83
    classes vs. structures, 82

creating instances of a class, 64
defining a class with access level, 76
extensions, 72
generics, 81
inheritance in classes, 69
initialization and deinitialization, 64
properties, 66
    computed, 67
    lazy, 68
    observers, 68
properties and methods, 63
protocols, 70
subclassing, putting restrictions on, 78
subscripting, 80
CLLocation class, 175
CLLocationCoordinate2D, 178
CLLocationManager, 188
    determining multiple locations, 191
CLLocationManager.authorizationStatus, 190
CLLocationManagerDelegate protocol, 189
close method, camera view controller, 237
closed-range operator (…), 36
closures, 58-59
    as last parameter in function calls, 59
    as parameter in function calls, 58
    escaping and non-escaping, 250
    in keyword, 58
    parameters, 58
    stored in variables, calling, 59
Cocoa and Cocoa Touch
    Carthage and CocoaPods tools, 101
    Cocoa, 96
    Cocoa Touch, 96
    design patterns in Cocoa, 91
    target-action mechanism, 158
Codable protocol, 124, 143
    autosynthesis of conformance to, 177
    CLLocation not in conformance with, 177
code
    connecting to SettingsTableViewController UI in Selfiegram app (example), 196
    connecting to UI in selfie viewer, 167-171, 172
        map view, 181
    guidelines for designing, creating, and naming, 61
    licenses for, 101
code signing, 15
    using Fastlane's match tool, 329-333

collections, 31-34
  arrays, 31
  dictionaries, 33
  improvements in Swift 4.0, 24
  of mixed type, Any type in, 52
  tuples, 32
color literals, 218
colors
  changing background color of app launch
    screen, 220
  changing in application themes, 218
command line, 103
  Fastlane working through, 323
  Xcode's command line interface, 322
commands, running in Xcode debugger, 306
comments, 27
commit editingStyle: forRowAt indexPath:, 155
comparison operators, 30
completion handler
  calling with nil passed in, 238
  closure for capture view controller, 241
completion handler property, 234, 270
computed properties, 67, 248
  adding in extensions, 74
  defining, 67
  working with, 67
configureView method, selfie viewer (example),
  169, 182
Connections inspector (Xcode), 167
Console view (Xcode debug area), 306
constants, 23, 28
constraints, 99
  adding for map view in view controller, 180
  fixing for label and text view in selfie detail
    view controller with map view, 180
  for label and switch in Settings view UI, 194
  setting for stack view, 265
  using to position text field and label in selfie
    viewer, 165
content modes (UIImageView), 166
  Aspect Fill content mode, 264
control flow, 34-39
  if statements, 34
  loops, 35
  switches, 37-39
controllers, 92
  controller classes, 93
convenience initializers, 65
conversion (types), 47

loss of precision in, 48
values that can't be converted, 48
Coordinate struct, 191
  conformance to Codable and Equatable
    protocols, 177
  creating in Selfie class (example), 176
copying structures, 82
Core Animation framework, 228
Core Data framework, 117
Core Graphics library, 98
Core Location framework, 97, 176
  communication with location hardware, 188
count property, arrays, 32
created property, 125
createNewSelfie method (example), 158, 240
  calling location manager to determine loca-
    tion, 190

D

Data object, 139
data stores
  building SelfieStore (example), 127-130
  Core Data framework, 117
data tasks, starting or resuming, 258
DateComponentsFormatter, 151
dates and time
  adding date formatter to selfie viewer, 169
  setting notification delivery with DateCom-
    ponent, 206
debug area (Xcode), 13, 304
debug navigator (Xcode), 11
  debugger guages, 309
debugging, 299-312
  using the Xcode debugger, 299-308
    breakpoints, 300-303
    controlling program flow, 307
    inspecting code, 304-307
Decodable protocol, 124, 143
default case (in switches), 37
default implementations of protocols, 74
default value (dictionaries), 51
defer keyword, 59
  code in a defer block, 59
  using to close image context, 133
deinit method, 65, 88
deinitializers, 65
delegates, 94
  applications and, 97
delegation, 71, 93-96

working with delegates in Swift, 94
delete method, SelfieStore (example), 141
deleteRows(at: with:) method, 156
deleting selfies (Selfiegram example app),
    155-157
    delete action, 226
deliver (Fastlane), managing your app's pres-
    ence on App Store, 339-341
dequeueReusableCell method, 149
design patterns in Swift, 91-96
    delegation, 93-96
    MVC (model-view-controller), 92
designated initializers, 65
detail view controller (Selfiegram app), 119
detectFaceLandmarks method, 277
developer certificates, 15
dictionaries, 33
    default value returned if key can't be found,
        51
    subscripting, 80
dispatch group, 258
distributing apps, 16
do-catch block, 86
    not needed for try? and try! statements, 87
Documents folder, 137
    Files app browser for, 138
documentsFolder computed property, SelfieS-
    tore (example), 136
done function, 271
doneButtonTapped method (example), 172
double length pseudolanguage, 293
Double type, 40
    adding to Int type, 47
Downloads for Apple Developers page, 4
drawing eyebrows, 271-274

E

EditingViewController, 266
    completion handler property, 270
    done function, 271
    eyebrows property, 269
    overlay properties, 269
editor (Xcode), 6
    assistant editor, opening along with story-
        board, 167
    jump bar, 7
    main editor and assistant editor, 7
editor selector (Xcode toolbar), 9
else if and else branches (in if statements), 35

email, sharing activities via, 224
empty sets, creating, 43
empty strings, creating, 40
Encodable protocol, 124, 143
English language, 283
    multiple variants of, 288
enum keyword, 44
enumerations, 44
    changing to different value of same type, 44
    in Swift vs. other languages, 45
    shorthand version of name, using, 44
    storing associated values, 45
    throwing an error, 84
    using switch statement to match values, 44
    with default values or raw values, 46
equality operators, 30
Equatable protocol, 177
error handling, 84-87
    enumeration throwing an error, 84
    for deleting selfies from SelfieStore (exam-
        ple), 156
    for location manager determining locations,
        190
    functions throwing an error, 85
    in calling capture view controller, 241
    in Swift 1.0 or Objective-C, 84
    overlay errors, creating, 246
    SelfieStoreError (example), 127
    showError method in Selfie List UI (exam-
        ple), 148
    throwing an error, 84
    try! statement, 87
    try? statement, 86
    wrapping functions, methods, and initializ-
        ers in do-catch block, 86
Error protocol, 84
escaping closures, 250
event-driven programming, 97
events, 97
    creating breakpoints for specific types of,
        303
exhaustive switches, 37
expandMap function (example), 184
expectations, 254
explicitly typed variables, 28
extension keyword, 73
extensions, 72
    providing default implementations of proto-
        cols, 74

using to make a type conform to a protocol, 74

F

facial detection code, 268
    (see also Vision framework)
failable initializers, 66
fallthrough keyword, 38
Fastfile, 322
    contents of, 327
Fastlane, 321-328
    configuring a Fastfile, 327
    doing a build, 325-327
    installing, 323
        via direct download, 324
        via Homebrew, 324
        via RubyGems, 324
    setting up a project, 324
    tools, 322
    using Fastlane's tools, 329-341
        boarding, adding testers to TestFlight, 337-339
        code signing with match, 329-333
        deliver, managing your app's presence on App Store, 339-341
        discovering other tools, 341
        generating screenshots with snapshot, 333-337
fastlane directory, 325
fatalError function, 241
file URLs, 136
FileManager class, 137
fileprivate (access level), 75
    classes defined as and their members, 76
    for property setters, 78
    private vs., 77
Files app (iOS), 138
final keyword, 78
    final classes, 248
    making SelfieStore class (example) final, 128
first responder, 173
flatMap, 216
Font Squirrel, 215
fonts, custom, 214-217
    adding to Xcode project, 215
    checking loading of, 218
    downloading from Font Squirrel, 215
    informing iOS of in info.plist file, 217
    loading using precise name, 216

for-in loops, 35
    closed-range operator in, 36
    iterating over sets, 43
    stride function in, 36
Foundation library, 96
frame (UIView), 98
French language, localizing Selfiegram app (example) for, 287-290
functional testing, 314
functions, 53-58
    capturing a value and using it multiple times, 57
    closure as parameter, 58
    functions and return values passed by value, 55
    guidelines for writing and naming, 61
    parameters with default values, 55
    passing parameters by reference, 55
    passing parameters to, 54
    receiving and using other functions as parameters, 56
    return values, 53
    returning multiple values or tuples, 33, 54
    returning other functions, 56
    throwing errors, defined with throws keyword, 85
    throwing errors, wrapping in do-catch block, 86
    using as variables, 56

G

generators, functions acting as, 58
generics, 81
    creating specific, nongeneric types from, 82
    defining, 81
genstrings command-line utility, 286
gesture recognizers, 184, 233
getImage method, SelfieStore (example), 139
getters and setters for computed properties, 67
Git, 118
    private repository for using match, 332
GitHub, repo for code examples, 111
graphics contexts (iOS), 273
guard statements
    guard keyword, 60
    wrapping font checks in, 218
gym, 326
    building your app with, 326
    chaining with other actions in a lane, 327

H

half-range operator (<..), 36
hashable types, 43
Heroku platform, 337
Homebrew, 323
    installing Fastlane via, 324
HTTP status messages and codes, 257
HTTPS protocol, 258

I

IBAction method, locationSwitchToggled, 198
id property, 125
identifier property (segues), 170
identifiers for UI elements in storyboard, 289
if statements, 34
    checking whether optional variable has a
        value, 49
    else if and else branches, 35
if-let statements, 50
image computed property, implementing for
    Selfie object (example), 125
image contexts, 273
image overlays, 245-261
    creating overlay model for Selfiegram app
        (example), 245-252
    testing the overlay manager, 252-261
        downloading overlay images, 258
        downloading overlay information, 256
        returning available overlays, 255
        writing the tests, 252
image picker delegate, 159
image pickers, 157
    capture view controller as replacement for,
        234
    replacing with capture view controller call,
        240
image properties for EditingViewController,
    269
image request handler, 277
image views
    content modes, 264
    user interaction in, 267
imageCache property, SelfieStore (example),
    136
images
    generating for testing SelfieStore (example),
        133
    image detection using Vision framework,
        274-279

immutable arrays, 32
implicit values, using for raw values in enumer-
    ations, 46
implicitly typed variables, 28
implicitly unwrapped optional variables, 49
import statement, 27
imports, 75
in keyword, 58
index paths, 145
    array of, in deleteRows(at: with:), 156
    canEditRowAt indexPath:, 155
    cellForRowAt indexPath:, 149
    using to delete selfies in Selfiegram app
        (example), 156
indices
    array, 32
    using to get elements out of sets, 43
    using to get values out of tuples, 32, 54
infix operators, 79
Info.plist file
    configuring location support, 186
    information about custom fonts, 217
inheritance, 69
    no inheritance in structures, 82
init method, 64
initializers, 64
    convenience and designated, 65
    creating for overlay manager, 249
    creating for OverlaySelectionView (exam-
        ple), 266
    for Selfie class (example), 126
    for structures, 83
    returning nil (failable initializer), 65
    throwing errors, wrapping in do-catch
        block, 86
inout keyword, 55
inspector (Xcode), 13
instantiateViewController(withIdentifier:), 241
Instruments app, 310-312
Int type, 23, 40
    extending, 73
    extending to conform to Blinkable protocol,
        74
    mapping to specific type of integer depend-
        ing on device, 40
Int64 type, 40
Int? type, 48
interface builder (Xcode), 16-18
    interfaces in iOS, 18

interfaces
    application, storyboards and nibs, 100
    modifying, 6
        (see also UIs (user interfaces))
internal (access level), 75
    default for methods and properties, 76
internationalization
    about, 283
    of Selfiegram app (example), 284-287
        generating the string table, 286
interruption handlers, 319
iOS
    Cocoa Trouch library for, 96
    device and AV orientation, 235
    events, 97
    Files app in iOS 11, 138
    fonts on, 214
    graphics contexts, 273
    informing of custom fonts in info.plist, 217
    interfaces in, 18
    managed environment, 137
    playgrounds for, 26
    responder chain, 173
    screen points, 98
    Selfiegram app (example) (see Selfiegram
        app)
    sharing functionality, 222
    swipe-to-delete behavior, 155
    view positioning by constraints, 99
iOS devices, 3
    orientation, 235
    running your code on, 15
iOS simulators, 14
iPad, Swift Playgrounds for, 24
is operator, 52
issue navigator (Xcode), 11
iTunes Connect, 16, 337
    managing your app's metadata on, using
        deliver, 340

J

JSON
    for Selfie objects (example), 143
    saving selfies in, 140
JSONDecoder class, 140, 142
JSONEncoder class, 142-143
jump bar (Xcode editor), 7

K

keyboard, dismissing, 173

L

labels
    creating outlet for label in selfie viewer, 168
    customizing appearance of, 220
    for function parameters, 54
    for Settings view table cells in Selfiegram
        app (example), 194
    for values in tuples, 33
    placing on visual effect view, 233
    positioning a label in selfie viewer, 165
lanes (Fastlane), 327
    running a lane, 328
languages, 283
    changing application language, 290
    configuring Selfiegram app (example) to
        support multiple, 284
    multiple variants of, 288
    pseudolanguages, 293
lastLocation optional property, 188
    setting to nil, 190
launch screen
    controlling and interfacing with through
        view controller, 221
    theming for an app, 220
layers in views, 228
layoutSubviews method, 230
lazy loading, 69
lazy properties, 68
    declared as mutable variables, 69
left-to-right languages, 283
let keyword
    defining arrays with, 32
    defining variables with, 23, 28
    in empty string declaration, 40
libraries
    importing into Swift code, 27
    library in Xcode utilities pane, 13
    main libraries in Swift, 96
licenses
    for code, 101
    for fonts, 215
listSelfies method, SelfieStore (example), 140
LLDB debugger, 299
    (see also Xcode, debugger)
    LLDB project site, 307
load method, SelfieStore (example), 141

Lobster font, 215
local notifications, 203
localization and internationalization (Selfie-
    gram app example), 283-296
    internationalization, 283
    localization, 283
    localizing Selfiegram to support French lan-
        guage, 287-290
    testing locales, 290-296
        previewing localizations, 294
        using pseudolanguages, 292
location computed property, 177
location information, adding to selfies, 175-191
    determining locations, 186-191
        configuring the app to support location,
            186
        talking to location hardware, 188-191
    showing the selfie's location, 179-183
    testing the new model, 178
    updating Selfiegram app model to add loca-
        tion support, 175-178
locationManager(didFailWithError error:), 189
locationManager(didUpdateLocations loca-
    tions:), 189
locationSwitchToggled method, 198
longitude and latitude properties (Coordinate
    struct), 176
loops, 35
    for-in, 35
    while, 36
lowercased method, 41

M
Mac computers, 3
macOS
    Cocoa library for, 96
    events, 97
    playgrounds for, 26
map views
    adding map view to selfie detail view con-
        troller, 180
    changing type to Muted Standard, 181
    creating outlet for map view in selfie viewer,
        181
    eliminating toggles from, 181
    making hidden, 181
MapKit framework, 181
maps
    flatMap and, 217

modifying selfie location map to expand on
    user taps, 183-186
showing for selfie locations (example), 175
Maps app, 175
Master-Detail App template, 115, 118
    segue between selfie list and selfie detail
        view controllers, 171
MasterViewController, renaming, 146
match, code signing with, 329-333
memberwise initializer, 83
memory management, 87-91
metadata
    retrieving from iTunes Connect for your
        app, 340
    submitting to iTunes Connect, 340
method stubs
    creating for overlay manager, 249
    creating for SelfieStore class (example), 128
    filling out for SelfieStore (example), 136-143
methods
    access control, 76
    deinitializer, 65
    final, 78
    in a class, 63
    in extensions, 73
    initializer, 64
    throwing errors, wrapping in do-catch
        block, 86
MKMapView, 180
model-view-controller pattern (see MVC pat-
    tern)
models (in MVC), 92
    building the Selfie app model, 123-143
        Selfie object, 123
    creating overlay model in Selfiegram app
        (example), 245-252
    model classes, 93
    updating Selfiegram app model to add loca-
        tion support, 175-178
modules, access control, 75
mutable arrays, 32
mutable variables, lazy properties declared as,
    69
mutating functions, naming, 61
MVC (model–view–controller) pattern, 91-93
    controllers, 92
    models, 92
    text editor example, 92
    view controller design and, 100

views, 92

N

navigation controller delegate, 159
navigation controllers, 119
    for camera view controller, 231
navigator pane (Xcode), 10
newSelfieTaken method (example), 191
nib files, 100
    .xib file extension, 100
nil, 34
    implicitly unwrapped optionals and, 50
    in optional chaining, 50
    initializers returning, 65
    meaning "no value" in Swift, 48
    optional variables set to, 89
    resulting from type conversions, 48
    returned from methods throwing errors and
        try? statement, 86
nil coalescing operator (??), 51
non-escaping closures, 250
nonmutating functions, naming, 61
notifications, 203-209
    avoiding spamming users with, 206
    creating for Selfiegram app (example),
        203-208
    local vs. push, 203
    localizing title in Selfiegram app (example),
        285
    testing, 208
NSColor object, 218
NSError object, 84
NSLocalizedString function, 284
NSString.localizedUserNotificationString, 285
NSTableView class, 146
NSValue class, 185
numberOfRowsInSection method, 149

O

Object Library, 17
object-oriented development in Swift, 63-107
    classes and objects, 63-82
    design patterns, 91-96
    error handling, 84-87
    memory management, 87-91
    structures, 82
    structuring an app, 97-101
    Swift libraries, 96
    Swift Package Manager, 101-106

ObjectID (in Xcode comments), 289
Objective-C
    accuracy setting for locations, 189
    communication to MapKit and Maps app
        handled by, 185
    Foundation library, 96
    nil in, 48
    Swift's interoperability with, 22, 159
objects, 63
    creating, 64
    in sets, 43
    initialization and deinitialization, 64
observers, 68
OmniGraffle drawing tool, 114
open (access level), 75
    classes defined as, 76
    public vs., 76
operators, 30
    overloading and custom operators, 78-80
optimizations, 309
optional chaining, 50, 95
optional variables, 48
    checking for a value, using if statement, 49
    checking for a value, using if-let statement,
        50
    Coordinate property, adding to Selfie class
        (example), 178
    declaring as implicitly unwrapped, 49
    lastLocation property, 188
    returned by failable initializers, 66
    returning from try? statement, 86
    set to nil value, 49, 89
    unwrapping using ! character to get value,
        49
    using for UITableViewCell styles, 152
    using guard statement to unwrap, 60
Organization Identifier setting, 116
Organization Name setting, 116
orientation computed property, 235
orientations on iOS, 235
outlets
    creating outlet for image view in selfie
        viewer, 168
    creating outlet for label in selfie viewer, 168
    creating outlet for map view in selfie viewer,
        181
    creating outlet for reminder switch, 202
    creating outlet for switch in SettingsTable-
        View Controller, 197

creating outlet for text field in selfie viewer, 167

different ways to create, 168

Overlay struct, 245, 250

overlay UI (Selfiegram app example), 263-281

building the UI, 263-266

connecting it to the app, 279-281

creating the overlay view, 266-268

hooking up the UI, 266

presenting the overlays, 268-279

drawing eyebrows, 271-274

initial setup, 268-271

Vision framework and image detection, 274-279

OverlayInformation struct, 246

overlayListURL class property, 248

OverlayManager class, 246

shared instance of, creating, 247

starting on downloading overlay assets, 281

OverlaySelectionView class (example), 266

closure handler property, 266

initializer for, 266

overlay property, 266

OverlayStore.swift file, 246

override keyword, 70

overriding methods, 70

ownership of objects, 87

P

package manager (Swift) (see Swift Package Manager)

package manifest (Package.swift file), 103

parameters

closure as function parameter, 58

default values for function parameters, 55

functions used as parameters to other functions, 56

in closures, 58

labels associated with function parameters, 54

passing by reference, 55

passing to functions, 54

variable number of (variadic), 23, 55

parent class, 69

performance, 309-312

profiling using Instruments, 310-312

resource usage shown by debugger gauges in Xcode, 309

permissions

checking for the camera, 159

for camera access, adding to info.plist, 162

for location hardware access, 186

for user notifications, 204

photo library, using instead of the camera, 159

photoOutput property (capture session), 234

photoOutput(didFinishProcessingPhoto photo:, error:) method, 239

playgrounds, 24-26

support for rich text markup in comments, 27

pointers, 84

postfix operators, 79

preferences, storing using UserDefaults class, 197

prefix operators, 79

prefix or suffix of a string, checking, 42

prepare(for segue: sender:) method, 170, 279

preview mode (assistant editor), 294

previewLayer property, 228

PreviewView class, 228, 232

print function, 23

privacy of users, apps respecting, 187

private (access level), 76

classes defined as and their members, 76

fileprivate vs., 77

making properties read-only, 77

Product Name setting, 116

profiles (performance) in Instruments, 310-312

project navigator (Xcode), 11

projects, setting up Fastlane for, 324

properties, 63, 66

access control, 76

computed, 67

final, 78

in a class

accessing using self keyword, 64

in extensions, 73

lazy, 68

observers, 68

read-only, rendering with private setter, 77

static and class, 248

stored, 66

protocols, 70

advantage of using, 71

conformance to, autosynthesis of in Swift 4, 177

conforming to other protocols, 72

creating classes conforming to, 71

creating, Blinkable protocol example, 71
default implementations, providing with
extensions, 74
optional, no support in Swift, 75
using extensions to make a type conform to,
74
provisioning profile, 16, 330
pseudolanguages, 293
public (access level), 75
classes defined as, 76
open vs., 76
push notifications, 203

Q

Quick Help comments, 27
Quicksand font, 215

R

range operators, 36
ranges
iterating over, with for-in loops, 35
using in switch statement cases, 37
raw values in enumerations, 46
using implicit values for, 46
recognizers, 183
redrawImage method, 272
reference counting, 87
reference types, value types vs., 83
refreshes, overlay information, 260
Release mode, 304
reminders, 201-202
repeat-while loops, 37
report navigator (Xcode), 11
requestLocation method, 191
resignFirstResponder function, 173
resource use of an app, 309
responder chain in iOS, 173
retain count, 87
retain cycles, 88
rich text markup in comments, 27
right to left pseudolanguage, 293
right-to-left languages, 283
Ruby scripts interacting with Xcode and App
Store, 322
RubyGems, installing Fastlane via, 324
Run button (Xcode toolbar), 8
run loop, 97
running your code, 13
on a device, 15

on iOS simulator, 14

S

save method, SelfieStore (example), 141
scenes, 100
schemes (Xcode)
changing application language, 290
scheme selector, 9
choosing iOS simulator, 14
scroll views, 264
using with stack view, 265
search navigator (Xcode), 11
security, HTTP vs. HTTPS protocols, 258
segues, 100
between view controllers, 170
creating manual segue, 264
#selector macro, 158
self keyword, 64
self.isUserInteractionEnabled = true, 267
Selfiegram app (example)
adding and deleting selfies, 155-163
deleting selfies, 155-157
taking new selfies, 157-163
adding location info to selfies, 175-191
determining locations, 186-191
showing selfie's location, 179-183
testing the new model, 178
updating the model, 175-178
building Selfie List UI, 145-154
improving the UI, 151-154
building settings view, 193-200
building the model, 123-143
Selfie object, 123-126
SelfieStore, 127-130
testing SelfieStore, 130-136
custom views and view controllers, 227-243
calling capture view controller, 240-243
camera view, 228-231
camera view controller, 231-240
image overlays, 245-261
creating the overlay model, 245-252
testing the overlay manager, 252-261
localization and internationalization,
283-296
internationalization, 284-287
localization to support French language,
287-290
testing locales, 290-296
overlay UI, 263-281

building the UI, 263-266
  connecting it to the app, 279-281
  creating the overlay view, 266-268
  hooking up the UI, 266
  presenting the overlays, 268-279
reminders and notifications, 201-209
  adding a reminder to settings, 201-202
  creating notifications, 203-209
setting up the app, 111-121
  creating the Xcode project, 115-118
  designing Selfiegram, 112-115
  renaming views, 120
  structure, 118
theming and sharing selfies, 213-226
  custom fonts, 214-217
  making the theme, 217-222
  sharing selfies, 222-226
viewing and editing selfies, 165-173
  editing selfies, 172-173
  selfie viewer, 165-172
semver (semantic versioning) system, 105
sender property (segues), 170
serialization/deserialization
  changes in Swift 4.0, 24
  of Selfie app model into JSON format, 124
session (capture), 229
setCameraOrientation method, 230
setNeedsLayout method, 230
sets, 42
  creating, 43
  hashable types in, 43
  iterating over, with for-in loops, 43
  modifying, 43
  purpose of, 44
  using index to get elements from, 43
setSession function, 229
setters (for properties)
  computed properties, 67
  fileprivate access level, 78
  private access level, 77
settings bundles, 195
settings view, building for Selfiegram app
  (example), 193-200
  adding reminder to settings, 201-202
  building the Settings UI, 193-197
  connecting settings view controller into
    hierarchy, 195
  implementing the settings, 197-200

making selfie creation code respect user
  settings, 198
SettingsKey enumeration (example), 197
sharing selfies (Selfiegram app example),
  222-226
  from selfie list view controller, 224
  sharing from detail view controller, 223
showError method, 148
signed code, 15
SIL font license, 215
singletons, 127
  OverlayManager class, 247
  standard singleton, intefacing with user
    defaults, 197
Snapfile, 336
snapshot tool (Fastlane), generating screenshots
  with, 333-337
social media channels, sharing, 222
sorted function, 58
source files, access control, 75
Spanish language, multiple variants of, 288
SplitViewController, configuring, 148
stack views, 265
static methods, 177
static properties, 248
  creating for SelfieStore class (example), 128
statically typed languages, 28
status display (Xcode toolbar), 9
Stop button (Xcode toolbar), 8
stored properties, 66
storyboard files, 100
  localizing, 289
storyboard ID, 240
storyboards
  creating and displaying view controller
    from, using code, 240
  launch screen, changing background color
    of, 220
  Main.storyboard file, 16
  opening storyboard and assistant editor
    together, 167, 172
stride function, 36
  stride(from: through: by:) form, 36
  stride(from: to: by:) form, 36
string interpolation, 42
String type, 40
  Apple documentation on, 41
strings, 40
  changes in Swift 4.0, 24

changing case of, 41
combining, 40
comparing using == operator, 41
conversions to other types, 47
counting characters in, 41
creating, 40
differences from arrays in Swift, 41
generating the strings table, 286
localization in Selfiegram app (example), 285
making available for localization, 284
searching, 42
switching on, 38
translating to French for Selfiegram app (example), 290
strong references, 89
structures, 82
    as value types, difference from classes as reference types, 83
    declaring using struct keyword, 83
    differences from classes, 82
subclasses (custom), adhering to requirements of parents, 268
subclassing, 73
    putting restrictions on, 78
subscript keyword, 80
subscript operator, 32-33
subscripting, 80
substring functionality, 24
substrings, 41
Subtitle cell style, 152
suffix of a string, checking, 42
super keyword, 70
superclass, accessing functions of, 70
Swift, 3
    language basics, 21-61
        code snippet example, 22
        collections, 31-34
        comments, 27
        control flow, 34-39
        defer keyword, 59
        functions and closures, 53-59
        goals of the language, 22
        guard keyword, 60
        guidelines for designing, creating, and naming code and APIs, 61
        imports, 27
        operators, 30
        playgrounds, 24-26

    types, 39-53
    variables, 28-30
    version 3 vs. version 4, 24
    versions 3.0 and 4.0, 21
Swift Open Source project, 21
swift package generate-xcodeproj command, 106
swift package init --type executable command, 103
Swift Package Manager, 101-106
    advantages of using, 102
    running through the command line, 103
swift package resolve command, 106
swift run command, 106
Swift Standard library, 96
swipe-to-delete behavior (iOS), 155
switches, 37-39
    fallthrough keyword in, 38
    switching over CLLocationManager.authorizationStatus, 190
    using to match enumeration values, 44
    using with associated values stored in enumerations, 45
switches (UI), 194
    creating outlet and actions for, 197
    creating reminder switch, 202
    getting state from user defaults and using to set appearance, 198
    onOff property, 198
symbol navigator (Xcode), 11
system notifications, 203

T

table views, 119
    appearance styles for cells, 152
    deleteRows(at: with:) method, 156
    improving for Selfie List UI to show age of selfies, 151
    in Selfies List UI (example), updating methods for, 149
    in Settings view for Selfiegram app (example), 194
    index paths, 145
    instructing to reload all data, 173
tableView(_ canEditRowAt indexPath:), 155
tableView(_ commit editingStyle: forRowAt indexPath:), 155
takeSelfie method (example), 238
tap gesture recognizer, 183, 233, 267

tap handlers, 266
target-action mechanism, 158
team, associating projects with, 15
templates (Xcode)
    Master-Detail App template, 115
    template chooser, 4
Terminal app
    opening files, 104
    running Swift Package Manager in, 103
test navigator (Xcode), 11
testCreatingSelfie function (example), 134
testDeletingSelfie test case (example), 135
testDownloadedOverlaysAreCached test, 254
testDownloadingOverlays test, 254
TestFlight, 16
    adding testers using Fastlane boarding tool, 337-339
testGettingOverlayInfo test, 253
testing
    Inculde Unit Tests and Include UI Tests settings, 117
    locales in Selfiegram app (example), 290-296
    location information in SelfieStore (example), 178
    location test selfie, showing the map, 182
    notifications, 208
    overlay manager, 252-261
        downloading overlay images, 258
        downloading overlay information, 256
        returning available overlays, 255
        writing the tests, 252
    Selfies List UI (example), 150
    SelfieStore (example), 130-136
    UI tests, 313-319
testLoadingSelfie test case (example), 135
testSavingImage test case (example), 134
text fields
    creating outlet for, 167
    editing text field in selfie detail view controller, 172
    positioning a text field in selfie viewer, 165
textLabel in cells of table view, 149
themes, 213
theming Selfiegram app (example), 213-222
    custom fonts, 214-217
        creating a theme file, 215
    making the theme, 217-222
throwing an error, 84

throws keyword in function definitions, 85
tint color, changing for an application, 218
title property, implementing for Selfie object (example), 125
toolbar (Xcode), 8
    editor selector, 9
    Run button, 8
    scheme selector, 9
    status display, 9
    Stop button, 8
    view selector, 10
trigger, setting to test recent code changes, 208
try! statement, 87
try? statement, 86
tuples, 32
    function return values, 54
    using switches with, 39
Twitter, 222
type aliases, 247
type casting, 52
types, 39-53
    defining for function parameters, 54
    defining for function return values, 53
    enumerations, 44
    extending, 72
    in arrays, 31
    in collections, 34
    in dictionaries, 34
    of variables, 28
    operator overloading and custom operators, 79
    operators and, 30
    optional variables, 48
    protocols as, 71
    sets, 42
    strings, 40
    testing for and downcasting using is and as operators, 52
    type safety and conversion, 46-48
    value types and structures in Swift, 83

U

UI prefix, Cocoa Touch classes, 96
UI tests, 313-319
    compiling and running using snapshot, 337
    UI testing classes, 313
    writing, 314-319
        basic test, 314
        checking if elements exist, 318

handling UI interruptions, 319
    recording UI actions, 315
UIActivity object, 222
UIActivityViewController, 222
UIAlertController class, 149
UIAppearance class, 213, 219
UIApplication class, 97
UIApplication object, 93
UIApplicationDelegate class, 97
UIBarButtonItem, 158
UICollectionView class, 146
UIColor object, 218
UIDeviceOrientation, 235
UIFont class, extending to load custom fonts, 215
UIGestureRecognizer, 184, 233
UIGraphicsBeginImageContext, 273
UIGraphicsGetImageFromCurrentImageContext, 274
UIImage object, 124, 126, 250
    CGImage vs., 278
    immutability of data, 271
UIImagePickerController, 157
    configuring, 159
UIImagePickerControllerDelegate, 157, 159, 242
UIImageView, 228
    content modes, 166
    creating outlet for image view in selfie viewer, 168
    placing in selfie viewer, 166
UIKit library, 27, 96
    responder chain, 173
UIKit.UIImage library, importing into Selfie app, 124
UINavigationControllerDelegate, 159, 242
UInt8 type, 40
    subscripting, 80
UIResponder objects, 173
UIs (user interfaces)
    adding reminder switch to settings view in Selfiegram app (example), 201
    building Selfie List UI (example), 145-154
    building Settings UI for Selfiegram app (example), 193-197
    building UI for custom camera view controller, 231
    connecting code and UI for selfie viewer, 167-172

    connecting for camera view controller, 234
    connecting SettingsTableViewController UI to code, 196
    customizing appearance using themes, 213-222
    for camera preview view, 232
    modifying selfie detail view controller UI to show location, 179-183
    overlay UI in Selfiegram app (example), 263-281
    using storyboards for, 101
UIScrollView class, 264
UISwitch class, 194
UITableView class, 145-146, 264
UITableViewCell, appearance styles, 152
UITableViewController, 100, 146, 193, 196
UITableViewDataSource, 145
UITableViewRowAction, 225
UITapGestureRecognizer, 233
UIView object, 98
    frame and bounds, 98
    layers in, 228
UIViewController, 18, 99
UIVisualEffectView, 233
UIWindow object, 98
Unicode characters, 40
    in string comparisons, 42
unowned references, 90
updateReminderSwitch method (example), 206
updateReminderUI(enabled: active:) method (example), 207
uppercased method, 41
URLs
    asset URL functions, 249
    creating cache URLs for image overlays, 248
    creating data URLs for image overlays, 247
    file URL, 136
    HTTPS, 258
URLSession class, 257
user interaction in image views, 267
user notifications, 203
UserDefaults class, 197
    saving user preferences with synchronize method, 198
UserNotificationCenter, 204
UserNotifications library, 203
utilities pane (Xcode), 11
    inspector and library sections, 13
UUID (universally unique identifier), 126

V

value types, 83
var keyword, 28
variables, 28-30
    assigning value to, 29
    closures stored in, 59
    declared with let keyword, 23
    declaring type explicitly, 28
    defining with let or var keyword, 28
    optional, 49
    passing as inout parameter, prefacing with
        &, 56
    releasing ownership of, 89
    storing functions in, 56
    types, 23, 46
Variables view (Xcode debug area), 305
variadic parameters, 55
version control in projects, 10, 118
versioning, Swift packages, 105
video layer, 228
view controllers, 18, 99
    controlling and interfacing with launch
        screen through, 221
    for Selfiegram app (example), 118
    segues from one to another, 170
    SelfieListViewController (example), 146
view selector (Xcode toolbar), 10
viewDidLoad function, 147
    adding bar button for adding new selfies,
        158
    adding location switch settings, 198
    for EditingViewController, 270
    image detection code, 279
    overriding for AVCaptureDevice.Discovery-
        Session, 235
    updating reminder switch, 208
views, 18, 98
    creating overlay view, 266-268
    custom views and view controllers, 227-243
        calling capture view controller, 240-243
        camera view, 228-231
    hierarchy of, 99
    in MVC pattern, 92
        view classes, 93
    moving around and resizing, 232
    renaming for Selfie example app, 120
    scrolling, 264
    stacked, 265
viewWillAppear method

CaptureViewController class, 280
    SelfieListViewController (example), 173
viewWillLayoutSubviews method, 237
Vision framework, 268
    and image detection, 274-279
Visual Effect with Blur view, 232
visual effects, adding as mask on top of views,
    233
VNFaceLandmarkRegion2D, 276
VNSequenceRequestHandler, 278

W

waitForExpectations(timeout: handler:), 254
weak keyword, 89
weak references, 88
while loops, 36
windows
    application window, UIWindow, 98
    setting tint color in main window of appli-
        cation, 218
wireframes, 112

X

Xcode, 3
    adding Fonts group to a project, 215
    certificate generation for developers, 15
    command-line tools, checking if installed,
        323
    controlling via command line, 322
    creating a new project, 4
        for Selfiegram example app, 115-118
    creating playgrounds, 25
    debugger, 299-308
    downloading, 4
    information on variables, 29
    interface, 6-13
        debug area, 13
        editor, 6
        navigator pane, 10
        toolbar, 8
        utilities pane, 11
    interface builder, 16-18
    iOS simulators, 14
    recording functionality for test functions,
        316
    rich text markup subset in Quick Help, 27
    support for multiple versions of Swift, 21
    Swift Package Manager and, 102
.xcodeproj file, 325

XCTestCase class, 131
XCUIApplication, 313

XCUIElement, 313
XCUIElementQuery, 314

About the Authors

Dr. Jon Manning is the cofounder of Secret Lab, an independent game development studio. He's written a whole bunch of books for O'Reilly Media about iOS development and game development, and has a doctorate about jerks on the internet. He's currently working on *Button Squid*, a top-down puzzler, and on the critically acclaimed award winning adventure game *Night in the Woods*, which includes his interactive dialogue system Yarn Spinner. Jon can be found on Twitter at @desplesda (*http://twitter.com/desplesda*), and online at *http://desplesda.net*.

Dr. Paris Buttfield-Addison is cofounder of Secret Lab (*https://secretlab.com.au*), a game development studio based in beautiful Hobart, Australia. Secret Lab builds games and game development tools, including the multi-award winning ABC Play School iPad games, *Night in the Woods* (*http://www.nightinthewoods.com*), the Qantas airlines *Joey Playbox* games, and the Yarn Spinner narrative game framework. Paris formerly worked as mobile product manager for Meebo (acquired by Google), has a degree in medieval history, a PhD in Computing, and writes technical books on mobile and game development (more than 20 so far) for O'Reilly Media. Paris particularly enjoys game design, statistics, blockchain, machine learning, and human-centred technology research. He can be found on Twitter at @parisba (*https://twitter.com/parisba*) and online at *http://paris.id.au*.

Dr. Tim Nugent pretends to be a mobile app developer, game designer, tools builder, researcher, and tech author. When he isn't busy avoiding being found out as a fraud, he spends most of his time designing and creating little apps and games he won't let anyone see. Tim spent a disproportionately long time writing this tiny little bio, most of which was spent trying to stick a witty sci-fi reference in, before he simply gave up. Tim can be found on Twitter at @The_McJones (*https://twitter.com/the_mcjones*), and online at *http://lonely.coffee*.

Colophon

The animal on the cover of *Learning Swift* is a fairy martin (*Petrochelidon ariel*), a member of the swallow family that breeds in Australia. This migratory bird winters through most of Australia, though some reach New Guinea and Indonesia.

The fairy martin averages 12 centimeters in length and weighs up to 11 grams. It is dumpy with a square tail; adults are iridescent blue on their back with brown wings and tail and a whitish behind. Its pale rump distinguishes this species from other Australian swallows. Males and females have similar coloring, but younger birds have duller coloring and paler foreheads and fringes. The fairy martin has a high-pitched twitter and a *chrrr* call.

During breeding season—from August to January—fairy martins gather in tens of nests; the largest known colony contained 700 nests. They traditionally nest near cliff faces, natural holes in dead trees, riverbanks, or rock crevices, but are increasingly found in man-made sites such as culverts, pipes, bridges, or buildings. Both sexes help build the nests, which consist of up to 1,000 mud pellets and are lined with dried grass and feathers. Fairy martins breed in clutches, which usually consist of up to four or five eggs.

Fairy martins feed in large flocks, catching flying insects in the air or in swarms over water. This is a highly gregarious species that often gather in large groups that include tree martins.

Many of the animals on O'Reilly covers are endangered; all of them are important to the world. To learn more about how you can help, go to *animals.oreilly.com*.

The cover image is from *Wood's Illustrated Natural History*. The cover fonts are URW Typewriter and Guardian Sans. The text font is Adobe Minion Pro; the heading font is Adobe Myriad Condensed; and the code font is Dalton Maag's Ubuntu Mono.

Learn from experts.
Find the answers you need.

Sign up for a **10-day free trial** to get **unlimited access** to all of the content on Safari, including Learning Paths, interactive tutorials, and curated playlists that draw from thousands of ebooks and training videos on a wide range of topics, including data, design, DevOps, management, business—and much more.

Start your free trial at:

oreilly.com/safari

(No credit card required)

www.ingramcontent.com/pod-product-compliance
Ingram Content Group UK Ltd.
Pitfield, Milton Keynes, MK11 3LW, UK
UKHW052230190325
456491UK00009B/139